PLAYING FOR GOD

NORTH AMERICAN RELIGIONS

Series Editors: Tracy Fessenden (Religious Studies, Arizona State University), Laura Levitt (Religious Studies, Temple University), and David Harrington Watt (History, Temple University)

In recent years a cadre of industrious, imaginative, and theoretically sophisticated scholars of religion have focused their attention on North America. As a result, the field is far more subtle, expansive, and interdisciplinary than it was just two decades ago. The North American Religions series builds on this transformative momentum. Books in the series move among the discourses of ethnography, cultural analysis, and historical study to shed new light on a wide range of religious experiences, practices, and institutions. They explore topics such as lived religion, popular religious movements, religion and social power, religion and cultural reproduction, and the relationship between secular and religious institutions and practices. The series focus primarily, but not exclusively, on religion in the United States in the twentieth and twenty-first centuries.

Books in the series:

Ava Chamberlain, *The Notorious Elizabeth Tuttle: Marriage, Murder, and Madness in the Family of Jonathan Edwards*

Terry Rey *and* Alex Stepick, *Crossing the Water and Keeping the Faith: Haitian Religion in Miami*

Jodi Eichler-Levine, *Suffer the Little Children: Uses of the Past in Jewish and African American Children's Literature*

Isaac Weiner, *Religion Out Loud: Religious Sound, Public Space, and American Pluralism*

Hillary Kaell, *Walking Where Jesus Walked: American Christian Holy Land Pilgrimage*

Brett Hendrickson, *Border Medicine: A Transcultural History of Mexican American Curanderismo*

Annie Blazer, *Playing for God: Evangelical Women and the Unintended Consequences of Sports Ministry*

Playing for God

Evangelical Women and the Unintended Consequences of Sports Ministry

Annie Blazer

NEW YORK UNIVERSITY PRESS

New York and London

NEW YORK UNIVERSITY PRESS
New York and London
www.nyupress.org

Roferonces to Internet websites (URLs) were accurate at the time of writing. Neither the author nor New York University Press is responsible for URLs that may have expired or changed since the manuscript was prepared.

Library of Congress Cataloging-in-Publication Data
Blazer, Annie.
Playing for God : evangelical women and the unintended consequences of sports ministry / Annie Blazer.
pages cm. — (North American religions)
Includes bibliographical references and index.
ISBN 978-1-4798-9801-5 (cloth : alk. paper) —
ISBN 978-1-4798-1813-6 (paper : alk. paper)
1. Christian athletes—Religious life. 2. Church work with teenagers—Catholic Church.
3. Femininity—Religious aspects—Christianity. I. Title.
BV4531.3.B566   2015
259.088'796—dc23   2015004164

For my parents

CONTENTS

ACKNOWLEDGMENTS

I am deeply fortunate to have had professional and emotional support throughout this project. First and foremost, I must thank the athletes and coaches who opened their lives to me during my two years of fieldwork and after. Without your honesty and willingness to embrace an outsider/scholar, this book would never have been possible. In particular, I would like to thank Fellowship of Christian Athletes (FCA) and Athletes in Action (AIA) for unfettered access to their archives; the director of the FCA summer camp in Forest Grove, Oregon, for facilitating my week of fieldwork (and the volleyball players there who treated me as part of their small group); the coordinator of AIA's fall 2008 women's basketball tour for integrating me with the team; and the leadership of the Charlotte Lady Eagles for their willingness to have a predoctoral anthropologist present for a season. I am truly grateful for the experiences I shared with the evangelical women in this book. Anthropologists often claim that fieldwork isn't fieldwork unless it changes you, and I know that I came out of this experience with more compassion, more understanding, and more empathy for conservative Christians than I previously thought possible. I hope that the many women and men who shared their athletic and religious lives with me can see themselves in this book.

My graduate school adviser at the University of North Carolina at Chapel Hill, Randall Styers, pushed me and supported me throughout this project. His expertise on professionalization, publishing, and surviving academia was truly invaluable, and his guidance during graduate school and beyond has contributed much to this project and to my career. Yaakov Ariel, Julie Byrne, Lauren Leve, Diane Nelson, and Thomas Tweed provided careful comments and useful criticisms, and I am grateful for their expertise. I also gained much from graduate seminars at UNC and at Duke University with Carl Ernst, Laurie Maffly-Kipp, Michael Hardt, and Barbara Herrnstein Smith. My graduate school colleagues fostered an atmosphere of collegiality, sharing everything from grant proposals to conference papers and job applications. In particular, Kathryn Lofton, Chad Seales, Rabia Gregory, Shanny Luft, Ben Zeller, Nora Rubel, Reid Neilson, Jeff Wilson, Isaac Weiner, Brandi Denison, John-Charles Duffy, Bennie Reynolds, Kathleen Foody, and Brannon Ingram have been a valuable support network for navigating academic life.

I joined the faculty of Millsaps College in Jackson, Mississippi, as a visiting teaching fellow after leaving UNC. My departmental colleagues there—Steven Smith, James Bowley, Darby Ray, and Lola Williamson—proved to be phenomenal allies as I continued work on this project. I am grateful to members of the faculty who read chapter drafts as part of the Works in Progress faculty writing group.

I was very fortunate to move from Millsaps to Princeton University to take a fellowship at Princeton's Center for the Study of Religion for 2010–2011. While at Princeton, I encountered an amazing network of dedicated scholars who invested their time and energy in reading and offering suggestions on my burgeoning manuscript. Members of the North American Religions seminar, led by Jessica Delgado, and the Religion and Culture seminar, led by John Gager, read chapters in progress and provided constructive criticisms. My co-fellows at CSR (the third floor mafia)—Jessica Delgado, Phil Haberkern, Manu Radhakrishnan, and Grace Yukich—provided comic relief, happy hour company, and diligent readership for even my roughest drafts. Additionally, my summer writing compatriots (Deadline Oriented Productivity Experiment: it works!) Janet Vertesi, Michaela DeSoucey, Nicole Kirk, Judith Weisenfeld, and Kathryn Gin joined forces with the CSR fellows to push each other in summer productivity. I am forever grateful for the support and encouragement of this fine group of scholars.

Upon leaving CSR, I joined the faculty of Centenary College in Shreveport, Louisiana, as an assistant professor. My department chair, David Otto, was a dream colleague and fully supported my research endeavors. I wish to thank him, my research assistant Kendall Hughes, and my faculty writing group—Amy Hammond, Will Broussard, and Mark Miller—for pushing me to make my time at Centenary productive and rewarding.

I joined the faculty of the College of William and Mary as an assistant professor in 2012 and am grateful to my Religious Studies colleagues—John Morreall, Marc Raphael, Julie Galambush, Maureen Fitzgerald,

Kevin Vose, Michael Daise, and Alex Angelov—for their welcome and support. I was fortunate to connect with junior faculty in other departments who provided much needed support during the final stages of this project. In particular, Eric Han, Fabricio Prado, Fahad Bishara, and Rose Buckelew were by my side for hours upon hours of writing around my kitchen table, and their company and community were invaluable.

Summer support from the Wabash Center for Teaching and Learning in Theology and Religious Studies and from the College of William and Mary allowed me to dedicate two summers to manuscript revisions. I developed a valuable support network through involvement with the Wabash Center's 2012–2013 workshop for pre-tenure faculty at colleges and universities; in particular, the workshop leadership—Tom Pearson, Paul Myhre, Patricia O'Connell Killen, Reid Locklin, Jeff Brackett, and Carolyn Jones Medine—provided intellectual nourishment through their ongoing support of my scholarship and career. The American Academy of Religion's Religion, Sport, and Play Group were another supportive peer network. I also thank students at Millsaps College, Centenary College, and the College of William and Mary who enrolled in my seminars on Religion and Sport; their thoughtful questions and comments helped me evaluate and improve the undergraduate teachability of this manuscript.

This book has benefited greatly from the editorial handiwork of Jennifer Hammer at NYU Press, who contacted me while I was still a graduate student and has nurtured this work through its many stages of development. I am indebted to the North American Religions series editors—Tracy Fessenden, Laura Levitt, and David Harrington Watt—who saw promise in my work and encouraged me to push this project in critical and sophisticated directions. Anonymous reviewers provided important feedback that has strengthened this book; the remaining imperfections are due to my own shortcomings.

Finally, I owe the greatest debt of thanks to my friends and family, who have kept me sane and laughing through my roller coaster of fieldwork, graduate school, job-hopping, and manuscript writing. I am deeply grateful to the Anderson family for housing me during my two months of fieldwork in Charlotte, North Carolina. Dinners around the Anderson table gave me something to look forward to every day in Charlotte, and I consider myself very lucky to have been able to count on Cathe and Bill for friendship and support. In Carrboro, my strongest advocates were often my friends, and my years in the Triangle were made richer and fuller through the strong and lasting friendships I formed with Ellie Blake, Michael Shick, Aisling Doyle, Dana Moseley, Karl Schmid, Robbie Mackey, Brice and Reece McGowen, Hunter Simpson, Stefan Mlot, Jay Shukla, Christi Ginger, Stephanie Shoemaker, Courtney Kotsionis, Gali Beeri, Charles Olbert, Jose Boyer, Cole Goins, Nick Gaskill, Shilpi Paul, Claire Anderson, Heather Mallory, Joanie Solsman, and Kelley Gill. These friends provided respite and laughter during my days in North Carolina and open homes to visit as I traveled in the years since. The restaurant staffs at Queen of Sheba and Panzanella made sure my evening shifts waiting tables were never boring, the Fly Five helped me move my body, and Lori Burgwyn took pity on this grad student and let me volunteer at Franklin Street Yoga in exchange for free classes. In Mississippi, the Bachelorettes (Lizzie Wright, Rachel Jarman, and Amanda Rainey) made Jackson feel like coming home, Brent Fogt was always available for pizza and beer, and the local music scene welcomed this midwesterner with open arms. In Shreveport, Wendee and Keith Myers were always up for a few games of Dominion on a weekday, writers and musicians joined me in forming Salon du Shreve, and the religious studies majors brought their good humor and their good cooking to my house once a month for some raucous potluck dinners. In Richmond, Joe Norkus took a risk on this bass player and formed Candy Spots, my trivia team made every Monday night an adventure, and my circle of women provided much-needed emotional support through tough times. In particular, I am grateful to Erin White and Bitsy and Tyler Brown, who took care of me when a knee injury knocked me out of commission two weeks after my move to town and have been caring friends ever since.

Long before I considered a career in higher education, my parents and siblings believed in me and had confidence in my success. Christine Blakeney, David Breck, George Glazer, Janice Spodarek, John and Charlotte Breck, Matt and Kathleen Breck, Joe Breck, James Glazer, Michael Glazer, and Blake Glazer (plus my other F2s and F3s) are just about the best family I could imagine. This book is dedicated to my parents: thank you for nurturing my intellectual creativity, for supporting me on my academic journey, and most especially for your love. I owe you much more than a book.

Introduction

Practicing Faith

Sports Ministry and Evangelicalism in America

"God turned my life upside down this semester. I moved out West with my fiancé for a job, and now I don't have that job or the fiancé anymore and I'm back here in North Carolina. I had been trying to do it all alone, and eventually God was like, 'No. You don't get to do this anymore,' and he took it all away from me." Taylor, a former Athletes in Action (AIA) staff member and University of North Carolina gymnastics alum, was speaking to a group of about thirty Christian college athletes at the weekly AIA sports ministry meeting on the campus of UNC–Chapel Hill.[1] Her tone was angry, but she became calmer as she told the group, "It was a humbling experience. I guess I just wanted to share that there will be times in your life when you will be angry, and that is okay." The event was the final meeting of the fall semester, and the campus minister, Tom, had invited Christian athletes to share and reflect on stories of praise, lament, or thanksgiving, the major themes of the book of Psalms.

Even though Taylor's story was not about sport, sport was not incidental—she was an athletes talking to athletes, and they shared the experiences of the effort, dedication, joy, and disappointments that accompany that identity. Dana, another female athlete at the AIA meeting, echoed Taylor's sentiments, emphasizing her own difficulty in maintaining her relationship with God. Dana was a senior graduating that spring, one of only three or four seniors at the meeting that evening. She told the group:

> At the beginning of this semester, I felt a great distance between me and God. I know that he doesn't go anywhere, that he doesn't change, so I knew it was my fault. But, I was real angry at him because I didn't know how to get back to him. But then, when I actually started listening to what

he was telling me and doing what I knew he wanted me to do—read my Bible, pray, et cetera—then I got back to him. So, I guess this is a little bit of a lament and a little bit of thanksgiving.

Many evangelicals describe their relationship with God as "personal," and in the cases of Taylor and Dana, this personal relationship entailed daily maintenance through activities like prayer, reading the Bible, and attending ministry sessions like AIA. Dana blamed herself for feeling distant from God, and Taylor interpreted her job loss and breakup as indications that God was disappointed in her failure to maintain her part of their relationship. Sports ministry opened a space for these athletes to reflect on their religious challenges.

Tom and his wife, Ann, began directing UNC's AIA chapter in 1983. At the time, campus AIA chapters were a relatively new idea. Athletes in Action is a branch of Campus Crusade for Christ and describes its vision as "a Christ follower on every team, in every sport and in every nation." The organization trains athletes and coaches to be evangelists. According to its website:

> Athletes and coaches around the world who are experiencing this life-changing relationship are telling the story of Jesus—to their teammates and fellow coaches, to hurting and needy people through their words and acts of compassion and kindness, and to millions of people through the media. Over 650 staff members and 7,500 volunteers in 94 countries boldly proclaim Jesus Christ and deeply equip believers to lead and urgently mobilize ambassadors of Good News and Good Will in the fulfillment of the Great Commission.[2]

For many evangelicals, "Good News" refers to the message of salvation through Jesus Christ, and the "Great Commission" refers to a section of scripture wherein Jesus appears to his disciples and commands them to travel to all nations teaching his message of salvation.[3] Evangelical organizations like AIA rely on the premise that the only way for humans to achieve salvation, and therefore assure their eternal happiness after death, is through a heartfelt belief in the reality and power of Jesus Christ.

Though AIA was not as prevalent when Tom and Ann began their work at UNC, by 2013, there were more than a hundred sports ministry organizations in the United States that involved tens of thousands of athletes, coaches, and fans. There is now a sports ministry organization for nearly every imaginable sport, from basketball and soccer to surfing and rodeo. The two largest sports ministry organizations remain the multi-sport ministries of Fellowship of Christian Athletes (FCA) and Athletes in Action, which have yearly operating budgets of $70 million and $20 million, respectively.[4] Each year, AIA hosts around thirty national and international tours for athletic teams, involving nearly 800 athletes who play against hundreds of teams and compete in front of audiences totaling in the tens of thousands. In 2012, FCA reported that more than 52,000 athletes and coaches attended its 363 summer camps, showing an increase of about 10,000 attendees over five years.[5] That same year, AIA had staff at nearly 200 college campuses and with thirty-five professional sports teams, and FCA had a campus presence at more than 9,000 middle schools, high schools, and colleges.[6]

For these thousands of Christian athletes, sporting settings are rarely solely about sport; sport is one dimension of their lives that they balance with their religious obligations. Taylor's and Dana's stories illuminate how sports ministry can provide a space to reflect on religious beliefs and practices. This book argues that the effects and consequences of evangelical engagement with popular cultural forms like sport are not predictable in advance, and that, in the case of sports ministry, the opportunity to use sport as religious practice was also an opportunity to rethink and reframe evangelical orthodoxy. This dynamic is particularly revealing in studying female Christian athletes because these women have often turned to sports ministry to reflect on issues of gender and sexuality that affect their lives as evangelical women and as athletes. Sports ministry has opened a site for religious self-reflexivity, and particularly for evangelical women who play sports, this self-reflexivity has contributed to subtle, complex, and largely unintentional shifts in understandings of evangelical orthodoxy.

American Evangelicalism and the Emergence of Sports Ministry

Today's evangelicals emerged from fundamentalist Protestantism as a distinct cultural group in the 1940s and 1950s. In 1942, a group of conservative Christian leaders gathered in St. Louis and formed the

National Association of Evangelicals based on a doctrine called "engaged orthodoxy." Engaged orthodoxy called on evangelicals to interact with non-Christians politically and culturally. This approach differed dramatically from fundamentalist strategies of the previous generation that emphasized purity through isolation.[7] Evangelicals established national organizations such as Youth for Christ in 1944 and Campus Crusade for Christ in 1951. The Fuller Theological Seminary, founded in 1947, was the first of many explicitly evangelical institutions of higher learning, contributing to a growing population of educated middle-class conservative Christians. The periodical *Christianity Today*, first published in 1956, targeted this emergent population of evangelical Christians. The success of these organizations evidenced an increasing number of Americans who engaged conservative Christianity and American culture simultaneously.

Evangelicals see themselves as *in* but not *of* the world.[8] This means that they understand the world as temporary and corrupted, and take it as their mission to reach as many people as possible with the message of salvation through Jesus Christ. They tend to adhere to an ideological unity through core religious beliefs.[9] In the simplest possible terms, these beliefs include the inherent sinfulness of humans, the power of God to intercede in human affairs, salvation through Jesus Christ, and the urgent obligation to share this information with others. They understand the Bible as the infallible word of God that can exercise power over people's hearts and minds.

Evangelical denominations in the United States experienced notable growth in the 1970s and 1980s in contrast with a concurrent decline in mainline Protestant church membership. Robert Putnam and David Campbell's recent research on religions in the United States found that while 23 percent of Americans could be categorized as evangelical in 1973, this number grew to 28 percent in 1993, but fell to 24 percent in 2008. They wrote, "Despite the mountains of books and newspaper articles about the rise of evangelicalism, in absolute terms the change was hardly massive, except by comparison to the collapsing mainline Protestant denominations."[10] Putnam and Campbell's research offers an important insight on the role of evangelical Christianity in American culture. Though evangelicalism did not expand greatly in terms of real numbers, evangelicals increasingly influenced American politics and popular understandings of American religiosity. Sociologists Michael Hout and Claude Fischer have gone so far as to argue that popular associations with the term "Christian" reflect primarily evangelical ideas on salvation and moral behavior.[11] In the 1970s and 1980s, sex and family became central political issues, and the Republican Party emerged as the party opposed to both abortion and gay rights. According to Putnam and Campbell, over the course of the late twentieth century, the Republican Party became culturally associated with religion, particularly conservative Christianity. Their survey data show that Americans see the Republican Party as "religion-friendly" and the Democratic Party as "religion-neutral." Though evangelicals experienced very little change in real numbers of adherents, they were instrumental in aligning conservative Christianity with conservative politics.[12]

Some evangelicals dislike the term "evangelical." For some, this word implies a zealous believer focused entirely on proselytizing to others. Rejecting this word does not mean that the salvation of others is less important to these evangelicals, but it does mean that methods of high-pressure witnessing have fallen out of favor. Sociologist Christian Smith's data, collected in the 1990s, show a tendency among evangelicals to refer to themselves as simply "Christian."[13] Contemporary evangelicals may push this a step further. For example, Angie, a Christian athlete and professional soccer player, told me, "When people ask me what religion I am, I say I am a believer in Christ. I am a Christ follower. For a lot of people, the term 'Christian' can be overwhelming or negative." Angie's language reflects a trend that Smith and others have identified—some evangelical Christians are uncomfortable with the label "evangelical," and for evangelicals like Angie, even the label "Christian" carried negative connotations. In this book, I use the term "evangelical" to refer to Christians who prioritize outreach to non-believers and adhere to a narrow definition of salvation. I use the term "conservative Christianity" to refer to those who share theological qualities and a conservative political outlook with evangelicals but may prioritize different practices.[14]

Very quickly after their emergence as a coherent group in the 1940s and 1950s, evangelicals established a compatible relationship with popular culture, turning to popular cultural forms like television, film, music, fiction, and sports to promote their idea of salvation to a larger American audience. This engagement demonstrates a double impulse.

Evangelicals were interested in using popular culture to communicate with those outside evangelicalism and increase interest in conversion. Media engagement like the development of Christian television shows and networks helped to shape evangelical self-understandings by positioning evangelical spokespeople as broadcasting to an audience of nonbelievers. Later, in the 1990s, popular novels like the *Left Behind* series explained evangelical salvation through a thrilling end-of-the-world adventure. Authors Tim LeHaye and Jerry B. Jenkins intended these books to reach an audience outside their tradition and included introductory descriptions of evangelical beliefs.[15]

At the same time that evangelicals engaged popular culture with the intention of reaching a nonbelieving audience, they carved out a separate wedge of popular culture for an explicitly Christian audience. This occurred, for example, in the development of Contemporary Christian Music, now its own category of production and consumption within the music industry. Contemporary Christian Music sounds very much like its secular counterpart; the primary difference is lyrical content that includes Christian themes. Likewise, the Christian video game industry produces games modeled after successful secular games but infuses them with Christian themes. Christian bookstores provide shopping experiences based on the American mall, yet the products and decor assure shoppers that they are in a religious environment. Evangelicals have been producing and consuming popular culture products like these for more than sixty years and are adept at integrating new media forms into their production and consumption patterns.

Sports ministry emerged from this dual impulse to use popular culture to reach a nonevangelical audience and to create specifically evangelical popular culture spaces free of worldly influence. Before the formation of the first sports ministry organizations in the 1950s and 1960s, Youth for Christ (YFC) featured athletes at its stadium-style rallies. Most famously, at YFC rallies in the 1940s, Jack Wyrtzen included the spectacle of world record–holding track star Gil Dodds sprinting for the audience. These rallies boasted attendance of 20,000 to 30,000 people. After his athletic performance, Dodds would deliver his story of becoming a Christian, saying things like, "Running is only a hobby. My mission is teaching the gospel of Jesus Christ."[16] Youth for Christ used this narrative to call for others to convert to evangelical Christianity.

According to YFC spokesperson Billy Graham, "We used every modern means to catch the attention of the unconverted, and then we punched them right between the eyes with the Gospel."[17] Clearly, Gil Dodds's presence was an attempt to use sport for evangelical outreach.

It was the magnetism of athletic celebrity that inspired Don Mc-Clanen to form Fellowship of Christian Athletes and Dave Hannah to form Athletes in Action. Both of these men were struck by Americans' admiration of sports stars and saw a potential to use that admiration to convert others. Both organizations recruited professional athletes who were Christian and helped those athletes become comfortable talking about their faith in public settings. Additionally, these organizations began forming separate spaces for evangelical athletes that mirrored secular sporting spaces, with FCA offering athletic training camps, and AIA forming traveling sports teams. Both of these settings included athletic activities like drills, training, and games, but evangelical Christianity was present throughout in the form of group prayer, Christian symbols on uniforms, and spiritual guidance from experienced evangelical athletes and coaches.

This dual trend of encouraging Christian athletes to use the secular spaces of sport for witnessing and of forming separate evangelical spaces for training and competing continued and expanded over the course of the late twentieth century. More sports ministry organizations emerged in the 1970s that targeted specific athletic populations. Baseball Chapel formed in 1973 and placed chaplains with all Major League teams within its first two years. Pro Athletes Outreach formed in 1974 and targeted professional football players. Both of these organizations have grown significantly since their formation. By 2013, Baseball Chapel was hosting chapel services in every Major League, Minor League, and Independent League city in the United States, as well as boasting a significant international presence in Latin America and Japan.[18] Pro Athletes Outreach continued to provide ministry services for professional football players (and their wives) and organized opportunities for professional football players to speak to high school and junior high coaches and players.[19] Over the course of the 1980s and 1990s, sports ministry organizations formed that targeted female athletes or youth sports, such as FCA's branch for professional women's golf that held weekly meetings for touring golfers. Upward Sports, the largest Christian sports league for youth athletics in the world, officially formed in 1995 after ten years of offering a local basketball camp in Spartanburg, South Carolina, that integrated athletic and religious lessons.[20] In many parts of the United States, Christian sports camps offer the best (sometimes the only) youth athletic training available.

The extent of these national organizations is striking, but these numbers only hint at the growth of sports ministry at a local level. As more and more athletes grew up affiliating their athletic and religious experiences, careers in sports ministry seemed increasingly viable options. Athletes who are unable or unwilling to pursue careers as professionals are able to coach or play for Christian teams at multiple levels—from youth club teams to Christian high schools and colleges to semiprofessional and professional Christian teams. Coaching positions at explicitly Christian colleges and universities are especially appealing career options for Christian athletes. In 2011, there were more than 500 coaching positions and more than 100 sports administrative positions at just thirty-three Christian colleges.[21] Additionally, many contemporary megachurches (churches with weekly attendance rates of more than 2,000) have an athletic staff. In 2011, more than half of the twenty largest megachurches in the United States featured sports programming prominently on their websites and employed full- and part-time athletic staff. Five of these churches also had on-site fitness centers, employing personal trainers and fitness class instructors. Full- and part-time staffs ranged from one director overseeing a volunteer staff to a full-time directorial staff of ten with six part-time employees and twelve or more seasonal part-time staff.[22]

Fifteen Christian colleges offer degrees in sports ministry, and many more offer courses or extracurricular training in the field.[23] Colleges have reported varying numbers of participants; for example, in 2008, Belhaven College in Jackson, Mississippi, had three or four students who were majoring in sports ministry, whereas Malone College in Canton, Ohio had twenty-five to thirty. These numbers have remained steady over the past few years.[24] Several Christian colleges require a primary degree in Bible but allow students to pursue a secondary major or emphasis in sports ministry. For example, Moody Bible Institute offers a sports ministry major that includes classes such as History and Philosophy of Sports Ministry, Organization and Administration of Sports Ministry, and Issues and Trends in Sports Ministry.[25] Many of these students were high school or college athletes who, upon graduating from these programs, pursue advanced degrees in ministry, careers in sports ministry organizations, or church athletic staff positions.

As these numbers show, there are multiple opportunities for careers in sports ministry. This book focuses on participation in sports ministry organizations, but it is important to note that what Christian athletes learn in sports ministry, they take with them to careers as coaches, administrators, and church staff members.

Becoming Athletes of God

When sports ministry originated in the 1950s and 1960s, Christian athletes' primary mission was to showcase evangelical Christianity to their audience. With the formation of the Fellowship of Christian Athletes in 1954, sports ministers began to conscientiously recruit celebrity athletes and market these men as paragons of masculinity and Christian devotion. FCA founder Don McClanen and AIA founder Dave Hannah both explicitly intended their organizations to promote manliness, strength, and the evangelical message of salvation. They wanted to use Americans' cultural admiration of athletic mastery to create a platform for Christian athletes to talk about their faith.

In the 1970s, however, when sports ministers began to explore athletic pleasure and pain as indications of God's involvement in sport, they came to understand their bodies as God's forum for demonstrating satisfaction or dissatisfaction with the believer. Christian athletes developed two key terms for describing their embodied sensations: "Christlikeness" and "spiritual warfare." These ways of talking about sport made physical sensations of pain, fatigue, mastery, and muscle memory, as well as emotions like frustration, vengeance, pride, and joy, signs of God and Satan struggling in and through the believer's body. Christian athletes identified the body as the primary site of interplay between good and evil, and this emphasis on the body shifted sports ministry's emphasis away from recruiting celebrity athletes.[26] Though sports ministry originally focused on men and masculinity, the emergent emphasis on individual embodied sensation allowed athletes with limited celebrity potential, like women and youth athletes, to actively participate. By the

1990s, women and youth athletes constituted the largest participant populations within sports ministry organizations.

Sport remains a realm of masculinity, and women who play sports, particularly at an elite level, confront gender expectations and gender contradictions in ways that may never arise with other kinds of activities.[27] For women in sports ministry, attention to the body has forced a reckoning with evangelical mainstays on gender and sexuality. This book offers a case study of how evangelical engagement with popular culture created the possibility for reevaluating orthodoxy from inside the tradition. Engagement with sport provided another toolbox for evangelical female athletes; when they actively sought to combine their athletic and evangelical identities, sport allowed them to develop a new kind of religious self-reflexivity that opened up a range of sometimes complementary, sometimes contradictory understandings of what it could mean to be an evangelical woman in contemporary America. Women in sports ministry bridge and negotiate a complicated set of identities: evangelical woman, elite sports competitor, and Christian athlete. They live out their gender and sexuality in athletic and religious contexts and have thought about, discussed, and often modified evangelical mainstays in ways that have significantly enlarged their range of potential behaviors and practices while still maintaining their sense of belonging to a tradition that they find meaningful. They do not do this alone, but in dialogue with secular athletes, male athletes, and lesbian athletes.

The evangelical mainstay on homosexuality maintains that same-sex attraction is contrary to God's will and that same-sex intimacy is sinful. Evangelical orthodoxy on marriage presents hierarchical gender roles—male headship and female submission—as part of God's plan for human happiness. As the female Christian athletes who now dominate sports ministry reflected on these theological claims from the point of view of athletes, they developed a more complex understanding of them. By redefining femininity as a conglomeration of both traditionally feminine and traditionally masculine traits, they became able to imagine that God intends women to be strong leaders as well as supportive nurturers. Partly through this redefinition and partly through their frequent and intimate interactions with a variety of athletic women, female Christian athletes are unlikely to outright condemn lesbianism, and they demonstrate a willingness to question dominant evangelical stances on its sinfulness. Within heterosexual relationships, female Christian athletes use their redefinition of femininity to build dating relationships and marriages based on gender equality, while at the same time upholding marriage as a central part of evangelical life.

Sports ministry participants have reassessed and modified evangelical stances on gender and sexuality in subtle and unpredictable ways. This has not created heterodoxy, but the opportunity for religious self-reflexivity has expanded and complicated orthodoxy. Evangelical mainstays that designate differences between men and women, God's expectation of heterosexual love, and marriage as God's plan for enacting those differences and that love do not disappear from the worldviews of female Christian athletes, but through sports ministry, they are able to discuss and modify these positions, maintaining them in altered forms. This book explores how Christian athletes do the ongoing work of maintaining religious belief while also engaging the shifting terrain of American popular culture. The encounter between evangelicalism and sports has led to a flexible evangelicalism that allows for a far wider range of beliefs and practices than the founders of sports ministry imagined.

Two facets of evangelical theology that come to the fore in sports ministry are attention to the supernatural (the enduring belief that God's will pervades the entire human realm and that all events or experiences are part of a divine order) and attention to differences between men and women (the idea that men and women are fundamentally distinct and that each sex has its own temptations and its own obligations toward the opposite sex, family, and community). As the following story illustrates, sports ministry provides an opportunity for Christian athletes to reflect on and engage these evangelical tenets with sometimes surprising results.

In April, with final exams right around the corner, UNC's AIA chapter met for the last few times. For Dana, graduation would follow finals, and she used the meeting to express concerns about her future. The college years would mark the end of her career as an elite athlete, so she was embarking on an identity shift. A second shift in her life was a breakup with her long-term boyfriend. She told the group, "I've been in a relationship with this guy for a year and a half, but I knew he wasn't a strong Christian. He was a believer, but he wasn't walking." Some evangelicals use movement metaphors like "walking" or "path" to describe maintaining an active and personal relationship with God. "For months now," Dana continued, "I've been wrestling with the dilemma of whether to break up or not, and finally I just asked God to do it. I just said, God, take this relationship out of my life. And He did." *Really?*

In sports ministry meetings, as in the locker room and on the field, athletes who have a prominent position on their team command an audience, and younger or second-string athletes often asked for, rather than delivered, advice. Sporting prestige and talent have a strong influence on sports ministry social dynamics. Because Dana was a senior, she spoke with authority on her struggles, and the younger athletes listened. Tom, the AIA campus minister, returned to Dana's story throughout the night. He used it to encourage the other athletes to believe that God has a plan for each of them. "God has a plan for Dana," he told everyone, "and once you submit to God's will, you will become peaceful and happy."

This theme reemerged at the following week's meeting. The final meeting of the semester was senior night, and Dana, one of the few seniors, was the first to share. Her story followed a common pattern within evangelical Christianity. She described herself as "raised in a Christian home," but then told of a struggle that she felt caused a distance between herself and God. "I came to college, and I really wanted to fit in on my team. I ended up having a really wild freshman year—lots of drinking and partying. That year, I really hit rock bottom." At this point, Dana sounded close to tears. "I knew that I had to turn to God about it," she continued. "I talked last week about the relationship that I was in and how I prayed that God would take it away. My ears had been closed. I needed to listen closer to God. And now, now that I've been listening, a feeling of great peace is over me." In this statement, Dana reiterated Tom's thoughts from the week before. She continued, "I've been searching for a job, but I'm not stressed about the future. I thought I wanted to move away, but it's clear to me that God intended I take a job in Research Triangle Park [about twenty miles away]. I bought a car—I never thought I would be able to do that. I'm happily single. God really does have a plan." She then shared her favorite Bible verse, Jeremiah 29:11 (NIV), "'For I know the plans I have for you,' declares the Lord, 'plans to prosper you and not to harm you, plans to give you hope and a future.'"

Dana's story is interesting for a number of reasons. It followed a format familiar to many evangelicals: a worldly or secular influence drew the believer away from God (in Dana's case, the partying with her team during freshman year); the believer made a conscious decision to realign with God (given the setting, the implication in Dana's story is that attending AIA meetings was an important part of that realignment); and following this reconnection to God, the believer experienced mental and material well-being (a feeling of peace, a job, a car). This story also emphasized a key tenet of evangelical faith—divine providence, the idea that God has a plan for humans. In Dana's story, God appears as both all-knowing and all-loving. God had clear intentions, and following God's intentions resulted in happiness and well-being. However, God was unable to force this plan upon Dana and depended on her actions to put it into effect. Stories like this emphasize that the decision to submit to God's plan is an essential aspect of a believer's religious life.

Further, Dana's story is interesting because it is very rare for believers to describe singleness as part of God's plan.[28] In every evangelical setting that I investigated, heterosexual marriage was an assumed part of a full religious life. I generally heard Christian athletes refer to singleness as a temporary state that would ultimately be resolved through submission to God's plan, implying that God planned a heterosexual marriage for every believer. Dana's assertion that she was happily single *and* in line with God's plan subtly challenges the normativity of heterosexual marriage.

One reason that being happily single challenges evangelical theological mainstays is that evangelicals often use marriage as a metaphor for the correct relationship between a believer and God. The next senior who spoke at the AIA meeting was Dave, a curly-haired rower on the crew team who was hoping to attend seminary in the fall. "I want to talk to you about my relationship with God," he began. "I really believe that God comes for us not because of anything we do, but because God somehow must. It's part of God's nature to desire a relationship with us. I've been thinking about a metaphor I see throughout the Bible of God's people being like a bride with God or Jesus as the groom."

Dave was holding a Bible in his hands and would gesture with it while he was speaking. "God wants that kind of relationship, a relationship of marriage importance, with his people," he continued. "But what I see in the Bible is that God's people are like an adulterous wife, unfaithful and whore-like. Yet, despite these serious faults, God always comes to you and reconciles you to him. For example, in Hosea, God commands

Hosea to take an adulterous wife so that Hosea can better understand God's relationship with humans." Dave paused and looked up at the group of Christian athletes. "I think this shows God's relationship with all humans. It's not because of anything we do that God comes for us, but because he is a good husband, basically. All I can offer God is the sins of my life. And he comes for me anyway."

For Dave, the metaphor that best encapsulated God's relationship with humans was that of an unfaithful marriage. It is important to explicate several facets of this metaphor. First of all, the believer is the female half of this heterosexual marriage. This metaphor would likely have had far different connotations if the believer were the husband, with God as the bride. Dave's metaphor relies on deeply held gender beliefs that privilege men as powerful actors and associate women with weakness, failure, and sexual infidelity. In Dave's story, Dave himself was the woman, and this kind of gender-bending is worth noting. Dave identified himself as an unfaithful wife, with God as his good husband. However, if Dave is like many evangelical men, he also intended to become a good husband himself one day. This means that Dave had access to both of the characters in his analogy: the whorish woman *and* the loving husband. For evangelical women, however, the character of the good husband would be more difficult to access, and the whorish wife would be the resonant identity. This may help to clarify why Dana's claim of being happily single *as part of* God's plan is revolutionary. It challenges this central gendered marriage relationship that many evangelicals see as the most apt analogy for the correct relationship between God and humans. Singleness as part of God's plan undermines both characters in Dave's analogy and specifically deprives God/men of the power to forgive/accept the unfaithful believer/wife.

After Dave shared his story, Tom, Ann, and an AIA student leader rose to pray for Dana and Dave. Tom presented them both with Bibles and delivered a prayer that affirmed marriage as part of God's plan for evangelicals. He said, "I pray that when God gives you a spouse that it be a godly marriage, and that when you have kids that you raise them to know the Lord so that, at the end of your lives, you can look back with no regrets." In this short prayer, Tom undermined both Dana's and Dave's challenges to evangelical mainstays. A "godly marriage" did not include unfaithfulness, and singleness was not part of God's plan. To not be married and to not have children was regrettable and out of alignment with God's intentions.

Athletes in Action's senior night demonstrates two major preoccupations within evangelical culture: maintaining a correct relationship with God, and gender as an organizing principle for the world. Female Christian athletes have negotiated these preoccupations through the masculine domain of sports. Using sport as a tool for divine connection has allowed female Christian athletes to rethink their gender understandings. Like Dana's subtle challenge of declaring herself happily single, other female Christian athletes have used the practices, embodied experiences, and central narratives of sports ministry to reassess femininity, sexual desire, and marriage. Through reevaluating theological mainstays from within their tradition, women in sports ministry have expanded their understandings of orthodoxy, and their ability to do so demonstrates that the outcomes of religious engagement with popular culture are not predictable ahead of time.

Studying Faith in the Field

When I began studying sports ministry in 2006, I visited the headquarters of both FCA and AIA. Fellowship of Christian Athletes' institutional home is in Kansas City, Missouri. In an imposing building near enough to the highway that the FCA logo can be seen by passing motorists, the headquarters includes the production team for FCA's member magazine, *Sharing the Victory* (previously titled *Christian Athlete*), the upper levels of the organization's administration, and a team of workers that produce summer camp curricula and resources for local FCA chapters. When FCA established its headquarters in Kansas City in 1979, the city was home to the national offices of the National Collegiate Athletic Association (NCAA). Though the NCAA relocated to Indianapolis in 1999, FCA remained in Kansas City. Over the course of my visits to FCA's headquarters, I amassed a collection of photocopied publications and had conversations with a number of FCA employees. It was during my first visit that I learned that FCA was perhaps most proud of its summer camps and treated summer as the beginning of the year, launching a theme and a key Bible verse each summer that served as the foundation for all other materials developed for use in the following school year.

Clearly, attending an FCA summer camp would be essential for my study of sports ministry. I identified two camps on the West Coast to visit the following summer. As a preliminary investigation, I attended one day of an FCA summer camp in Watsonville, California, in June 2007. This gave me an idea of the daily structure of camp as well as its social organization. Each day of camp was packed with workouts (both as a full camp and in smaller teams), small-group Bible studies in sport-specific "huddles," and full-camp worship sessions both at midday and in the evening. Later that summer, I attended a weeklong camp in Forest Grove, Oregon. This FCA camp brought together around eighty high school athletes of multiple sports for five days of athletic and religious training. Campers would rise early for fifteen minutes of contemplative Bible study before morning exercises, and throughout the day they continued to align and combine evangelical Christianity and sport. The majority of sports ministry participants are women, and most FCA summer camps reflect this demographic. However, the camp that I attended in Oregon offered a football program that greatly increased male attendance, resulting in nearly equal numbers of male and female participants. The 2007 summer camp curriculum, "Game Ready," presented sport as part of spiritual warfare. In the fall of 2007, I returned to FCA's headquarters in Kansas City to talk with the curriculum developers about their choices in putting together the "Game Ready" programming.

About a month after my first visit to the FCA headquarters, I traveled to Xenia, Ohio, to visit the headquarters of Athletes in Action. The AIA World Training and Resource Center is far more expansive than FCA's office building. Athletes in Action's headquarters also includes an expansive sports complex of two softball fields, two soccer fields, a baseball field, a football field with a track, and a ropes course. The property, which was first used for the Ohio Soldiers' and Sailors' Orphans' Home during and after the Civil War, also includes housing for nearly 300. Whereas FCA's headquarters overlooked a major highway near a major urban center, AIA's Xenia facilities were set in a rural environment, surrounded by the cornfields and rolling hills of central Ohio. During my visit to AIA's headquarters, I was able to meet and talk to many administrators, including former AIA president Wendel Deyo, the man responsible for relocating AIA away from the headquarters of its parent organization (Campus Crusade for Christ, then in California) to the independent facility in Ohio, where Deyo had been serving as an AIA minister with the Cincinnati Bengals.

AIA gave me full access to its archives. Though it was not published as consistently as FCA's member magazine, AIA did produce a publication entitled *Athletes in Action Magazine*, much of which chronicled the adventures of the organization's traveling teams. Though AIA had a significant presence on many college campuses, it was clear to me that its administrators were most proud of these traveling teams. I had been regularly attending AIA's weekly meetings on the campus of UNC–Chapel Hill but knew that in order to explore AIA more fully, I would need to travel with one of its touring teams. Soon after its founding in 1966, AIA made a name for itself with its traveling men's basketball team, so a basketball tour seemed a logical choice.

I arranged to join the AIA women's basketball team in fall of 2007 for their tour of games against college teams in the northeastern United States. The team was made up of ten women who had played basketball at the college level and were pursuing basketball careers either as professional players or as coaches. The women ranged in age from twenty-two to thirty; four of them were African American, four were white and native-born, and two were white and from foreign countries. The ten players were accompanied by six other women: two coaches, a trainer, two spiritual advisers, and an AIA blogger who documented their tour for the AIA website. These women also demonstrated a range of racial and ethnic backgrounds. The head spiritual adviser was African American; the assistant coach, a Canadian, was white; and the trainer, head coach, assistant spiritual adviser, and blogger all were white and native-born. Former AIA basketball players and other AIA staff members joined the group for parts of the tour. All in all, the team played nine games in fifteen days with only a week together to train before hitting the road. During this tour, I was present for practices, games, Bible studies, hotel breakfasts, and hours upon hours of riding in vans—in short, the grueling schedule of a competitive traveling team.

Because AIA and FCA are the two oldest and largest sports ministry organizations and have had a presence in the sports world for more than fifty years, they have dramatically influenced the larger field of sports ministry. Inspired by the initial success of these organizations in recruiting athletes as evangelical witnesses, sport-specific ministry organizations formed and proliferated. To represent this phenomenon, I identified a women's Christian soccer team in Charlotte, North Carolina, the Charlotte Lady Eagles, as my final field site. The Charlotte Lady Eagles are a subsidiary of Ministry Athletes International (MAI), a sports ministry organization that focuses solely on soccer. According to its website, "Missionary Athletes International was founded on the simple premise that, through the common enjoyment of this worldwide sport, we would be able to build relationships that allow us to share the Good News."[29] As mentioned earlier, "Good News" is a common evangelical phrase that refers to the message of salvation through Jesus Christ. MAI owns four professional and semiprofessional soccer teams: the Chicago Eagles, the Southern California Seahorses, the Charlotte Eagles, and the Charlotte Lady Eagles. These teams compete in secular leagues against secular teams, they travel abroad to work with international soccer teams, and they run training camps for youth athletes.

I spent a competitive season with the Charlotte Lady Eagles in the summer of 2008. Some of the women who played that season had been with the team since its inception in 1998, and some were still in college and spent the summer with the team in order to improve their skills for their college season. The Lady Eagles drew women from across the country and from abroad. It was the only women's team of its kind in the United States: an explicitly Christian team in an elite secular league. In 2009, the year after I conducted my fieldwork, Women's Professional Soccer (WPS) formed, filling a gap in professional women's soccer made when the Women's United Soccer Association (W-USA) suspended its operation in 2003, and many of the women from the Charlotte Lady Eagles went on to play for WPS teams. During my fieldwork, semiprofessional soccer was the highest level of competitive soccer available to women in the United States, with the exception of Olympic-level competition. The season I spent with the Charlotte Lady Eagles was my longest field visit, and I achieved a higher level of rapport with the women on that team than in my other field studies. Women on the Charlotte Lady Eagles were comfortable sharing struggles that went to the heart of evangelical identity, namely, issues of gender and sexuality. After completing my fieldwork, I maintained contact with many of the athletes I encountered and have followed up with them in phone calls and Facebook conversations over the ensuing years.

These three field sites represent a significant cross section of sports ministry in America—FCA camps for high school athletes on the West Coast, the AIA women's basketball team competing in the Northeast, and a semiprofessional Christian soccer team in the South—and focus on the largest population within sports ministry: women.

When I conducted research at a field site, I always had a pen and notebook in my hands. I jotted down details and phrases intended to later jog my memory of what was going on. I reserved several hours every evening for typing up thorough accounts of the day's proceedings, using my notebook jottings to guide my recollections. I found my notebook strategy to be much less intrusive than a tape recorder and so made handwritten notes during conversations and informal interviews. These, too, I typed later in a more thoroughly fleshed-out way.[30] There are pros and cons to this approach. The main drawback was that I was forced to paraphrase much of what I heard, with a few short, direct quotations to anchor the tone of what was said. The benefit to my approach, however, was that I had greatly increased access to my subjects' interactions. In previous fieldwork for a different project, I had observed how my subjects would edit themselves when they were aware of a tape recorder, and I would often hear the most interesting information in the minutes after I stopped recording. In my sports ministry field sites, Christian athletes often carried Bibles with them everywhere. In the locker room and on the sidelines, it was common to see team members with open books, underlining or scratching marginalia in their Bibles or devotional texts. Therefore, my notebook and pen were not out of place, and I was easily able to blend in. Of course, my subjects knew that I wasn't scrawling in a Bible, but my notebook fit in more easily than a tape recorder could have. At times I was unable to take notes on a conversation, particularly during meals. Whenever this happened, I would, if possible, withdraw for an hour to type notes on that conversation from memory. The end result was several inordinately large computer files containing as much detail as I could muster.

Field notes, and the later use of field notes in a project such as this, are always filtered through the point of view of the author. The anthropologist has a certain kind of credibility ("I know because I was there") that is different from the credibility of historians or archaeologists.[31] At the same time, my perspective as a young, white, female nonathlete and an atheist scholar certainly impacted my records of events, conversations, and social interactions. In an attempt to be as transparent as possible about my social location and perspective, I have chosen to include first-person narratives in this book.[32] This approach is intended to invite the reader to see what I saw and to be honest that my eyes provide only one perspective. I have prioritized the words of my subjects whenever possible, and I hope that the many athletes, coaches, and sports ministers who opened their lives to my scrutiny can see themselves in this work.

This book is a study of what scholars have called "popular religion," "lived religion," or "everyday religion": the ideas and practices that constitute religion in the lives of ordinary believers.[33] When I use the term "Christian athlete," I am referring to an evangelical athlete involved in a sports ministry organization, which is an organization that actively promotes combining sport and evangelicalism. I use the term "elite athlete" or "elite sports" to distinguish between the recreational athlete and the athlete pursuing sport as a primary career. In this book, I consider Division I college, semiprofessional, and professional levels to be elite sports. Participation in elite sports is limited, and those who compete at this level are expected to consistently prove that they are qualified to do so. This book is not about church softball leagues, though participants at that level could also be called Christian athletes. The athletes and coaches featured in this book perceived their athletic activity as a religious obligation, an understanding that intertwines evangelical Christianity and sport. For them, sports were a way to connect with the divine, and therefore they understood their athletic experiences as religiously meaningful.

Knowing God through Sports

When anthropologist Susan Harding studied fundamentalist Baptists in the 1980s, she came to the conclusion that "speaking is believing."[34] By this, she meant that her subjects used linguistic practices like witnessing to experience their faith and strengthen their beliefs. She argued that the act of speaking one's beliefs out loud to an outsider was not merely about convincing the nonbeliever; the practice of witnessing also solidified beliefs for the speaker. In this way, the ideas that the believer put into words (the sinfulness of humanity, God's love for humans, and heartfelt belief in Jesus Christ as a means to experience that love and salvation) became more than beliefs; they became knowledge. This insight is help-ful because this book addresses the development and implications of religious knowledge within sports ministry.[35]

One significant difference between Harding's subjects and mine is that the conservative Christians in this book are athletes, and they see their athletic life as compatible with—even essential to—their religious life. Starting with Harding's argument that speaking gives a believer con-fidence in the validity of his or her beliefs, the question for this book becomes: How do Christian athletes, whose primary activity is not speaking but playing, experience what Harding calls "belief that indis-putably transfigures you and your reality, belief that becomes you"?[36] How do they experience the sort of belief that they find indisputable, belief that they can use as their linchpin for making sense of the world?

I argue that Christian athletes experience transfiguring belief through sport itself. The embodied actions of training, practicing, and compet-ing serve to anchor and strengthen Christian athletes' certainty of the distinctiveness of their religious tradition, the existence of an all-loving God with a perfect plan and an evil counterpart that desires human fail-ure, and their ability to experience a connection with the divine. Part I of this book presents a thorough exploration of how using sport in this way had the unintended consequences of undermining traditional witness-ing strategies and elevating individual religious experience as the most important aspect of sport.

Chapter 1 examines conversion and witnessing as primary evangeli-cal practices. I briefly turn to the history of sports ministry to illustrate how these practices have changed over time, and I use my fieldwork to show how contemporary sports ministry has expanded the work of witnessing and the practice of conversion. Contemporary sports minis-try relies on "witnessing without words" (demonstrating one's salvation through good sportsmanship rather than testimony) and recommitment (confirming one's decision to convert by reenacting a conversion mo-ment), and these elements destabilize the membrane between evangeli-cal insiders and outsiders. After all, the unsaved can be sportsmanlike, and recommitment seems to undermine the once-and-for-all rhetoric of evangelical salvation. I describe how Christian athletes struggle to redefine witnessing and recommitment in ways that maintain their un-derstandings of evangelical distinction and moral superiority.

While witnessing remains a primary goal for the leadership of sports ministry organizations, sports ministry participants have become much more likely to frame their goals as experiential. Innovations in sports ministry in the 1970s allowed Christian athletes to elevate individual religious experiences over numerical witnessing goals. While sports ministers originally privileged athletes' witnessing because athletes had access to large audiences, contemporary Christian athletes are more likely to think of their circumstances as special because of the intimate physical pleasure they experience through sport. Focusing on athletic activity as pleasing to God in itself paved the way for some Christian athletes to reexamine evangelical orthodoxy on witnessing and to use their embodied sensations to rethink what kinds of behaviors and mindsets constitute serving God. Chapter 2 turns to athletic intimacy to investigate the embodied knowledge that Christian athletes can develop through sport.

As individual religious experiences became a normative element of sports ministry training, the language of Christlikeness and spiritual warfare became central. Many evangelicals describe the devil as a real force for evil, and chapter 3 turns to Christian athletic understandings of the world as a never-ending battle between God and Satan enacted through athletes on the playing field. Christian athletes strive for Christlikeness as a way to defend themselves against the temptations of Satan; they see fatigue, frustration, and soreness as Satan's tools to weaken the athlete, who in turn uses the Christlike qualities of determination and meaningful suffering to avoid unsportsmanlike behavior or other wrongdoing. Though pain and injury would seem to undermine God's care for the athlete, Christian athletes narrate these as evidence of God's involvement in athletic life and present athletic setbacks as instances of God trying to tell them something. The ubiquity of this language shows that these narrative tools constitute important methods that Christian athletes use to make sense of their lives.

The Christian athletes in this book very rarely used the phrase "I believe" unless they were talking to nonbelievers. To each other, they would say, "I know." Take, for example, Dana's narrative that opened this chapter. She said, "I felt a great distance between me and God. I know that he doesn't go anywhere, that he doesn't change, so I knew it was my fault." This is a statement not of belief but of knowledge, of shared knowledge. When Dana said, "I know that he doesn't go anywhere," she implied, "I know that *we all know* that he doesn't go anywhere." This statement referred to the shared knowledge base that Dana used to draw her conclusion, "so I knew it was my fault." To be a believer means to enter into this shared knowledge community and to use that established knowledge to draw conclusions about how one should conduct oneself in the world. Part II of this book is about that process, the process of living out the implications of one's religious knowledge. As such, this book responds to two epistemological questions. Part I explores the question, how do Christian athletes know what they know? And part II asks, what are the effects of that knowledge?

In addition to being a stronger noun than "belief," "knowledge" carries another set of connotations that are applicable to this study. The verb "to know" is used in some biblical translations to signify sexual relations, hence the colloquialism "to know in the biblical sense." This set of connotations is valuable to keep in mind. The athletes in this book used their bodies, not their words, as the primary element of their Christian identity. As part I of this book shows, sports ministry's focus on the body created a sense of intimacy with God, what my subjects referred to as "oneness," "connection," or "Christlikeness." They gained knowledge of God through their bodies, and because the body was the site of this knowledge, the implications explored in part II are implications that directly relate to bodies: gender and sexuality.

Evangelical female athletes are enmeshed in a theological worldview that emphasizes inherent gender differences between men and women. But at the same time, they are aware that playing sports is in itself a challenge to long-standing gendered descriptions of women as passive, weak, or delicate. Within sports ministry, evangelical women have, over the course of the past generation, expanded godly femininity to include strength, action, and leadership, while maintaining a sense of the importance of traditional feminine nurturing. As chapter 4 shows, these athletes employ different self-display choices in different contexts, revealing femininity as a social construct requiring ongoing performance. They also work very hard to maintain a sense of essential gender difference, and this contradiction has opened a space for evangelical female athletes to reflect on their religious tradition's expectations regarding women's bodies.

Chapter 5 investigates the tension between homosocial sporting environments and evangelical orthodoxy regarding homosexuality. Evangelicals have long been proponents of sex-segregated environments for religious education, and sport mirrors this separation. However, combining religious and athletic homosocial spaces brings attention to the body while condemning sexual attention in general and homosexuality in particular.[37] Evangelical condemnation of homosexuality stems from the idea that God intends heterosexual love and marriage for every believer and that God has the power to alter a person's sexual desires to bring believers into alignment with this plan. For women in sports ministry, many of whom have had positive interactions with out lesbians or have known evangelical women who experience same-sex attraction, the issue of human sexuality is complicated and has fostered feelings of extreme ambivalence as they attempt to reconcile evangelical orthodoxy on God's power and plan with their own athletic lives.

Chapter 6 explores marriage as an unstated evangelical requirement. Evangelical Christians have developed a substantial literature on marriage roles and gendered behavior in the household. Much of this literature promotes traditional gender hierarchy as God's intention for a Christian marriage. I explore how Christian athletes negotiate evangelical marriage practices while maintaining an athletic career and how they use their experiences as athletes to reflect on, reinterpret, and ultimately expand orthodoxy regarding marriage roles. This chapter returns to a major theme of the book: Christian athletes use the forms of knowledge they develop through sports ministry to redefine and renegotiate other aspects of their lives.

Sports ministry's focus on witnessing, individual religious experience, and the discourses of spiritual warfare and Christlikeness can produce an intimate knowledge of what it means to be a Christian athlete. This intimate embodied knowledge has allowed female Christian athletes to engage and modify orthodoxy by redefining godly femininity, increasingly accepting lesbianism, and renegotiating marriage expectations. These unintended consequences show that religious engagement with popular culture can produce new religious tools that do the very real work of maintaining religious belief, but not always in predictable ways.

PART I

Knowledge

1

Making the Save

Conversion and Witnessing

"You are afraid. You are afraid of what God can do with your life," Andrew scolded me, clearly frustrated. We had been sitting and talking over an open Bible for nearly two hours. It was my second day of fieldwork at a Fellowship of Christian Athletes summer camp for high school athletes in Forest Grove, Oregon. Andrew was the weight-training coach and worked with each of the athletic groups on weight lifting and conditioning skills. That morning, I had joined the track team for his training session, and he included exercises meant to be specifically helpful for me. Andrew was a patient weight room instructor and worked individually with each athlete, giving the men and women equal attention and spending time with me, a visitor and not an athlete, on proper form and execution.

He impressed me. He was confident, respected, and hardworking. He worked with professional football and soccer players, yet treated fifteen-year-old cross-country runners as if their training was just as important. I watched the athletes respond to his instruction, push themselves, and feel pleased when he thought they had done well. I felt this myself as I struggled to complete the push-ups and pull-ups along with the track athletes. And when he told me, "Good job," I couldn't help but glow with self-satisfaction. So, when Andrew found me in the cafeteria and said, "I'd like to talk to you about your project," I was flattered and immediately sat down. Two hours later, we had discussed the meaning of Jesus's resurrection, the problem of evil, and the evangelical definition of salvation. For Andrew and evangelicals like him, the Old Testament is a long prediction of Jesus's coming, and the New Testament is evidence of God's love and perfect plan for all humans. He painstakingly walked me through connecting verses, openly anticipating that "Aha!" moment when I would finally realize that this applied to me.

Andrew and other camp leaders treated the Bible as the absolute authority. Campers carried their FCA-issued Bible, emblazoned with the title "God's Game Plan," everywhere with them. Each night at camp meeting, the camp director called out the names of the campers who had left their Bibles behind and brought them to the stage to perform "I'm a Little Teapot" or some equally embarrassing and humorous feat. I wasn't surprised that Andrew employed the Bible as evidence for his claims—God loves you, has a wonderful plan for your life, and sent Jesus so you could experience salvation and eternal life. I was surprised at his intensity, persistence, and growing frustration. In the weight room, I responded to his instruction easily and without question, but during this conversation, I was resistant.

"But, how can you explain suffering in the world if God loves people and has a wonderful plan for their lives?" I asked.

He replied, "Suffering comes from man, not from God."

"But, what about suffering that doesn't come from humans, like hurricanes and natural disasters?"

"Look, sometimes God allows bad things to happen, but he does this for a reason." Andrew was growing increasingly frustrated with my inability to comprehend this point. "Let me ask you a question," he continued. "If your life was perfect, would you be looking for God?"

"So, God uses suffering to communicate with people?"

"That's right. You need to recognize that you need God before you will look for him."

I told Andrew that I remained skeptical, but I appreciated his taking the time to explain this to me.

He sighed, exasperated with my failure to accept this instruction. "I'm not talking to you right now for my own benefit; this is for you. I hope that I'm planting a seed in you that will grow. What you do with what we talked about tonight has eternal consequences."

As I closed the Bible in front of me and we stood to walk to the camp meeting, I felt shaky. Andrew had dealt with my hard questions deftly and with great confidence. Also, I had great respect for him after our morning weight-lifting session and wanted him to respect me. I felt like I had let him down.

My conversation with Andrew remained on my mind as I continued my fieldwork with evangelical athletes over the next year and a half.

Other athletes also told me that God uses suffering to reach out to humans, and this helped them explain injuries, loss, and athletic setbacks. And Andrew's description of witnessing (telling others about the evangelical Christian idea of salvation) as planting seeds was by far the most prevalent metaphor that I encountered. However, one reason my conversation with Andrew stuck out was because it was comparatively rare. I had expected to constantly experience witnessing given the fieldwork I had planned. But conversations like the one recounted here occurred only a handful times over the course of my fieldwork, and this was the only conversation directed individually at me and framed in terms of my personal salvation.

Witnessing and conversion are two primary, defining characteristics of evangelical Christianity. Believers can often identify a conversion moment when they first made a decision to openly profess their faith and live differently. Following conversion, evangelical leaders encourage new believers to become witnesses, to tell others of their conversion and specifically about how their lives changed after professing faith in Jesus Christ. While these practices are common in evangelical Christianity as a whole, in sports ministry, witnessing and conversion take on a slightly different tone. As sports minister Greg Linville put it in a published resource for Christian athletic organizations, "The profound truth is that if a true conversion is desired, rather than just a decision, a sports ministry that keeps a person engaged over the years may be better than a one-time evangelistic event and should be pursued by any church desiring long-term substantial growth."[1] Sports ministers like Linville take a longer view of conversion, downplaying the importance of first-time commitments in favor of spiritual development over time.

Through examining the history of sports ministry and its contemporary practices, we can see that conversion and witnessing are not static, but open-ended and various. Conversion is often followed by recommitment, and witnessing is no longer a predominantly verbal practice. The blurry edges to these concepts represent a significant struggle within sports ministry as believers who feel compelled to witness can have substantial difficulty determining if their witnessing strategies are effective. Athletes are used to measurable, quantifiable goals, and the blurriness of conversion and witnessing has fostered dialogue about how to maintain belief in the distinctiveness of evangelical Christianity and the superiority of one's own morality, as well as how to effectively convey one's beliefs and morality to outsiders.

Andrew's approach to witnessing—direct confrontation through conversation—has declined in favor of what many Christian athletes call "witnessing without words." Today's Christian athletes see conversational witnessing as minimally effective and describe their primary method as behavior based—convincing others of the veracity of their beliefs through exemplary comportment on and off the field.[2] This change in witnessing strategies emerged from the Christian athletic encounter with what I call "the problem of winning." In order for Christian athletes to attract an audience to listen to their message of salvation, the athletes have to win; the losing team is much less likely to draw an audience. The pressure to win creates a moral dilemma as Christian athletes struggle with how to behave on the field—should they do everything possible to win, including bending the rules, or should they try to be models of sportsmanship even if this means losing? The problem of winning is, at its heart, a question of how to witness and reflects the core struggle of combining evangelical Christianity and sport.

Performing Salvation: Conversion as a Formative Evangelical Experience

The day after my cafeteria conversation with Andrew, I spoke with the camp director, Sean. Sean was a man in his early thirties. He and his wife had a two-year-old son who was with them at camp with a broken leg. It was common to hear Sean refer to his son's wheelchair as a "race car," and he generally impressed those at camp as a good father and a good role model. Sean's approach to conversion differed from Andrew's. For Sean, the Bible and logical reasoning were not effective means of convincing a nonbeliever. He told me, "I want to make God real for these kids, and the way to do that is through the things that are important to them, like sport. Tonight's the altar call, and I tell you, I don't really care how many kids raise their hands, how many kids make commitments. I'm just interested in taking them one step closer."

An altar call is an evangelical practice in which a minister or a lay religious leader invites members of an audience to come forward to the front of the crowd. The action of walking to the front of the gathering is a public display that one is becoming "saved"; the audience member who walks forward is making a commitment to Jesus Christ and to the beliefs of evangelical Christianity. When Sean referenced kids "raising their hands" or "making commitments," he was talking about this evangelical practice of publicly identifying oneself as a new believer. Like many sports ministers, Sean saw sport as a way to connect with nonbelievers, and he was dedicated to the power of sports ministry to convey primary evangelical teachings like the importance of conversion.[3] Though Sean de-emphasized decisional commitment ("I don't really care how many kids raise their hands"), he was still firmly invested in a conversion model. The unspoken ending to his sentence would be, "I'm just interested in taking them one step closer [to conversion]."

Sean attributed his understanding of the primary tasks of sports ministry to the book *Focus on Sport in Ministry* by Lowrie McCown and Valerie Gin. According to McCown and Gin, every person can be placed along a spiritual continuum, from -10, indicating no belief in God, to 0 or X, indicating a change of allegiance from nonbelief to belief, to +10, an ideal state of Christlikeness. According to their description, "A person described by a '-3' has a positive attitude toward Christ, but as yet has made no commitment to follow Him. Further up the axis, . . . an individual at the 'X' acknowledges that Christ is the way to Life and makes a radical change of allegiance from living for himself to living for Christ. This is the midpoint of the continuum."[4] McCown and Gin present this spiritual continuum as a theory with significant implications for sports ministry:

> The vast majority of sports ministry groups today, however, do not see evangelism as a process. They instead focus on the middle portion of the continuum, with particular emphasis on the point of conversion. But if the focus is solely on that single point of conversion, the "X," we may not fully see what we are doing as effective ministry. In practice, we evaluate ministries based on the number of conversions, the number of people who have come to Christ. We believe that if attendees at a sports camp have walked an aisle, prayed a prayer to accept Jesus, or raised a hand, we can now determine whether they have made a commitment to Christ. Our typical standard of evaluation is based on numbers and logic. Of course, it is much easier to measure someone reaching the point of con-

version than it is to measure someone moving up from a "-5" to a "-3" on the continuum. Nevertheless, it is very possible to have an effective ministry that may never see people come to Christ at the "X" point yet is still helping them journey from a "-10" to a "-8" or from a "-5" to a "-3."[5]

So, when Sean told me he wasn't interested in how many kids raised their hands or committed, but he was interested in moving them one step closer, he was invoking McCown and Gin's spiritual continuum as a measure of successful evangelism rather than a traditional measure of counting commitments.

The conversion experience itself was not as important to Sean as sports ministry's ability to set up opportunities for kids to see God as real. He explained:

> I just want people to be real. Being a Christian isn't easy. Jesus promised us hard times. I mean, any logical proof I give you for God, you can poke holes in. But then, you don't want to be able to put your thumb on God, because that would mean that God isn't very big. If you can feel that God is real, I mean really feel it, then you just know that he has a plan for you and that you are important in his eyes.

For Sean, feelings could serve as evidence that God is real and cares for humans. While these feelings may emerge in an altar call situation, he saw other situations as equally effective in moving people along their spiritual continuum. Playing sports, the ups and downs of winning and losing, could give rise to the feeling of a greater power at work, and through sports ministry, those feelings could translate into knowledge of God's reality and power.

"It's a generational thing. People my age and younger don't care about the altar call nearly so much anymore," Sean said.[6] That night, however, the altar call proved to be one of the most significant moments of camp. Even though Sean, McCown and Gin, and others downplayed the importance of conversion in favor of a continuum approach, conversion remained central to the self-identity of evangelicals at camp. We gathered that evening for the camp meeting, and the worship band opened the gathering with praise songs. There were the daily activities of embarrassing campers who had left their Bibles in the cafeteria or on the field.

Some of the college athletes, the leaders of small groups called "huddles," performed a skit based on the *Rocky* movies. Then, Jeff, one of the college athletes, read an emotionally moving poem about his mother dying of cancer. Much of the room was in tears as he broke down during his reading, and the applause that followed was thunderous.

As Jeff walked off to a flurry of hugs and handshakes, an obese man in a baseball jersey took the stage as the night's main speaker. He began with comical stories about his family, leading to a lesson that God, like a father, provides rules to protect his children. According to the speaker, these rules exist not because God is mean or unfair, but because God has a strong desire to help you live in the best possible way. The speaker held up the Bible and proclaimed it "a guide so you'll never be destroyed," invoking God as a benevolent rule provider. Because of this emphasis on rules, guides, and destruction, the speaker was able to present conversion as a weighty undertaking with serious consequences. He described a personal relationship with Jesus Christ as part of spiritual warfare—fail to convert and you go to hell, convert or recommit and you are signing up for a lifetime of struggle against the tactics of the devil. He told the campers that being a Christian is not easy, but it is incredibly important:

> Lindsay Lohan, Paris Hilton—they don't have full and lasting lives. When Peter was walking on the water toward Jesus and he took his eyes off Jesus, Jesus didn't let him drown. He helped him up. Jesus never came to judge. He came to set you straight. If you have a cold, NyQuil can take care of the symptoms. But, we're not talking about outward symptoms. We're talking about your heart. Are you prepared to meet Jesus today?

I glanced over and saw the lead singer of the worship band praying at the side of the stage with his eyes closed and palms outstretched. He was smiling, and I imagined that he was looking forward to what would happen next.

"Right now, you are facing danger," the speaker continued. "Every coach will tell you that you are facing danger. This is a jump for eternity—hell waits for those who fail to believe in Jesus when he is introduced." He told the audience members to close their eyes and called for a raising of hands. "How many of you have a desire to know him?" he called out. The majority of campers raised their hands, and the huddle leaders gathered at the foot of the stage as the speaker invited campers making first-time commitments to approach. "Heaven is cheering you on right now!" he said.

Approximately twelve of the eighty or so campers walked to the foot of the stage to meet their huddle leaders. As the huddle leaders embraced these new converts, the speaker called for those wishing to recommit their lives to Jesus, and nearly everyone responded. As I watched from my fifth-row vantage point, almost the entire population of the camp gathered at the front of the stage. Campers formed circles with their huddle leaders and tearfully prayed for new converts and for their own recommitments. The band returned to the stage, and music swelled over the scene—groups of campers crying and praying. The room felt emotionally charged as campers responded physically to the experience—hugging, laying on hands, lifting hands, calling out.

These gestures demonstrated their emotional state, and they later narrated these emotions as embodied knowledge of God's active involvement in the altar call. They used phrases like "God moved my heart" and "I felt the Spirit inside me." This kind of description linked their bodily sensations to certainty of God's presence. Just as Sean described earlier, feelings and sensations transformed into indisputable knowledge through the practices of sports ministry.

The idea that embodied sensation can contribute to religious certainty is not new.[7] Émile Durkheim's seminal work *The Elementary Forms of Religious Life* notes this relationship, arguing that the physical activities of a ritual are a shared communal experience that strengthens a community's and an individual's sense of identity. He wrote, "Thus a rite is something other than a game; it belongs to the serious side of life."[8] The FCA camp relied on this understanding. Though the ritual of the altar call was embedded in a context of sporting games, the event belonged to the serious side of life for those who committed or recommitted that evening.

The following day, campers and huddle leaders continued to describe the night's intensity as evidence of the existence and emotional investment of God: "I just know that God was there and was working with all of us. It was like there was a celebration in heaven and we could feel it." One huddle leader said, "Real. I just know God was real." For Christians at the camp, the emotional and physical experience of the altar call served to cement God's reality and presence. Feelings were evidence for the existence of God, God's interaction with individuals, and God's plan for humans, and Christians at camp identified these precepts not as "beliefs" but as "knowledge."

One striking facet of the altar call was the prevalence of recommitments and the relatively small number of first-time commitments. Part of the explanation for the small number of first-time commitments was the camp itself: athletes drawn to evangelical sports camps are likely to be familiar with evangelical traditions like altar calls and therefore likely to have already made first-time commitments. For example, I spent significant time with the volleyball huddle while at camp, and the seven high school girls in the huddle had made public commitments at altar calls previously, and all of them walked forward to demonstrate recommitment.

Conversion experiences are central to evangelical theology; evangelicals understand the declarative conversion moment as the first stage in establishing a personal relationship with Jesus Christ. The altar call activity of FCA camp—with campers standing and walking to be physically close to their huddle leaders—gave commitment and recommitment an emotional and physical density, and the physical performance made the commitment public. This sort of physical ritual fit easily at an evangelical sports camp where the camper-athletes already understood physical action as an integral part of their identity. Recommitment was a double acknowledgment of one's own conversion and of the importance of conversion in general. It is performative in the sense that religious studies scholar Catherine Bell describes performance as "a type of event in which the very activity of the agent or artist is the most critical dimension and not the completion of the action."[9] In this context, this means that the action of recommitment is more important than the outcome of salvation because, after all, salvation was marked at one's first-time commitment. Recommitting reenacts that salvific moment and allows the believer to access the feelings and sensations of becoming saved. This is one way that believers continue to know that God is real; they have opportunities to refresh the emotions that guided their certainty in the first place.

Following the highly emotional altar call, the volleyball huddle gathered in the room of one of their huddle leaders, Becky, for a late-night conversation. With recommitment on their minds, campers began to tearfully confess hardships and struggles that had made them doubt God. One camper described her frustration with failing to make a club team she had tried out for. "I tried to ignore God and go it alone, tried to make myself happy. But I wasn't happy. I doubted him really until tonight." The other girls expressed empathy both with not making the team and with doubting God. Another camper told the group how her mother had been diagnosed with breast cancer the previous year. "It was really hard on me. But I just know that God has a plan because my mom survived even though Jeff's didn't." Almost everyone in the room was crying at this point. Another camper told of her experience on her high school's dance team. "I've been really struggling with comparing my body to other girls and feeling insecure. Also, I've been dating this guy who's not a Christian. I mean, he goes to church, but," she shook her head, "you can just tell about people. At first, I was really clear about setting boundaries, but I let up over the course of the year and ended up going way further than I wanted to. Now, I know that wasn't right and I have to do something about it."

These confessions reveal a range of concerns that the girls saw as obstructions in their relationship with God and obstructions to their certainty of God's reality and power. Campers construed experiences as trivial or as serious as not making a team to being diagnosed with cancer to dating as challenges to faith and understood that evening's recommitment as a remedy to heal their relationship with God. Their readiness to admit a sense of distance from God and even a sense of doubt regarding God's existence and intentions reflects anthropologist Susan Harding's findings in her study of fundamentalist Baptists. According to Harding, "The membrane between disbelief and belief is much thinner than we think. . . . Believers and disbelievers assert there is no middle ground: you are either one or the other. You cannot both believe and disbelieve. But that is precisely what it means to be 'under conviction.'"[10] The Baptists whom Harding studied used the phrase "under conviction" to describe a relationship with God that needed to be improved. They felt "convicted" about a behavior or a feeling and sought to resolve this in order to reconnect with God. Given Harding's analysis, a Baptist under conviction might tell a very similar story to the girls in the FCA volleyball huddle—something happened in my life that drew me away from

God, but now I realize that, and I am recommitting so that I can be close to God again.

Recommitment does the religious work of confirming an evangelical belief structure wherein salvation is a matter of personal choice, and that choice informs all other aspects of an evangelical's life. Recommitment may in fact be a more important ritual than conversion; recommitment underscores one's identity as saved while at the same time opening space for confessions and resolutions of doubt and struggle. Sean, the camp director, may be able to use McCown and Gin's spiritual continuum theory to acknowledge that people do not just move from farther away from to closer to Christ; they might shift in the other direction as well. In this way, conversion is not as cut-and-dry as that night's speaker had made it seem when he said that conversion was a choice for all eternity.

For the majority of these campers, altar calls were comparatively rare experiences, and they often described summer camp as a "mountaintop experience," a singular and special occasion very different from daily life. How, then, can believers sustain faith in their salvation when they leave the mountaintop? How can they maintain the core evangelical belief that conversion is the most important choice that humans can make and that all humans who fail to make this choice are damned? How can they continue to know God? One answer is witnessing, telling others about one's own conversion with the hopes of convincing them to commit their lives to Jesus.

Speaking Salvation: The Injunction to Witness

Witnessing has a long history within the Protestant tradition, but for contemporary evangelical Christianity, the most relevant historical development occurred in the 1950s with the mass production of witnessing materials on a previously unimaginable scale.[11] In 1951 on the campus of UCLA, Bill Bright, inspired by Youth for Christ, began Campus Crusade for Christ (now called Cru in the United States).[12] Bright defined his ministry as "aggressive evangelism." This was different than "friendly evangelism," a tool used by other evangelistic groups to gain the trust and respect of a colleague before sharing the gospel. Aggressive evangelism prioritized the proclamation of belief and the story of one's conversion as the first pieces of information that Christians should share about themselves. In order to assist his organization's members in this task, Bright developed a twenty-minute presentation for staff to memorize called "God's Plan for Your Life." According to ministry scholar Richard Quebedeaux, "As far as Bill was concerned, this how-to-do-it approach worked, and it became the model for almost all subsequent evangelistic and training materials published by the movement. It was pragmatic."[13] It also reflected the prevailing economic strategy of mass production and mass consumption.[14] Bright was tuned into this economic logic and saw evangelical Christianity as a marketable product. In fact, Bright was inspired to clarify his "pitch" after hearing a sales professional speak at a ministry staff conference in 1956.[15]

Bright created a mass-producible and mass-consumable version of the gospel, first in the form of a memorized verbal speech, and later in print materials. He developed a condensed version of "God's Plan for Your Life" in a booklet called *Have You Heard of the Four Spiritual Laws?* (1965), and the organization states that this is the most widely distributed religious booklet in history, with 2.5 billion copies printed to date.[16] To paraphrase, the four spiritual laws are (1) God loves you and has a wonderful plan for your life, (2) humans are sinful and are separated from God, (3) Jesus Christ is God's only provision to connect with God, and (4) in order to connect with God personally and be assured of eternal life in heaven, one must accept Jesus Christ as Lord and Savior. This can be accomplished by reading "The Sinner's Prayer," which is included at the end of the pamphlet.[17] A variety of evangelical organizations use the four spiritual laws today, often referring to them as a simple gospel message.[18]

The genius of *Have You Heard of the Four Spiritual Laws?* is its high degree of portability and simplicity, making it a prime example of standardization and mass production. The booklet treats salvation as a step-by-step process that can and should be the same for everyone. According to religious studies scholar David Harrington Watt, the booklet "reveals popular evangelicalism's close ties to the advertising ethos of American commercial culture and its emphasis on the this-worldly rewards of Christianity."[19] John Turner's work on Bill Bright emphasizes the impact of contemporary media on Bright's evangelical plan, noting that *Have You Heard of the Four Spiritual Laws?* may have been successful because "perhaps in the era of television, a brief advertisement for Jesus closed an evangelistic sale better than a wordy discourse."[20] Witnessing is a practice centered on conversion, on encouraging another to make a decision to become a Christian, and the language of decision making brings together conversion and consumption. Bright and others perceived evangelical Christianity as a product on the market and turned to successful production and advertising strategies to refine witnessing.

Sports ministry emerged shortly after Bill Bright's evangelical innovations, and the influence of advertising techniques is clear in sports ministry founders' descriptions of their projects. Don McClanen's idea for the Fellowship of Christian Athletes in 1954 was born of celebrity sales power and the standardization of the gospel message. He wrote letters to a number of athletes whom he knew to be Christian to recruit them for his new organization. He told them, "If athletes can endorse shaving cream, razor blades, and cigarettes, surely they can endorse the Lord, too. So my idea is to form an organization that would project you as Christian men before the youth and athletes of this nation."[21] This letter-writing campaign highlights two important assumptions McClanen made. First, he imagined the gospel as a product to be consumed by the public. Second, he saw a need to present Christianity as masculine by relying on male athletic spokespeople. Early sports ministry targeted and recruited men by presenting a masculine side to religious devotion.[22]

While combining athletics and masculinity was not new, what was new was the conflation of religious outreach and salesmanship.[23] In the mid-1960s, Dave Hannah, founder of Athletes in Action, employed advertising and celebrity endorsement language in his vision for an athletic branch of Campus Crusade for Christ. As Joe Smalley recounts in his history of AIA:

> The idea for the project came to Hannah one day as he watched a Campus Crusade music group share an evangelistic message through its performance. Hannah thought out loud, "Why couldn't an athletic team be used in the same way? Athletes are used to sell everything from candy bars to cars. Why not have them tell about something far greater—the message of Jesus Christ?"[24]

Sports ministry founders Hannah and McClanen noticed the rise of athletic endorsements in the television industry and envisioned using America's hero worship of athletes to further an evangelical agenda.

The 1950s postwar economic boom and the advertising power of television foregrounded buying and selling. This allowed religious leaders like Bright, Hannah, and McClanen to envision evangelical Christianity as a product on the market that would benefit from celebrity endorsement. According to advertising theorist Pamela Odih, the advertising strategies of the time "invited consumers to constitute their identities through the purchase of products whose stories and images echo historically specific grand narratives."[25] The use of sporting celebrity to sell products gestured to the grand narratives of capitalism, including "competition, achievement, efficiency, technology, and meritocracy."[26] As sport and culture theorists continually point out, sport constitutes a cultural nexus that reflects the economic values of production and consumption while, at the same time, emphasizing individual achievement and physical excellence. According to Barry Smart, for example, "A culture of individualism places emphasis on personal effort, achievement, toughness, and strength. . . . The institution of modern sport is a culturally significant repository for these values, an institutional setting in which such values are continually reaffirmed and accorded popular acclaim."[27] Sport appealed to evangelicals because sporting celebrities were icons of masculinity with incredible sales power. McClanen and Hannah recruited these men to be witnesses, and over time, their organizations and sports ministry as a whole developed pedagogical tools to make athletes into effective witnesses.

As the following story illustrates, contemporary sports ministry continues to include training on how to witness. Midafternoon on the first day of their team retreat, the Charlotte Lady Eagles gathered around an unlit fire pit to listen to Amanda explain how to know God personally. The semiprofessional Christian soccer players had heard this message before. Many of them had been raised in Christian families and had played or coached for Christian colleges, and all of them were spending their summer playing for an evangelical soccer team. Despite their familiarity with the message, they listened closely to Amanda, a veteran goalkeeper and model evangelist.

Amanda began, "How do you know God? Through accepting Jesus." She emphasized that this acceptance of Jesus was a starting point, and thereafter Christians should continue to grow in their faith and in their knowledge of God's power:

God is asking you to believe and to trust him. The Bible helps build your trust. I accepted Christ when I was six, but at fifteen, I really opened to the Word. It's a constant process, but the first thing you have to do is accept Christ into your heart. Think about when you decided, I want to be a soccer player. That was a choice, and that choice means choosing to practice and be surrounded by other players. When you reflect on how far you've come since you first made that decision . . . God knocks on your heart and we have to open the door. If you say to him, "You've got to show me," I promise you, he will. Just like you didn't see the benefit of those foundation moves at first, but now you know that they helped you grow in your sport.

Amanda's parallel between advancing one's knowledge of sport and advancing one's knowledge of Christianity holds in more ways than one. Amanda framed her story this way to demonstrate to a group of elite athletes the extent of change that was possible after converting to evangelical Christianity. This comparison worked in this context because her audience had made definite decisions to be soccer players and dedicated vast amounts of time and energy to pursuing soccer careers. However, Amanda's comparison also referenced a similarity in *how* one gains knowledge of soccer and how one gains knowledge of God—through practice.

During the summer I spent with the team, the Charlotte Lady Eagles attended sports ministry training twice a week to learn about and discuss various aspects of life as Christian athletes. Sports ministry training taught the Lady Eagles to support their beliefs with Bible verses, to formulate their own testimony, and to understand their sporting identity as an extension of their Christian identity. One of the most important components of this training was witnessing, which Amanda and others called "telling your story." A believer's story is a narrative that tells of life before converting to Christianity, the experience of accepting Jesus, and what life was like afterward. Within the context of the Lady Eagles, it was fully appropriate for one player to ask another, "How did you come to know the Lord?" In fact, players used this as an icebreaker when getting to know each other.

Delivering one's testimony is a learned and constructed activity that follows particular rules. Amanda led a sports ministry training session on how to construct a testimony after the team had returned from retreat. She first defined testimony as "how the gospel changed your life." She then asked the team to brainstorm in small groups about other definitions of "testimony." One player, Lex, said, "It's obviously about how God worked in your life, and it's to give him glory for how he's changed you." Lex's explanation points to the centrality of change within the narrative and the speaker's obligation to convey the importance of God's role in this change.

Amanda then defined a courtroom testimony as "a statement by a witness to prove that something is true." She said, "We use our testimony to prove that Christ is true." She drew a large V on the board and labeled the far left side with her birth date, labeled the bottom of the V with "90 years," and left the right side blank. According to Amanda, the V represented a time line of a person's life extended beyond death. She told the group, "Somewhere on there, you made a decision to walk with Christ. Draw a line and put a dot there." She turned to face the group, "If you haven't made that decision, use today's date. If you're not sure, we can make that official today, if you want." She turned back to the board, "When you understand what happened to you before you accepted Christ, you can make it tangible to the gospel." By this, Amanda meant that believers must recognize the changes in their lives following their acceptance of Jesus. These changes then become evidence of God's involvement in their lives.

Amanda gave the players a handout entitled "My Story." It was divided into three sections for the players to complete: "Before Jesus," "The Transition," and "With Jesus." Amanda encouraged her teammates to understand their lives according to this format. She concluded her lesson by telling the group, "We're always going to be attacked by Satan. As life continues and you move to a new place—for example, graduating from college—and you look back on your awesome years as a college athlete; now is a time of seeking. Having Christ will give you that path. You do have a testimony, but you will continue to have testimonies. We have to incorporate the gospel in order to evangelize. It's important to understand the gospel in its fullness in order to create your testimony."

For evangelical Christians like Amanda, the gospel is the single most important piece of information in the Christian faith. They credit sincere belief in the resurrection of Jesus with the ability to change people, and those with the most authority in the Lady Eagles' community were those most practiced at delivering the gospel message and chronicling changes in their own lives. Because this was an athletic community, the majority of changes that players discussed were changes in athletic or on-field behavior: giving up swearing, no longer feeling a desire to retaliate, becoming accepting of injury or loss, or being able to play through fatigue or soreness. Players verbalized these changes, and some were expert at telling the story of how their athletic lives changed with conversion. Telling and retelling these stories reinforced knowledge of God's reality and power, evidenced with changes in their athletic lives.

The Lady Eagles primarily told these stories to each other, not to opposing teams or to audiences gathered at their games. Telling these narratives within the group was practice for sharing these stories with nonbelievers. Witnessing to each other was a way to gain confidence for future interactions with outsiders in much the same way that practicing passing and scoring was a way to gain confidence for future interactions in games. In telling and retelling their stories to each other, these Christian athletes developed a robustness of belief, confirming their commitment with each retelling.

During the summer I spent with the Lady Eagles, I saw relatively little witnessing to outsiders. One player, Tess, worked at Starbucks and would usually have a Christian book with her to read if it was slow during her shift. She hoped her coworkers would ask about it so she could have a conversation with them about Christianity. "But, I try to be really cautious," she told me, "because you don't want to be like, 'Have you heard about the love of Jesus Christ?' That's a turn-off." Tess's statement reflects a larger shift within evangelical Christianity away from the aggressive evangelism practices that Bill Bright promoted in the 1950s and 1960s. While Evangelical Christianity relies on witnessing for experiencing belief and for maintaining the centrality of conversion, in sports ministry, athletes no longer think of witnessing as a solely verbal practice. Sports ministry organizations have turned to "witnessing without words" to emphasize physical behaviors as their primary evidence of self-change and the power of God.

Displaying Salvation: Witnessing without Words

When Athletes in Action first formed traveling teams in the 1960s, their focus was a halftime gospel message delivered by team members. As a branch of Campus Crusade for Christ, AIA considered sharing the four spiritual laws an important part of these presentations. As time went by, host institutions progressively marginalized this practice. Over the course of the 1990s, AIA's testimony was pushed to the edges of the game and the court; host institutions moved AIA's presentation from halftime to postgame and from center court to the end zone or to a small room nearby, and at most games today, the AIA players are not allowed to witness at all. The athletes do, however, pass out programs containing team testimonies to the audience. According to an AIA basketball staff member, "Slowly, over the years, schools did not want to upset alumni or boosters who may be in the audience, so they would not allow us to share at halftime. Many would allow us to share after the game as a consolation and then after a time, even that stopped. These days it is rare that we are permitted to share." The progressive marginalization of witnessing had important consequences for how AIA's traveling athletes understood their obligations.

As the number of listeners and the practice of verbal witnessing declined, AIA shifted its emphasis to demonstrating intensity on the court. Athletes in Action historian Joe Smalley writes of a 1980 men's basketball tournament in Europe, "AIA would not be permitted to present its usual halftime evangelistic program, so all the team's talking would be done on the court. And the trip to Europe provided a unique opportunity to disclaim a deeply-imbedded European stereotype about Christianity—that Christians are 'sissies,' in need of a crutch."[28] On-court intensity replaced narrative witnessing as the key goal of athletic tours. Players emphasized on-court behavior (sportsmanship, toughness, endurance) as a way of demonstrating that Christians are worthy competitors and that evangelical Christianity is an avenue for athletic success.

One reason this shift made sense was because, as scholars of sport have noted, Americans tend to see sportsmanship as a moral category.[29] Some posit that sport has attained moral relevance in our society comparable to religious ethics. For example, James W. Keating, a scholar of sport and ethics, noted that a range of public figures from Nobel Prize winner Albert Camus to former president Herbert Hoover to Pope Pius XII all describe sport as an important ethical training ground. Keating calls this "a tendency all too common among the champions of sportsmanship—the temptation to broaden the concept of sportsmanship until it becomes an all-embracing moral category, a unique road to moral salvation."[30] Keating is highly critical of sportsmanship as a moral category, but he does illuminate a cultural tendency to conflate admirable sporting behavior with upstanding morality beyond sporting competitions.

Sport sociologist Jay Coakley's textbook, *Sport in Society,* points to a "character logic" in American sporting culture that supports experiences ranging from Little League to the Olympic Games. He notes that for more than fifty years scholars have been comparing athletes to nonathletes in hopes of validating the proposition that sports build character. Of this research, he says:

> These snapshot comparisons have provided inconsistent and confusing results. First, researchers have wrongly assumed that *all* organized competitive sports involve similar character-shaping experiences for *all* athletes. Second, they have wrongly assumed that the character-shaping experiences in organized sports are so unique that people who don't play sports are at a disadvantage when it comes to developing certain positive traits, attitudes, and behaviors.[31]

Coakley's astute recognition of the faulty assumptions that undergird this kind of research is unlikely to alter the overriding cultural assumption that sport builds character.[32] Because Americans have been culturally trained to see sport as morally relevant and sportsmanship as a moral barometer, sports ministry easily embraced on-field behavior as a form of witnessing and a way of demonstrating moral superiority. For contemporary sports ministry organizations, behavior on the playing field is at least as important as verbal witnessing.

This was not always the case. A major issue that arose very early in sports ministry had to do with winning. To garner an audience for evangelical Christianity, the athlete had to achieve the kind of athletic fame that comes through winning. Athletes in Action founder Dave Hannah noted that winning increased receptiveness to AIA's evangelical message: "I've consistently observed that, when our team is playing well, people seem to care more about what we say."[33] In a more overt statement of this phenomenon, Hannah pointed to winning as not only helpful but necessary for AIA's evangelistic success: "Who has better attendance—first-place or last-place teams? Who is featured in the newspapers more—the nation's finest or the also-rans? Who do people write about, talk about, pay to see? Winners! The better we are, the more people will watch us. The more people watch us, the more we will reach for Christ."[34] These statements clearly link evangelistic potential to athletic success.

This link is perhaps not surprising, but it is related to an enduring problem in sports ministry—*how* is one supposed to win? Can one combine athletic prowess and Christian behavior during the game and still win? In an article in FCA's member publication, *Sharing the Victory*, football player Brent Dennis described this conflict in one of its most obvious forms: the violently dangerous game of football. In an important football game during his junior year at the University of Tulsa, Dennis was struck by the conflict between violent sports and Christianity:

> Emotions were high and the hitting was fierce. Midway through the second quarter, under a heap of bodies, I heard the moan of an injured athlete. As we unpiled I realized it was Kerwin [Freshman of the Year] who was writhing in pain. I'd silently wished for this to happen but, when it did, I felt suddenly empty inside. Trainers and coaches poured onto the field. When Kerwin's helmet was removed I no longer saw him as a faceless enemy to be feared and conquered. He was half man, half boy, just like me . . . a 19 year-old who played this crazy game to get an education. He wasn't evil and I couldn't rejoice in his agony. I felt his anguish and was enraged by the insensitive jubilation of my teammates. . . . I have no absolute answers—only the awareness that a Christian athlete or coach who authentically seeks to serve the Lord must face into the dilemma of reconciling Christ's compassion with the killer instinct required to win.[35]

Dennis's dilemma reveals a tension between the desire to win (and therefore have an audience) and the desire to behave with Christlike compassion on the field, a behavior that may undermine one's ability to win.

This problem did not trouble every Christian athlete. For example, A. C. Green was a power forward for the Los Angeles Lakers in the 1980s who reconciled his faith with harsh playing. In an interview published in *Sharing the Victory*, he stated:

> God wants his people to be warriors. I don't mean getting into fights—I mean doing your best. I don't think any Christian should be passive. If

he is, he's heading for a lot of problems in his spiritual walk. I'm ready to battle when I step onto the court. I expect to fight. Not physically, but to get rebounds and score points. The Israelite warriors in the Bible were always ready to fight, to destroy their enemies and possess their land. It's that spirit that moves me.[36]

Whether one struggles with rough play like Dennis or embraces it like Green, the problem is the same—for celebrity evangelism to be effective, the athlete must win.

This conflict has not gone unnoticed by evangelical Christians. Shirl Hoffman, a sport sociologist and long-standing critic of sports ministry, has published numerous articles and books addressing the disconnect he sees between intense sporting competition and Christian character. Hoffman grew up affiliating sports and Christianity but, over time, came to question the validity of presenting competition as spiritually fulfilling. He describes a tennis match in his recent book, *Good Game: Christianity and the Culture of Sports*: "If either of us allows sympathy to overwhelm self-interest and begins placing our shots where the other can easily return them, we will have lost the spirit of the game. Sports are zero-sum in nature: I can only win if you lose. In committing myself to winning, I am at the same time committing to making you lose."[37] As Hoffman and others have noted, to fully engage in sporting competition, an athlete must be willing to embrace the "killer instinct," a quality Hoffman defines as "ridding yourself of sympathies for your opponent that might inhibit you in applying your full resources to furthering your own cause."[38] This is Hoffman's main critique of sports ministry: sports ministers deny that competition comes at the expense of sympathy.

Hoffman, who is well aware of sports ministry's history of embracing advertising strategies, writes, "The dynamics of selling Christ are not much different than the dynamics of selling basketball shoes. The celebrity pitching the gospel, like the celebrity pitching athletic shoes, must embody an attractive image, and in the athletic world this means that he or she must be a winner."[39] This means, "Intentionally or not, sport celebrities end up selling faith not on the merits of Christ's image or message but on the strength of their own."[40] Hoffman's critique is theological; he is concerned that aligning big-time sport and evangelical Christianity undermines evangelical doctrine.[41] Religion journalist

Tom Krattenmaker raises a similar point: "The problem with faith-based victory, and with victory-based faith, is that every winner eventually loses, and that every star that rises in the sports constellation eventually falls."[42] This reality has pushed contemporary sports ministry organizations to redefine witnessing.

Like the Charlotte Lady Eagles, contemporary AIA players saw learning to verbally share testimonies as an important component of their Christian athletic identity. But as one player, Abby, told me, "It's not enough to have a cross on your uniform anymore, you have to bring it on the court, really demonstrate that you're a Christian." A cross on a uniform may symbolize belief, but for Abby, it was through practical applications that one demonstrated the difference between Christian and non-Christian players. Abby said, "I'm not gonna shoot and hold my follow-through like I'm all that, because it's not about me. It's never about me. It's about him." For Abby, behavior rather than identification undergirded Christian athleticism. When she was able to demonstrate behaviors that she identified as Christian (like not holding her follow-through), she shored up her belief in Christian athletes as distinct and special. This distinction is at the heart of ideas about witnessing. For witnessing to perform the important religious work of maintaining belief and securing community, there must exist a clear understanding of a population that needs witnessing—people to listen to a testimony or to notice that Abby was behaving differently than they expected.

Athletes are bodily performers. And while the women on the AIA team and the staff certainly spoke about their faith a great deal—delivered testimony, discussed Bible verses, had long talks about spirituality and belief during innumerable hours traveling in vans—they were primarily speaking to each other, not to outsiders. They understood their primary evangelistic outreach power as athletic, embodied, and performative. Tina, the team chaplain, told the team several times, "Share the gospel every day, and, when you have to, use words."[43] After one game, some spectators approached Tina to compliment the AIA team on their intensity despite the fact that they weren't playing for any recognizable reward. She told the team, "You were a tremendous testament in your playing to that other team and to the crowd. . . . You did a great job of sharing without words last night." For evangelical athletes like these, athletic performance in itself was a form of witnessing.

One of the key missions of sports ministry is to use differences from the larger sporting world as a demonstration of moral superiority and as a form of witnessing, and differences in opinion most often arose over the most appropriate way to accomplish this goal. For example, one session of the Charlotte Lady Eagles' sports ministry training was dedicated to gamesmanship, the practice of using the rules to gain an unfair advantage over your opponent. In soccer, gamesmanship is fairly common, and players often accepted it as part of the game. Examples of gamesmanship include stalling by taking a long time to throw in a ball, remaining on the ground longer than necessary after a fall, or taking one's position at a slow pace. The Lady Eagles prided themselves on being different from the majority of soccer teams and being able to demonstrate that difference on the field. However, all of the players had previously played on teams that relied on gamesmanship, and they expected it from other teams. Cultural studies scholar Brian Massumi has noted not only that gamesmanship is a common practice in soccer but also that it is the skilled use of gamesmanship that creates a soccer star. "The star plays against the rules but not by breaking them. He plays around them, adding minute, unregulated contingencies to the charged mix. She adds free variations: 'free' in the sense that they are . . . unsubsumed by the rules of the game."[44] The Lady Eagles wanted to stand out from the larger soccer community because of their skill, but practicing gamesmanship, though generally accepted and even promoted in soccer generally, was not how they wanted to be identified.

One point of contention that the Lady Eagles discussed in sports ministry training was how to know when to use common practices that might be considered gamesmanship and when to avoid these practices even if it meant giving the other team the advantage. For example, taking the ball to the corner is a stalling practice. It is not against the rules, but it is frustrating for the defenders. One player, Tara, had her boyfriend visiting from out of town, and he was sitting in on the training session.

Tara's boyfriend, a former Eagle who now played on a secular team, spoke up. Everyone turned, and noticing the attention, he laughed and said, "Okay, I'll tell you the answer." The group laughed, but Tara's boyfriend was granted a measure of authority on the topic.

"I'll tell you one thing," he said. "As a forward, I would take it to the corner every time. But, as a defender, I get so mad at that player. It's part of the Eagles' organization to try to be different. If you do something that might be weird to them [the other team], then they're gonna start asking questions about why the Eagles do the things that they do. And the answer is that we're trying to be like Christ. If the ball goes out of bounds, you pick it up and hand it to the player [instead of waiting for the other player to go and get it]. And, yeah, it's more work. And, that's part of being on this team, doing the extra work."

The Eagles believed that playing soccer could be effective evangelism. However, this involved two somewhat contradictory impulses: playing fair and winning. As winners, they would be able to draw a larger audience and have a greater platform for their message. However, if they won by not playing fair, their message would lack validity. This is the problem of winning.

The sports ministry training leader, a former player named Summer, emphasized that intentionality matters as much as action. She said, "Anger is as bad as murder to God. Lust is as bad as adultery. There are rules, but it's what's in your heart and mind that Jesus sees and that can be judged. We can take this one step further. Jesus is looking at the hearts of men. This parallels the game with the rules that are in place. Yeah, we're not breaking the rules, but we can go further. These little things have an effect on how we're seen. You can trust that God will provide you with integrity if you take this a step further. It comes down to what's in your heart."

A goalkeeper, Leslie, asked, "Is there such a thing as a smart foul?"

This sparked some controversy. Jennie responded immediately, "No, not if it's intentional. No way."

Angie disagreed. "You can get a foul without hurting the other player. It can be strategic, not malicious, like a shirt tug. It can be done within the confines of the game."

"You shouldn't have to tug a shirt," Jennie shot back.

The starting goalkeeper, Ellie, broke in, "As Christians, we shouldn't do it, but as players, we're expected to."

Tara tried to bring the conversation back to intentionality. "If you're saying in your head, 'I'm trying to foul this person—'"

Ellie completed her thought, "It's wrong. But, it's also *smart*."

Tara tried another tactic, bringing the conversation back to distinction. "Yeah, it might be crazy to play that way [without fouling], but how many times did Jesus say that other people are going to think that his followers are crazy?" she asked rhetorically.

Nora, the team's six-foot-two forward, broke in, "So, a lot of times, I'll be the biggest player on the field." Everyone laughed, relieving some of the mounting tension. "Okay, most all of the time," she conceded. "So, on my college team, I'll get told to go in and commit a foul. But I always play to the ball. If I go in and get a yellow card [penalty], it was still my intention to win the ball."

Emily, the assistant coach, agreed, saying, "If your intention is to win the ball—fouls will be called, but it's your intention that matters."

Chelsea, a talented player from a well-regarded college team, brought up how difficult it is to keep one's intentions pure during competitive play. "I was playing once, and this girl subbed in. She would hit you and then run for the ball. I knew that they [the referees] weren't going to call her, so I had to play harder. It wasn't dirty, but you better believe I was going in harder on her than I was on the other forward. I mean, what do you guys think of that? Like, if she fell, I would help her up, but . . . ," she trailed off.

"You were right," Jennie assured her.

"Don't get it [sportsmanship] confused with not playing hard," Tara clarified. "It doesn't mean that we're not going to tackle and play hard."

"What if that means playing dirty?" Chelsea asked.

"I don't think we should play dirty," said Tara. The players had identified a disturbing gray area. There is no hard-and-fast line between playing aggressively and playing dirty.

Emily spoke up. "Chelsea, what you are describing was you protecting yourself."

Chelsea disagreed. "Honestly, I was thinking, 'Yeah, I'm going to hurt this girl.'"

Tara tried again to emphasize intentionality. "It's not to say that you're never going to do it. But, as a team, we should be unified in our commitment to not use the game to get an unfair advantage."

Andrea, a young, quiet player, tried to bring up a new way of approaching the problem. "Maybe we shouldn't keep the ball in the corner. Maybe we should trust God to bless that and not let them score. We can be a witness because of that."

Tara agreed. "There are aspects of gamesmanship that are geared at getting an unfair advantage. We can play teams fair and win. This is a stepping-off point for us to be different."

Relying on intentionality was troublesome for figuring out how to distinguish themselves from non-Christian athletes. Intentions are invisible, and the team wanted to use identifiable practices, like helping up a fallen opponent, to display difference to the other team and the fans. The Charlotte Lady Eagles and other sports ministry groups see sportsmanship as an important part of their mission. They recognize, as does sportsmanship scholar James Keating, that "to work daily and often intimately with one's competitors and to compete in circumstances which are highly charged with excitement and emotion, while still showing fairness and consideration, is evidence of an admirable degree of self-mastery."[45] When players are able to attribute this self-mastery to their faith in Jesus Christ, they can use this as evidence of God's power to act in the world as well as their own moral superiority.

Witnessing without words—using sportsmanship to demonstrate moral distinction—is the primary mission of many of today's sports ministry organizations. These practices function in much the same way as verbal witnessing. Witnesses are able to cement their own identity as saved, perceive a distinction between themselves and the unsaved, and use this identity and distinction as evidence for their religious beliefs. However, as the sports ministry session recounted here shows, it is incredibly difficult, perhaps impossible, to reconcile the desire to demonstrate compassion for one's opponent on the field with the desire to win.

Conclusion

For evangelicals, conversion is a defining moment in their religious identity. At altar calls, evangelicals physically perform conversion by walking forward as a public display of commitment. Sports ministry organizations actively encourage recommitment, and this is perhaps a more important practice than first-time commitment because it affirms the athlete's belief in conversion while also opening space for confessions of doubt and struggle. Following conversion, evangelicals are expected to formulate their testimony and share their story with others. As I hope this chapter makes clear, testifying is no longer understood solely along verbal lines. Christian athletes see their behavior on the field as potentially more effective witnessing, and many dedicate themselves to good sportsmanship rather than storytelling.

American evangelicals rely on distinction, on setting themselves apart from nonbelievers. As sociologist Christian Smith notes:

> Evangelicals see themselves as living an aberrant way of life from that of the surrounding world. . . . On television, in schools, on the news, and at work, evangelicals see and hear a set of values and lifestyle commitments that feel to them fundamentally alien and inhospitable. . . . [But] evangelicals feel compelled to struggle to remain involved with and relevant to the emerging mainstream American culture.[46]

Because distinction is important in evangelical culture generally, particularly in the form of moral superiority, and because sports are understood culturally as a moral enterprise, early sports ministers saw winning competitions as a powerful witnessing tactic. But very early in the development of sports ministry, athletes encountered the problem of winning—the problem of how to reconcile the need to win with the need to demonstrate on-field sportsmanship and compassion. This problem remains central in sports ministry today.

The appeal of combining sport with ministry continues to be a strong impulse for evangelical Christians. Sports ministry turned to "witnessing without words" as a response to the problem of winning. This turn, however, opened up another problem—how does one *know* if one is witnessing without words? One answer to this is Sean's explanation that the embodied experiences of sport can make God real for athletes. In the next chapter, I turn to these experiences to show that Christian athletes measure their success through sensations of athletic pleasure that they attribute to God's approval.

2

Transcendent Intimacy

The Embodied Pleasures of Sport

In the 1980s, FCA's member publication *Sharing the Victory* ran the "Sports Conscience Series," a group of articles "designed to encourage readers to grapple with some of the thornier issues in athletics." In these twenty articles spanning two years, sports ministers addressed difficult topics like "How to Treat a Superstar" and "When Your Heroes Become Zeroes." Overall, these articles reflected an ongoing concern in sports ministry that emphasizing winning was problematic. The authors warned time and again against getting caught up in sports mania. They cautioned that believing that winning matters above all else or treating sports celebrities as if they are more valuable than other Christians could lead to a "perilous worldliness" that linked religious authority with worldly success.

Sharing the Victory asked Neil Wolkodoff, one of the contributors to the series, "If you could wave a magic wand and make one change in athletics, what would it be?" He answered, "Redefine winning. Measure winning by how you utilize your God-given abilities. . . . You may only pole vault eleven feet but if that's your max, you've won in God's eyes. If your friend vaults fourteen feet but has potential to clear eighteen, he doesn't fit my definition of a winner."[1] Wolkodoff's redefinition of winning directly confronts the issues I identified in the previous chapter. By claiming that Christian athletes should focus their energy on self-improvement, he deprioritized winning and shifted the emphasis to athletic activity in itself.

Christian athletes are fond of quoting the Oscar-winning film *Chariots of Fire* (1981) to explain the value of athletic pleasure. The film, based on the life of Olympic sprinter Eric Liddell, depicts a conversation between Liddell and his sister. When she encourages him to give up sport and pursue a missionary career in China, Liddell responds, "I believe

God made me for a purpose, but he also made me fast. And, when I run, I feel his pleasure."[2] I often heard Christian athletes quote this passage word for word as evidence that athletes can feel God's pleasure during their athletic endeavors, making the cinematic account of Liddell's life a matter of real-life importance. Connecting athletic pleasure to God is key to understanding sports ministry—Christian athletes see their joy in sport as a message from God that God is pleased.

Though Christian athletes often interpret the claim by this Hollywood version of Eric Liddell—"When I run, I feel his pleasure"—as evidence that athletic activity can bring pleasure to God, one could also understand that quotation differently. He could be saying, "In order to feel God's pleasure, I must run." This second interpretation establishes a causal connection between athletic activity and the sensory experience of transcendent pleasure. Christian athletes use sport as a means to experience this pleasure, and they describe this feeling as a connection with God. While sport is not the only mechanism Christian athletes use to connect with God, their understanding of sport as a vehicle for divine connection makes playing sports important regardless of the outcome of competition. Understanding sport as a means to experience God's pleasure is very different from understanding sport as a means to gain an audience for witnessing; sport for the experience of divine pleasure emphasizes individual and private religious experience, not converting others.

If evangelicals evaluated the success of verbal witnessing by number of conversions, and they evaluated the success of witnessing without words by the impression they made on others, how do Christian athletes evaluate the embodied sensations of their athletic performance? How do they *know* that they are feeling God's pleasure? Turning to historical developments in sports ministry, we can see that, for Christian athletes, sporting pleasure became a way to experience, think about, and articulate sensations in their bodies as a form of intimacy with the divine. This chapter brings together two facets of "knowledge." When Christian athletes say that they know God personally, they often mean that they have certainty of God's power and reality. They may also mean that they feel connected to that power. And, when Christian athletes describe the feeling of being connected to God, this often takes on sexual overtones. This reveals a second facet of "knowledge": to know can also be used as a sexual verb and appears so in some biblical translations. Attributing athletic pleasure to God both solidifies the Christian athlete's knowledge of God's presence and frames that presence as sexually fulfilling.

The Making of an Athlete of God

To explore the related discourses of religious experience, athletic mastery, and sexual pleasure, it is helpful to turn to the first emergence of this kind of description within sports ministry. Wes Neal was the first and most prolific sports minister on this topic. Neal joined Athletes in Action's traveling weight-lifting team in the 1960s and traveled with AIA founder David Hannah and Olympic weight lifter Russ Knipp on a U.S. tour of churches and schools. The men would use their strength to lend authority to their evangelical message. According to Neal, "We would always bring the strongest kid in the crowd to the stage to try the lift. And, of course, he couldn't do it. So, then they would really listen to us." Though this strategy seemed to be effective in encouraging young men to listen to the gospel, Neal felt something was amiss. Athletes in Action presented lifting weights and sharing the gospel as two separate things, and even though they happened one right after the other, the two actions did not seem to affect each other very much. In Neal's words, "I didn't know how to lift weights God's way."

Over the next few decades, Neal dedicated himself to the task of understanding how to do sports God's way, and he became a prolific writer for Christian athletes. His first published work, *The Making of an Athlete of God,* appeared in 1972.[3] Soon after, he founded the Institute for Athletic Perfection and republished his materials as *The Handbook on Athletic Perfection: A Training Manual for Christian Athletes*, which has been reprinted several times, most recently in 2000. Neal also wrote *The Handbook on Coaching Perfection*, and his insights form the basis for Athletes in Action's recent publication *Game Day Glory*. In 2008, Neal released a DVD entitled *Doing Sport God's Way*.[4]

When Neal entered sports ministry in the late 1960s, he agreed with the Athletes in Action maxim that Christian athletes could and should be different from non-Christian athletes, but he noticed that his faith did not impact his athletic behavior. Neal grew frustrated with sports ministry's lack of attention to the struggles that are distinct to Christian athletes. He told me, "I wasn't any different from a non-Christian in my athletics. I was still nervous before competition. I still had all the same ups and downs as a non-Christian. We used to train at a gym in southern California, and a lot of the college football lifters would look up to us to try to learn about being a Christian athlete. Of course, we didn't know any more about it than they did."

One day, Neal was lifting weights at this gym, and he missed a lift. "I knew I would get pinned, so I had to push myself away from the bar. I was so frustrated that I smashed my fist on the platform." His fiancée, Peggy, approached him, asking, "Are you angry?" When Neal denied his anger, Peggy said, "Well, they all think you are," gesturing to the college football players. Neal told me, "I was so embarrassed and humiliated. I vowed that would never happen again." For Neal, this experience was evidence that something was lacking in his Christian athletic training. He did not think that his behavior was an accurate reflection of his beliefs and his identity as a Christian.

Gary Warner, editor of *Christian Athlete* in the 1970s, voiced a frustration similar to Neal's with the lack of change in his sporting behavior after his conversion to evangelical Christianity:

> My faith had no practical application to my competitiveness. I was the same old person between the base lines. I cursed, I lost control, I was obsessed with winning. I would manipulate and do whatever it took to win. I slid into bases with my spikes high, and if a baserunner did not get down to the double play, I had no qualms about putting the ball between his eyes. From the bench, I heaped abuse on opponents and referees. After all, this was competition. This was being an athlete. And no one modeled a Christian difference for me to see.[5]

Warner began to question why his faith did not affect the way he played sports. Like Neal, he was troubled by this disconnection.

Neal and Warner were not the only ones to notice that Christian athletes seemed largely the same as their secular counterparts. At the same time as these two men began to challenge the values of sports ministry, *Sports Illustrated* writer Frank Deford published a scathing critique of what he called "Sportianity."[6] According to Deford, Sportianity was a locker-room religion on the rise in professional leagues that involved a declaration of Christian beliefs yet did not require ethical improvements. He wrote, "In the process of dozens of interviews with people in Sportianity, not one remotely suggested any direct effort was being considered to improve the morality of athletics."[7] Deford conjectured that this lack of attention to sporting morality was connected to sports ministry's dependence on athletic celebrity. As he saw it, the ministry benefited from sports' promotion of the hero worship of winning athletes. Because sports ministry used the system for evangelism, sports ministers would be unlikely to seek significant changes in the organizing principles of competitive sport. "No one in the movement—much less any organization—speaks out against the cheating in sport, against dirty play; no one attacks the evils of recruiting, racism or any of the many other well-known excesses and abuses.... Sportianity seems prepared to accept athletics as is, more devoted to exploiting sport than serving it."[8] Deford clearly saw this as a problem.

Deford wrote three articles for *Sports Illustrated* on "Sportianity." In the second and third pieces, he tempered his critique somewhat and introduced "Sportians," who were interested in addressing moral issues in sport. In particular, he pointed to the article "Sports and War" that appeared in *Christian Athlete* in 1972, while Gary Warner served as editor. This article juxtaposed pictures of injured athletes and fallen soldiers in Vietnam, linebackers and the front line. The article decried emphasizing winning over team cooperation and cautioned against treating the world like a sporting competition:

> In the midst of the most complex time in our nation's history, we are witnessing a phenomenal growth of our athletic institutions. Sports has become the national conversation, complete with its own peculiar grammar and vocabulary. It has absorbed our passions in its fantasy world of winners and losers. Sports has proved compatible with our view of the world as a dichotomy of winners and losers. In fact, we seem to retreat into sport in order to deny the complexity and ambiguity that marks the political, social, and religious issues of our time.[9]

The article went so far as to argue that sports ministry needed to take seriously the conflation of sports and war in America and rethink

Christian involvement in both: "In fact, in light of Jesus a whole new conception of sports is demanded. Needless to say a re-examination of sports may be a bitter and traumatic task for a society as permeated with sports (and war) as is ours. I believe we can anticipate a conversion of spirit that will produce a new vision of what sports can be."[10] Rather than using sport as a platform for witnessing, *Christian Athlete* sought to bring Christian beliefs and practices to bear on actual athletic behavior.

Deford noted that the Christian athletic community ignored this critique, and he argued that sports ministry was more interested in celebrity sales-pitches than systemic change:

> While athletics does not appear to have been improved by the religious blitzkrieg, the religious people who work that side of the street seem to have been colored by some of the worst attitudes found in sport. The temper of athletic religion is competitive, full of coaches and cheerleaders, with an overriding sense of wins and losses, stars and recruiting, game plans and dugout chatter.[11]

Deford even goes to far as to suggest, "It might be a good idea right now to talk to the veteran GM in the sky about the possibility of a rebuilding year."[12] He pointed out that reliance on celebrities undermined any possibility of sports ministry pursuing ethical improvements for sport. Deford saw this as not only a disappointment but a failure of Christianity to live up to God's expectations. Perhaps Sportians, he suggested, should reassess their values.

Because winning is central to gaining cultural attention, Christian athletes who saw their evangelistic potential as tied to their win-loss record felt motivated to win at all costs. Sport sociologist Shirl Hoffman has noted that tying winning to evangelistic potential can lead a Christian athlete to understand that winning is God's will. He quotes Roger Staubach, who said after the 1972 Super Bowl, "I had promised that it would be for God's honor and glory, whether we won or lost. Of course the glory was better for God and me since we won, because victory gave me a greater platform from which to speak."[13] This sort of affiliation of winning and God's will is problematic for a number of reasons. It does not explain why Christian athletes might lose games. It does not take into account the fact that there may be Christian athletes on opposing teams. And it elevates a win-at-all-costs mentality that eclipses any discussion of the morality of athletic behavior.

At the time that Deford delivered his critique of Sportianity, a number of authors began to criticize the sporting establishment as a tool of capitalist oppression. Similar to "Sports and War" in *Christian Athlete*, Paul Hoch's 1972 Marxist critique of big-time sport argued that football in particular functioned as an "opiate of the masses," distracting the population from "the illicit violence in today's society—riots, student uprisings, bombings, crime in the streets, and revolutionary deeds. . . . By contrast, the clean, hard violence of football is refreshing and reassuring, because it is done according to rules."[14] Hoch posited that America's sporting establishment worked to justify military involvement in Vietnam. "It goes without saying that a worker who is so busy rooting for the Yankees that he forgets that his real wages are declining is a good bet to be so busy rooting for the Yanks in Vietnam that he forgets his son might get killed there."[15] Along these lines, Deford's *Sports Illustrated* article quoted Episcopal priest Malcolm Boyd on the dangers of combining Christianity and sport in a time of war: "It is this kind of trying [to win], the kind that this athletic religion teaches, which is killing off so many men, leaving widows. It is very dangerous right now to be trying harder. It is making us more machinelike instead of more human. We'd do better to learn how not to try so [hard]."[16] These critiques indicate a larger dissatisfaction with sport that permeated the counterculture of the 1970s.

Dave Meggyesy, pro-football player turned Marxist critic, was another voice who pointed out parallels between the ideologies of sport and war.[17] In the early 1970s, during a debate between several prominent coaches, athletes, and sportswriters, Meggyesy critiqued the sporting establishment, saying, "I love athletics, but the horror is what we do to each other in the name of the system." Gary Warner, who was in the audience, later described the event: "There was no debate. The rejoinders were platitudes and clichés and, at times, so childishly sophomoric that the audience broke into laughter. I wanted to cry. Upon leaving I determined that the ramifications of competition for the Christian had to be spoken to."[18]

Part of Warner's disappointment may have stemmed from how Meggyesy's comments challenged a definitive aspect of evangelical Christianity—being *in* but not *of* the world. Evangelicals sought to use sport as a platform for witnessing, but in using sport this way, they learned that it was difficult to combine their religion and sport without sacrificing the distinctiveness of evangelical Christianity. As Warner and Neal noted, there were no identifiable differences between Christian and non-Christian athletes. By engaging with sport without recognizing the "ramifications of competition for the Christian," Warner saw a blurring of the boundary between evangelicals and the secular world. According to Christian Smith, a scholar of American evangelicalism, "The implicit distinction between 'us' and 'them' is omnipresent in evangelical thought and speech, so much so that it does not often in fact draw to itself much attention. Yet it subtly and profoundly shapes evangelical consciousness and discourse."[19] For Warner and other sports ministers, maintaining a distinction between "us" and "them" entailed a careful examination of sport not as a witnessing platform but as a set of practices that might conflict with Christian morality. Out of this examination emerged a new way of thinking about Christian athletic practices, most famously articulated by Wes Neal.

Lifting Weights God's Way

Wes Neal told me about a televised interview he did in the late 1960s: "The host asked me about lifting and I used that question to share the four spiritual laws, [Campus Crusade for Christ's directions for personal salvation]. Afterwards, I felt that I had done wrong on that. I didn't respect his question. I used his question to talk about something else."[20] Neal experienced a crisis of conscience about using his athletic celebrity as an evangelistic tool. He felt that his identity as a Christian should infuse his sporting experience; it should be more than something he talked about after the game. His mission to infuse sport with Christianity led Neal to question and redefine the desired outcome of combining sport and evangelicalism. For Neal, sport was no longer solely a platform to reach others but an opportunity to use his athletic body to experience a connection with God. Sport could be a religious experience, and he saw this as perhaps even more valuable than using sport to draw attention to an evangelical message.

When Neal's goal for Christian athletics was no longer limited to evangelism, he came to understand his Christian athletic obligation as "to give every ounce toward something and to do it as unto the Lord." He called this a "Total Release Performance," and understood it as a sensation of Christlikeness, of being one with Jesus Christ.[21] He would later describe it using Psalms 150:1–6:

> Praise the Lord! Praise God in His sanctuary; Praise Him in His mighty expanse. Praise Him for His mighty deeds; Praise Him according to His excellent greatness. Praise Him with trumpet sound; Praise Him with harp and lyre. Praise Him with timbrel and dancing; Praise Him with stringed instruments and pipe. Praise Him with loud cymbals; Praise Him with resounding cymbals. Let everything that has breath praise the Lord. Praise the Lord.[22]

Neal interpreted the musical instruments in these verses as metaphorical. He wrote:

> Let the energy flow from within, reflecting His greatness. Praise Him through your stamina. Let the melody of your song before Him be seen in the quickness of your reflexes and dexterity of your fingers. Praise God through the rhythm of your strides. Shout His praise with perfect timing. Shout praises to the Lord with every fiber in your body.[23]

Neal described this use of sport as a "praise performance," "athletic perfection," and a "Total Release Performance"—"the total release of all that you are toward becoming like Jesus Christ in each situation."[24] For Neal, this experience was the ultimate goal of any sporting activity. Sport could foster a sense of intimacy and closeness with God, a feeling of being saturated with the love and power of Christ.

A Total Release Performance requires mental preparation. According to Neal, "It is your mind that the Holy Spirit engages most of the time," and his publications provide instructions for Christian athletes to cultivate a mental state conducive to interaction with the Holy Spirit.[25] He saw the mind as an access point for the Holy Spirit: "The word 'mind' refers to all of our senses which are alert to external objects—the primary organ being the brain. The human mind, acting independently, can produce great works. But it can also produce chaos. It was designed by God to work in a dependent way with His Holy Spirit."[26] Because

Neal understood the mind as a "meeting ground with God," many of his instructions involved creating a state of mind intentionally in tune with Jesus Christ: "I picture myself as Jesus—this is not heresy; there is no way that we *are* Jesus, but I see myself as Jesus living in me. I'm not copying his behavior, but I'm in a union with his spirit." Neal describes this union as a purifying renewal of the mind: "It's a combination of losing yourself and building yourself—less of me, more of Christ. . . . It's an awesome awareness." For Neal, isolated concentration on the Holy Spirit made mental clarity possible and, in turn, could allow an athlete to experience a Total Release Performance, an awe-inspiring awareness of renewed purity.

Focusing on Total Release Performance was an attempt to distinguish Christian athletes from non-Christian athletes, to identify a sensation that was accessible only to Christian athletes. Yet Neal's descriptions of athletic pleasure differ very little from secular weight lifters' accounts. For example, take bodybuilder Frank Zane's description of his experience of training with intense concentration:

> I proved to myself that if my concentration was keen enough, I could close the breach between myself and the exercise apparatus when I worked with it. I riveted my attention to the proper form of the exercise to the extent that no external environment existed for me. I became compatible with my workout. Distractions were filtered out. You have to personally get into it and work at it to experience what I mean. It transcends simple training. You float like a cork in a heavy sea.[27]

For Neal and Zane, the feeling of total release was possible through mental concentration. However, Zane and Neal offer different accounts for the origin and cause of these sensations. For Neal, total release is a gift from a pleased God; for Zane, it came from his own hard work and attention. For weight lifters like Zane, sports certainly provided an experience of extraordinary pleasure, but these athletes are less likely to narrate this pleasure as an experience of communion with God.

Christian athletes like Neal believe that God could and would help them improve in their sport. Neal emphasized that this resulted from mental intentionality, arguing that if an athlete opened his or her mind to Jesus, athletic training and performance would improve:

Your mind was designed by God to express your praise of Him. Your body was designed by God to express that praise in action. In your performance, as you praise God both mentally and physically, you will be doing the very thing for which you were designed. By performing the way you were designed, your athletic ability is developed to the maximum potential.[28]

Neal is careful to point out that developing to your maximum potential did not mean that you would always win; your maximum potential might not be as great as your opponent's. Nevertheless, Neal does argue that an athlete could never achieve his or her full potential without the help of Jesus Christ.

It is interesting to note that at the same time Neal was working on a theology of sport that cultivated an intense mental state, the weight-lifting community in general was dedicating a substantial amount of energy to exploring mental preparation as key to athletic improvement. A number of texts appeared in the 1960s that explored the notion of visualization—vividly imagining success as a way to achieve its actualization.[29] The book *Psycho-Cybernetics* (1960), by Maxwell Maltz, includes several examples of using visualization to improve athletic performance. For instance, under the heading "Imagination Practice Can Lower Your Golf Score," Maltz lists several professional golfers who practice in their imaginations as way to prepare for competition. According to one golfer, "If you would picture the end result—'see' the ball going where you wanted it to go, and have the confidence to 'know' that it was going to do what you wanted, your subconscious would take over and direct your muscles correctly."[30]

Visualization strategies also began to appear in sports ministry, and by 1969, Bill Glass included visualization in his address to the FCA national conference: "A large part of athletic success is in the mind of the athlete. The premise is that experiences vividly imagined have the same impact on the subconscious as experiences actually experienced."[31] Athletes who spent time mentally envisioning success at their sport were finding that this mental exercise significantly improved their on-field performance.

In the 1960s and 1970s, when Neal was developing his theology of sport, weight lifting was just becoming a recognized component of athletic training. Weight training was popular in post–World War II California and gained an international stage through the 1952 Olympics in Helsinki, where the American media made much of the U.S. weightlifting victory over Russia, the nation's Cold War enemy.[32] Gym franchises popped up across the country, and Americans began to see weight lifters not as muscle-bound freaks but as model athletes. Neal's background in weight training is important for understanding his theology of sport. He would have had access to the literature of the day that emphasized mental conditioning, and he first put his theological ideas into practice through lifting weights with fellow AIA members in his garage.

For those involved in California's weight-training community in the late 1960s and 1970s, Arnold Schwarzenegger was the unchallenged expert on all things gym and fitness related. Schwarzenegger had moved to the United States in 1968 and competed in the Mr. Olympia competition, the highest level of international professional bodybuilding, in 1969, when he took second place to Sergio Oliva. When Schwarzenegger returned to the Mr. Olympia competition in 1970, he won, becoming the youngest bodybuilder to ever do so, at the age of twenty-three. He continued to win the Mr. Olympia competition each year from 1971 to 1975 (his 1975 victory is chronicled in the documentary film *Pumping Iron*)[33] and came out of retirement in 1980 to win again. Schwarzenegger was the only bodybuilder to win the Mr. Olympia title seven times until Lee Haney broke this record in 1991, and he remains one of only two bodybuilders to win the competition five years after his last victory. (The only other person to do this was Schwarzenegger's longtime training partner Franco Columbo.) Schwarzenegger's expertise gained popular recognition through the 1985 publication of his book *The Encyclopedia of Modern Bodybuilding*, referred to colloquially as "The Bible of Bodybuilding."[34] Largely because of his weight-training expertise, George H. W. Bush recruited Schwarzenegger to serve as chairman of the President's Council on Physical Fitness from 1990 to 1993.

Schwarzenegger was one of the preeminent weight trainers when Neal was reworking the goals of sports ministry, and Schwarzenegger's understanding of the source of athletic pleasure is very different from Neal's. His autobiography includes a conversation with a training mate that illuminates the theological difference between how Christian athletes and non-Christian athletes interpret the pleasures of sport:

Helmut insisted that if I achieved something in my life, I shouldn't thank God for it, I should thank myself. It was the same way if something bad happened. I shouldn't ask God for help, I should help myself. He asked me if I had ever prayed for my body. I confessed I had. He said that if I wanted a great body, I had to build it. Nobody else could. Least of all God.[35]

Schwarzenegger attested that his muscular development and success in his sport was due to his own work. While Neal and other sports ministers acknowledged that independent success was possible, Neal argued that fully maximizing one's athletic potential was only possible with God's help.

Neal would have known that lifting weights requires mental dedication and intense concentration. To increase muscle mass, one must work a muscle to exhaustion, and this requires mental stamina as well as physical endurance. For example, in the 1970s, Jim Murray advised the new bodybuilding trainee that one can hold a weight in one's hand and curl it up, but that "isn't really bodybuilding. To get the full bodybuilding effect on the biceps, you must flex your arms deliberately, consciously contracting the biceps, all the while *thinking* biceps."[36] Schwarzenegger took this concept a step further. He wrote in his autobiography, "I was learning more and more about the mind, about the power it has over the body. It meant having complete communication with the muscles. . . . I locked my mind into my muscle during training, as if I'd transplanted my mind into the tissue itself. By just thinking about it, I could actually send blood to a muscle."[37] Schwarzenegger's emphasis on mental conditioning reveals how important this practice was for weight training.

Because Neal was a weight lifter, he was likely to see mental experiences as being just as important as beating one's opponent. For him, success in sport was not about the score; success was the feeling of connecting with Jesus Christ. This feeling, a Total Release Performance, was the goal, and Neal called this experience "winning."

He told me, "For example, I was in this tennis tournament where I was playing a sixty-year-old guy who had been a state champ in his youth. Everyone thought that I would clobber him, but he was creaming the daylights out of me."

Neal's wife, Peggy, knew Neal's principles and the terminology, and she called to him from the sidelines, "Wes, are you winning?"

"I told her, 'Yes. I am. I really am.' The guy must have thought I was crazy."

This anecdote reveals some of the difficulties Neal encountered in his developing theology. He wanted to redefine winning as experiential rather than comparative, but at the same time, he taught that his theology of sport could measurably improve athletic performance. A Total Release Performance was "winning," but it could also help you win in the traditional sense.

Neal's goal was to change the way Christian athletes understood their athletic goals. He wrote, "The perfect athletic performance is Jesus Christ living and performing through you. If you believe in Him (totally rely upon Him), you have taken the first step in experiencing the perfect athletic performance."[38] He clarified that it is only through heartfelt acceptance of Jesus Christ that an athlete is able use the principles he developed. "I can't teach this to a non-Christian. You would be counterfeiting if you tried to do it, and it wouldn't work." For Neal, the perfect athletic experience was not defeating someone else; it was a Total Release Performance, a sensation of intimate connection with Christ that allows the Christian athlete to transcend bodily limitations and experience an awesome awareness of God's reality and power.

Neal wrote, "Your athletic abilities are a gift from God. Since you are an athlete, it is logical for you to offer the best quality of your abilities to Him as an expression of your love."[39] Rather than a platform for evangelistic witnessing, this understanding elevated athletic activity as a praise and worship experience. In his descriptions of Total Release Performance, Neal referred to sensations of athletic pleasure that stem from training with intense concentration. He likely experienced this pleasure through weight lifting, and as the next section shows, the athletic pleasure that Neal endorsed is highly sensual, ecstatic, and often connected to pain.

The Spiritual Erotics of Pleasure and Pain

Pleasure is a significant component of athletic training and competition, and Christian athletes identify this pleasure as a gift from God. Gary Warner described athletic pleasure as a sensual connection between the body and the divine. He wrote of "breaking through 'the wall' away from the pain and entering a spiritual experience in which body and spirit intermingle in a joyous dance . . . that coming together, that intimate ecstasy when one senses he has arrived at the quintessential harmony of life. The truest beauty of sport comes when one isolates and enters this private, enchanted world."[40] Warner's language invokes sensual pleasure. For Warner, "intimate ecstasy" that emerges through sports is a spiritual experience of embodied pleasure, a deep tie between the flesh and the transcendent. Literature for Christian athletes on sport as religious experience continues to explore this tension between fleshly pleasure and divine connection.

As many athletes and sports ministers have noted, sport is never purely pleasing to the body—there is a strong sense of sport as difficult work, pushing the body to its physical limits in ways that are painful to experience and difficult to endure. As Shirl Hoffman noted, "Pain and discomfort are not incidental conditions of sport competition, they are central, the indispensable relish for mellowing the raw taste of pleasure."[41] In sport, the embodied sensations of pain and pleasure are linked—the pain of training is linked to the pleasure of mastery. Warner recognized that, in athletics, improvement is often tied to suffering. He wrote, "After being refined in the fire of pain, there were tangible results: my body toughened; my mind and body did new things together; I formed special relationships; I gained new skills; I had new appreciation for the gifts of others; I found a new identity."[42] For sports ministers like Warner and Neal, sport has an unparalleled potential to foster the kinds of sensations that can link humans to the divine—sensations of deep pleasure and purposeful pain.

The conflation of athletic pleasure and athletic pain can be found in most sports, but weight lifting in particular offers a provocative window on this relationship. Weight lifting emphasizes the individual dimension of sport. According to Neal, "In weight lifting, there's no opponent to distract you. Four hundred pounds is four hundred pounds any day of the week. You can't win because your opponent messed up." With no opponent to define oneself against, the weight lifter must rely on self-motivation and mental concentration. Weight lifting is also a sport that relies on, even requires, the conflation of pain and pleasure; the soreness that results from weight training is a valuable indication of progress.

Given his level of influence, it is helpful to turn to Arnold Schwarzenegger's description of purposeful pain as pleasurable:

Seeing the new changes in my body, feeling them, turned me on. It was the first time I'd ever felt every one of my muscles. It was the first time those sensations had registered in my mind, the first time my mind knew my thighs, calves, and forearms were more than just limbs. I felt the muscles in my triceps aching, and I knew why they were called triceps—because there are three muscles in there. They were registered in my mind, written there with sharp little jabs of pain. I learned that this pain meant progress. Each time my muscles were sore from a workout, I knew they were growing.[43]

Schwarzenegger articulates the sexual pleasure of athletic training—the changes he experienced turned him on. He is even more explicit about this feeling as sexual pleasure in the book *Pumping Iron* when he compares the feeling of blood rushing to a muscle, "the pump," to an orgasm:

A bodybuilder knows that when he pumps up his muscles it means growth. The muscles grow. So therefore he knows when he pumps up well, that is progress. And that satisfies him he cause he feels the progress in his body. Therefore the pump feels good. It's actually the best feeling a bodybuilder can have. It's a difficult thing to explain. Like sometimes we joke around and we get a good pump and we say you have to admit that a good pump is better than coming. Somebody off the street wouldn't understand that, but sometimes a pump is the best feeling you can have.[44]

Schwarzenegger's openly sexual interpretation of his athletic experience may seem extreme, but it does provide an indication of the intensity of athletic pleasure.

Scholars of religious experience have long called attention to the parallels between religious ecstasy and sexual pleasure.[45] The original meaning of the word "ecstasy" in the Greek translates as "being dislocated" or "being outside or beside," and scholars have compared religious ecstasy to other religious states like possession or trance wherein the person experiences or narrates feelings of being displaced from his or her body. Scholars Angelika Malinar and Helene Basu defined religious ecstasy as an "immediate and sensual experience of the absolute [divine]."[46] Ecstasy in religious contexts has a double-sidedness—an intense surrendering to the divine while at the same time experiencing a heightened self-awareness, what some scholars have called "overalertness."[47] It's easy to see the similarities between Warner's and Neal's descriptions of spiritual athletic pleasure and religious ecstasy. While sensual athletic pleasure and overalertness can occur in secular athletic settings, as bodybuilders Frank Zane and Arnold Schwarzenegger describe, the difference for Christian athletes is that they understand these sensations as gifts from God.

Explorations of intimacy with the divine have a long history in Christianity and appear frequently in the writings of female saints. Saint Catherine of Siena, who wrote in the fourteenth century, understood spiritual exercises like prayer as a method of uniting with Christ in a transformative intimacy. She wrote, "Because prayer, exercising her in the above way [by humility], unites with God the soul that follows the footprints of Christ Crucified, and thus, by desire and affection, and union of love, makes her another Himself."[48] Saint Catherine's description of a love union with God is an experience of intimacy with the divine that transfigures her into another Christ. This is not very different from Wes Neal's use of physical exercise to envision and experience what he described as a unity with Christ.

Another famous articulation of a love union with Christ appears in the writings of Saint Teresa of Avila, who wrote in the sixteenth century. Saint Teresa committed herself to a spiritual marriage with Christ and believed this union could bring on a transformation into Christlikeness. She described the sensation:

> This instantaneous communication of God to the soul is so great a secret and is so sublime a favour, and such delight is felt by the soul, that I do not know with what to compare it, beyond saying that the Lord is pleased to manifest to the soul at that moment the glory that is in Heaven, in a sublimer manner than is possible through any vision or spiritual consolation. . . . He will not separate Himself from her.[49]

Saint Teresa's description of intimate pleasure and joining with Christ demonstrates an erotic dimension to her relationship with Christ, whom she considered to be the bridegroom of her soul.

Emphasis on intimacy with Christ remains central for many contemporary evangelical women. Lynn Neal has pointed out in her analysis of contemporary evangelical romance novels that these novels place a relationship with God above all other relationships. She shows that for evangelical readers, God is the ultimate lover, and every love story resonates with God's unconditional love for humanity. Evangelical romance novels make God and God's love present in the lives of believing readers. "Instead of an angry judge or a distant relative, God emerges in these novels as a pivotal figure who would never stop loving these women."[50] These examples show that intimacy with Christ has a long tradition within Christianity, and this intimacy has often carried an explicitly feminine dimension.

Sport is an example of a human activity that indistinguishably mixes pleasure and pain. This may add to sport's potential to foster religious experience. Jeffrey Kripal has argued that the erotic has a parallel dimension of trauma and that this connection can lead a believer to interpret an experience as religiously significant. Using Rudolf Otto's definition of religious experience as simultaneously terrifying and invigorating, Kripal writes, "Intense human suffering and profound religious experience are not only compatible, then; they often require one another."[51] What is new about the intimacy promoted by Wes Neal is an explicitly masculine dimension, most notable in Neal's promotion of pain as an avenue to experience "total release" and unity with Christ.[52]

Submission to authority and the ability to push through pain are central components of Neal's advice for Christian athletes. He compared submitting to one's coach to Jesus's submission to God by sacrificing his body on the cross. If the athlete imagines him- or herself as Jesus, the coach takes on the role of God by demanding physical sacrifice. In Neal's *Handbook on Athletic Perfection,* he told athletes, "The chain-of-command is a biblical concept designed by God to help us function at our maximum effectiveness."[53] He told the story of not wanting to continue doing an exercise that was causing him pain:

> When my coach told me to continue practicing the lift that caused my shoulders to ache, I realized that my role in the chain-of-command was to obey his leading. It didn't matter if I agreed with his approach or not. As long as he was my coach, his responsibility was to give me instructions and my responsibility was to follow them.[54]

Neal encouraged the Christian athlete not only to follow the coach's instructions but to do so as an enthusiastic servant to the coach and, by extension, to God.

The reason my weight-lifting workout went so successfully when I returned to the platform to lift was because I looked upon myself as a doulos [servant] to my coach. I wanted my actions to be the instant and complete response to my coach's desire for me. I knew that by being obedient to my coach, I was also being obedient to God.[55]

In this way, Neal presented obedience and pain as two facets of Christlikeness that athletes should emulate in their practices and competitions.

Using the example of Christ's crucifixion, Neal explained that bodily sacrifice is an expression of love for God. He advised Christian athletes to imagine themselves as Jesus and therefore as capable of experiencing sacrificial pain for God. For example, he told me:

I have a cycling route that I do. At first, I really loved the downhills, but now, I've come to love the uphills. I love feeling the tension and agony in my muscles, and I push through the pain as a love expression for the Lord. As a Christian, I know that God uses a broken person, God uses an empty vessel. And, as I become dead to myself and filled with Jesus, I can push through the pain barrier.

Neal encouraged the Christian athlete to emulate Jesus's ultimate endurance of the pain and agony of crucifixion. He wrote, "It was the attitude of Jesus that brought Him through punishing physical torment that would have stopped other men in the starting blocks. . . . You must have Jesus's attitude in your athletic performance if you are to conform to his likeness [and maximize your athletic potential]."[56] According to Neal, Jesus's pain was part of God's plan, and therefore athletes should understand their own pain as God's plan for them to improve athletically and spiritually.

For Neal, and for many other evangelical Christians, Jesus's crucifixion is the central, organizing theological principle of Christianity. Jesus's death is the primary and most extreme example of the sacrifice that accompanies an allegiance to God. Neal used this understanding of the pain of crucifixion to frame his own athletic pain. He told me that he advises Christian athletes: "You are meant to present yourself as a living sacrifice. Sport can be an opportunity to express love for Jesus for what he did [by also engaging in a physical sacrifice]."

The simultaneously painful and purifying experience of weight training lends itself to spiritual interpretation, particularly for evangelicals who see Christ's suffering and death as the central theological tenet of their faith.[57] It is important to note that even though this experience often carries a sexual subtext that seems to align it with traditionally feminine religious experience, the purposeful pain that accompanies spiritual athletic pleasure firmly positions this experience within masculine understandings of sport. Sport as masculine self-torture connects the athlete's body to the suffering Christ, a pleasurable connection that simultaneously values purposeful pain and transcendent experience.

Pushing through the pain barrier is tied to a masculinizing sporting project that equates manliness, sacrifice, and suffering. According to sports sociologist Michael Messner, "Athletes who are 'playing with pain,' 'giving up their body for the team,' or engaging in obviously highly dangerous plays or maneuvers are consistently portrayed as heroes; conversely, those who remove themselves from games because of injuries raise questions about their character, their manhood."[58] Playing with pain and understanding pain as purposeful align Christian athletes with larger ideologies of sport that value bodily sacrifice. Sportswriters have noted that while this dimension of painful bodily sacrifice has long been normative for male athletes, female athletes increasingly experience the same pressures to play with pain for the sake of winning.[59] In my research, I found that female Christian athletes also turn to metaphors of intimacy to articulate their athletic experiences.

As the following story demonstrates, Neal's ideology of intimate transcendence remains influential for contemporary sports ministry participants. Around the campfire at the Charlotte Lady Eagles' team retreat, Tara played guitar and led praise and worship songs. As the singing ended, M.J., a staff member with the Eagles organization, stood to address the group. The firelight lent a somber dimension to M.J., who was normally full of friendly sarcasm. As she held a small book open in one hand, she began not with a Bible verse but with a story.

"Some of you know that I've been going through a rough time," she began. "On the way to the campfire tonight, I really had to pee, but I didn't want to be late, and somebody said to me, 'M.J., you just spent two months in Ethiopia. Just go pee in the woods.' And I thought to myself, 'Yeah, I'm really good at peeing in the bush. I'll just go in the woods.'

She paused and sighed. And of course, I peed all over my leg and had to go back to the cabin and change and I missed all the singing. And that's kind of how I feel right now—can't even pee right." There was laughter, but it was clear that this anecdote was leading to a more serious story.

M.J. went on, "My father is in jail right now. There have been some troubles in my family. My father was the pastor of our church, and he was caught having affairs with a number of women. I'm not sure what to think about this. The scandal was huge and my whole family is embarrassed and ashamed." M.J. continued to tell her story to the group and confessed questioning her faith. As noted previously, Christian athletes (and evangelicals in general) tend to use a predictable narrative frame for events in their lives. Challenging situations may lead a believer to feel distanced from God, but this distance can be corrected through faithful practices like prayer, Bible reading, and worship. M.J. did not follow this format. This was not a story of overcoming distance but one of experiencing that distance, of living in the confusion and unhappiness of a family event coming between her and God.

Over the course of my time with the Lady Eagles, I participated in a small-group devotional with M.J. and a few others, and M.J. and I became friends. We spent time together outside of the Eagles' events. I went to church with her and her roommate and would join them for glasses of wine on the porch of their house. On my birthday, she arranged an announcement over the loudspeaker at the soccer game that evening: "A special happy birthday to Annie bah-bah-bah-BLAZER!—resident anthropologist for the Charlotte Lady Eagles. Thank you for bringing us a little bit of culture every day." She was a thoughtful friend.

She was also a thoughtful investigator of religion. Her family experiences had led her to deeply question the value and effects of Christianity, and she emerged from this struggle with a sense of intimacy with the divine. During one small-group meeting, she explained to the group, "I had been bathed in the knowledge of the gospel since I was born, but it wasn't until I took the gospel inside of me that I was changed. Everything about me changed from the inside out, instead of wearing the gospel like a veneer over my life. *Knowing* the gospel isn't only about head knowledge, knowing *about* it. It is an intimate feeling of internalizing God's love, knowing it in the biblical sense."

M.J. compared knowledge of the gospel to sexual knowledge of a lover. For her, the most effective language for describing her relationship with God was the language of intimacy. This places M.J. in a long tradition of Christian women using sexual metaphors to describe their relationship with God or Christ. However, M.J.'s identity as a sports ministry leader and former elite athlete allowed her to see that sport itself could produce feelings of intimacy with the divine.

M.J. stayed on staff with the Eagles after the summer I spent with the team, but after a few years, she relocated to Clemson, South Carolina, with her new husband to start a family there. In Clemson, she and her husband were actively involved in ministry but no longer working specifically with athletes. During a phone call with M.J., who was speaking from her Clemson home, I asked her to reflect on the pleasures of sport. I expected her to reference the intimacy that she had spoken of during our time together with the Eagles, but instead, she brought up *Chariots of Fire*, and told me, "This guy who I worked with when I was with the Eagles, he would quote that part of *Chariots of Fire* where the lead guy—what's his name?"

"Eric Liddell," I told her.

"Yes, Eric Liddell," she agreed. "Eric Liddell tells his sister, 'When I run, I feel his pleasure.'" She paused after this quotation, then continued, "So, it's like that. You and God are participating in joy together. It's hard to describe what it feels like to have that connection with God. For me, it's an overwhelming feeling of knowing that I was made for exactly what I'm doing in that moment. And in that moment, God has never been more real. I almost feel like I can reach out and touch him. Everything is more real. There's a phrase in the Bible—'joy inexpressible.' It's like I couldn't really explain it if I wanted to."[60]

Religious studies scholars have long included inexpressibility as a component of religious experience. William James called it "ineffable," impossible to convey in words.[61] This sensation of pleasure beyond words shows up in descriptions of athletic mastery (zone or flow states) and sexual intimacy. M.J.'s feeling of overwhelming knowledge of God's reality is an example of the kind of certainty that Christian athletes derive from the embodied experience of playing sports and an example of how Neal's reworking of sports ministry's priorities allowed for individual religious experience to overshadow traditional kinds of witnessing.

Conclusion

From the 1950s to the 1970s, sports ministry underwent a significant shift and began to present attention to pleasure and pain as more appropriate priorities for Christian athletes than earlier ideas of Christian athletes as celebrity witnesses. As I have shown, this shift emerged from a critique of celebrity evangelism and a desire to address athletics at the level of intention and behavior rather than publicity. The resulting theology of sport, developed by Neal, aligned the sporting values of mental concentration, playing with pain, and obedience to the coach with the evangelical value of establishing a personal relationship with God.

As addressed in the previous chapter, one problem with using athletic celebrities for evangelism was the problem of winning. In order for athletes to gain the kind of celebrity that made them prominent witnesses, they had to win. This meant that they had to conform to the standards already present in the sporting world, even if these standards involved questionable morality. Given this, it is no surprise that Neal's work involved a redefinition of winning that no longer relied on sporting competition but instead relied on theological understandings of religious experience. For Neal and for Christian athletes who embrace his teachings, "winning" is not about points at the end of the game—it is not even about gaining an audience to evangelize. "Winning" is a personal religious experience, narrated as connecting to Jesus through sacrifice, pain, and pleasure.

Due in large part to the theological innovations of Wes Neal, contemporary sports ministry prioritizes embodied sensations as ways to discern God's intentions, God's pleasure, and God's ongoing battle with Satan over the souls of the converted. When Christian athletes feel connected to God, they often describe this as a feeling of "Christlikeness": an affiliation and proximity to Christ that grants them the power to push themselves in their sport. When Christian athletes feel a sense of distance from God, they often frame it as part of "spiritual warfare": Satan uses the athlete's frustration or fatigue to stand in the way of the pleasurable sensation of Christlikeness. These two discourses are key to understanding embodied experience in contemporary sports ministry, and the next chapter turns to female Christian athletes' use of this language, examining how narrative tools can maintain understandings of evangelicalism as valuable and of sport as a viable means to experience transcendent intimacy.

3

Spiritual Warfare and Christlikeness

Narratives of Bodies and Battlefields

"Beat me! Beat me!" Becky shouted as she sprinted alongside a camper finishing an endurance challenge at an all-camp competition. It was the fourth day of the Fellowship of Christian Athletes summer camp, and all the small groups, called "huddles," were competing against each other in a series of games and races. These contests were primarily fun, lighthearted games like wrestling in sumo suits or wheelbarrow races. This general atmosphere made Becky's shouted demand stand out, and I jerked my head away from my conversation to watch Becky and the camper sprint past.

The endurance challenge was the final event of the camp competition. Campers ran to the gym to get a ribbon, then ran to the auditorium to get another ribbon, then returned to the field where they had started. When one of the girls from the volleyball huddle would appear at the edge of the field, Becky, a college athlete and the huddle leader, would sprint alongside her yelling, "Beat me! Come on, beat me!" The exhausted high school girls would break into full sprints, grimacing as they tried to beat Becky to the final checkpoint. Once they sprinted through, Becky gave them a pat on the back, then ran back to the far side of the field to run along with her next camper. I was not the only one watching with awed admiration as Becky did this for all seven of her huddle members.

Becky's inspirational sprinting was powerful in the context of camp not only because of her loud demands that the campers defeat her but also because of her insistence that these high school athletes push their limits. She demonstrated to them physically that they could reach beyond their exhaustion and soreness to sprint, even though they were wiped out from four straight days of intense athletic training. At FCA camp and in sports ministry generally, athletes learned that their faith could be an athletic tool for pushing through exhaustion and soreness. Sports ministry frames athletic experiences like frustration or fatigue as Satan's tools to prevent athletic experiences of Christlikeness. As one camper put it, "I can feel the enemy in my head when I'm sore or tired. It's a big accomplishment to play through the soreness." Athletes at the camp narrated playing through soreness as defeating "the enemy," the ever-present Satan who longs to separate Christian athletes from Christ using sensations within the athletes' bodies.

Evangelical Christians use the discourse of spiritual warfare to address issues as varied as politics, education, sexual infidelity, and depression, to name a few. This discourse was not out of place at an evangelical sports camp; what was striking about its use in an athletic environment was the concrete and tactile application of the concept. Satan, the devil, or the "enemy" was not metaphorical but a force that generated specific and identifiable conditions like soreness, fatigue, or frustration. Anthropologists like Marcel Mauss have focused on embodied initiation rituals that occur during adolescence as extremely influential in developing individual and social understandings.[1] If Mauss is correct in his analysis of the body techniques acquired during adolescence, FCA camp provided high school athletes with a complex narrative for understanding their bodies that emerged from a physiological, psychological, and social matrix. Taking that matrix seriously means digging into the narrative tools that Christian athletes use to describe their world.

Becky's sprinting alongside her campers screaming, "Beat me!" lends itself to multiple interpretations. Certainly, she intended to push the campers beyond what they thought they were capable of. She also increased the intensity of the experience by adding a dimension of violence and punishment to her commands. But, for Becky and for Christian athletes like her, the most important aspect of the sprint was not the camper's satisfaction of learning that she could do more than she thought she could but the knowledge that, in that moment when she chose to sprint, she was fighting against Satan with her faith and her body. Becky had told the huddle earlier that week:

> Sport goes away. Spiritual warfare is real. The enemy is waiting for you to pull you down into the darkness. You have to be on fire for Christ, to be a light that others can run to. Other people will use the enemy's strength

to fight against you; you have to keep your eyes open and use your strong faith to keep clear about who your enemy is.

In this worldview, human existence is a battle between forces of good and evil, with the believer inextricably bound to the fight.

For many evangelicals, once one commits to Christianity, one is also committed to staving off the devil, an indefatigable enemy who will forever attempt to pull the Christian away from Christ.[2] Christian athletes often narrate their physical experiences as part of spiritual warfare. In this war, Satan uses fatigue, frustration, team conflict, and soreness to break down the athlete, who in turn uses the Christlike qualities of determination and meaningful suffering to connect to Christ and avoid unsportsmanlike behavior. Many of the Christian athletes I talked to saw their bodies as the most important site in the battle between Satan and believers, and they used their embodied experiences to affirm their belief in that ongoing battle.[3]

Though Becky was clear that this battle was bigger than sport ("Sport goes away"), many Christian athletes, including Becky, see sport as an important battleground. As noted in the previous chapter, sports ministry treats athletics as an opportunity to experience an intimate connection with Christ, and these experiences establish religious knowledge. Sport minister Wes Neal made athletic suffering meaningful by positioning this pain as an opportunity to connect with the divine. Exploring the twin discourses of spiritual warfare and Christlikeness can help explain how this theological understanding is enacted and experienced in the religious lives of Christian athletes. Spiritual warfare creates a closed system wherein every challenge, every obstacle, and every success can be attributed to either God's plan or the tactics of the devil. This narrative does not always hold perfectly, but when Christian athletes invoke it, the concept of spiritual warfare provides a powerful paradigm for explaining setbacks, elevating the importance of sport, and maintaining evangelical belief structures.

"Game Ready": The Political Resonance of Spiritual Warfare

At the beginning of each summer, FCA launches a new theme for its athletic camps. The theme in 2007 was "Game Ready," which corresponded to a key Bible verse, Ephesians 6:11 (HCSB): "Put on the full armor of God so that you can stand against the tactics of the Devil."[4] When I interviewed an FCA higher-up, he summarized the 2007 camp theme this way:

> So really, the whole "Game Ready" is, we want the image that, after everything we've done, the kids go back—all the videos, the testimonies, the Bible studies, the devotions—they go back and they say, I'm in a battle. I'm in the game. And, I have a choice to determine what team I want to be on. And, also I have an opportunity every day to be victorious or not. You know, and, it's going to be a struggle. It's going to be a battle. And, you just don't walk into games haphazardly and just think it's going to be, you know, malaise and whatever.
>
> But, instead, we want you to be ready. We want you to be focused, be prepared for that game that's before them. We feel that, as a ministry, our responsibility this summer was to equip them with the understanding that they are approaching a game. And, it could be a life-and-death situation, physically or spiritually.

In this description, the element of conflict is apparent—FCA intended to teach campers that they are embroiled in spiritual warfare. The ease with which the speaker moved between the concepts "battle" and "game" equalizes these two ideas in importance and urgency, making athletic experiences into military confrontations in the war against Satan and Satan's powers of worldly temptation.

For many evangelical Christians, embattlement is a central theological concept that colors their self-perception, their interactions with other people, and their relationship to the world at large.[5] Embattlement is the feeling of being constantly under threat; it is a sensation of being vulnerable to harm that triggers an urgent desire to protect oneself or to fight back. Spiritual warfare, as the overarching camp theme, encompassed embattlement in sporting competition as well as societal problems and individual struggles. According to one curriculum developer:

> Look at our youth. A lot of them are depressed. They're hopeless. They have no vision for their life, and they don't understand why. They come from broken homes, and they don't understand why. They have trouble

at school, they don't know why. It's because there is this battle going on. So, you kind of tiptoe around it or you can call it what it is. Satan is out to get you and ruin your life. It's kind of a call to arms. I mean, tap into that competitive mind-set—someone's pushing you. How are you going to respond? It's like, "I'm not going to be bullied."

Because FCA recognized that athletes are already familiar with competition and struggle, it structured this curriculum to highlight conflict as central to athletic and Christian success.

The organization's curriculum developers knew that war was a prevailing metaphor in sport and was also a reality in the contemporary world. Their reference to war reflected American political involvement on the global stage at that time. I asked two curriculum developers about the choice to focus on war and battle in the 2007 theme, and they responded:

> CURRICULUM DEVELOPER 1: I think there's several layers to that. I mean, one is, I can remember my coach saying, in looking at the entire season, each game is a battle, but the season is the war. Like, "We lost the battle. We didn't lose the war." I mean, war is such a relevant issue across the world right now. I don't think that was directly tied in, but it kind of—
> CURRICULUM DEVELOPER 2: It was happening.
> CURRICULUM DEVELOPER 1: It wasn't some obscure reference that nobody would understand.

Though connecting to ongoing global conflict was not FCA's primary goal for its camp curriculum, the United States' continued military involvement in Iraq and Afghanistan was common knowledge, and FCA was able to draw on cultural familiarity with military missions to increase the intensity of the idea of spiritual warfare.

Following the terrorist attacks of September 11, 2001, the Bush administration launched a series of military endeavors intended to quell terrorism and protect the American way of life. President George W. Bush continually presented military action as a dualistic battle between good and evil, us and them. Political science scholar Giorgio Agamben has noted that this rhetoric was part of the normalization of an omnipresent threat, establishing a constant "state of exception." Agamben's analysis is helpful for understanding spiritual warfare. Normalizing the state of exception (for example, airports' constant orange threat level) makes the emergency the rule and "the very distinction between peace and war . . . impossible."[6] Though normalizing the state of exception has been on the rise in Western politics since World War II, Agamben points out that the Bush administration was particularly adept at invoking a state of exception to justify its decisions after September 11, 2001. According to Agamben's analysis, Americans have accepted and continue to function under the pretense that we are in a state of exception, when in fact the exception has become the norm.

Embattlement has long been a central component of evangelical religious rhetoric, but post-9/11 political rhetoric connected embattlement to American identity. Born-again president George W. Bush frequently used the concept of embattlement to support military endeavors. Religious studies scholar Melissa Conroy analyzed Bush's rhetoric in an essay on American militarism:

> Bush has said, "There is no neutral ground—no neutral ground—in the fight between civilization and terror, because there is no neutral ground between good and evil, freedom and slavery, and life and death." This epic battle, so clearly delineated, stresses the absolute nature of differences between the two forces. It serves to create a harmonious idea of "America" by excluding a scapegoat, whose form is any force thought to threaten the beatific ideal image of America.[7]

As Conroy notes, the simplistic dualistic presentation of "us" against "them" served to elevate an ideal image of the United States and presented any threat to this ideal as an act of evil.

America as an ideal moral model has had great appeal for some evangelical Christians. Conservative Christian political involvement since the 1970s has often mobilized around America's potential (framed as not fully realized) to act as a moral beacon for the world. Partly because of its established presence in American politics, the Bush administration was able to use the language of America as a moral model in response to the attacks of 9/11.[8] David Harvey has argued that Bush's presentation of America's enemy allowed the Bush administration to invent and justify "preemptive strikes" on groups and countries construed as threats to freedom. Harvey stated that this formulation is a "catastrophic and . . . suicidal calculation" that functions by associating the war on terror with the apocalypse.[9] Religious studies scholar Clayton Crockett has agreed, noting that "the conflation of war and violence with biblical revelations and predictions of the Apocalypse and the second coming of Christ suggest that something is deeply wrong at the heart of the American Empire."[10] Perhaps what is deeply wrong is what religious studies scholar Jason Bivins identified as a threat to the democratic value of conversation. He wrote, referring both to conservative Christians and to political liberals, "Differences in religio-national destiny are issued as challenges, not to conversation partners in the work of democracy, but to the opposing team, whose utter defeat offers the only true consolation, the surest sign of victory."[11] Bivins's choice to frame this failure of conversation as a battle/game shows both the prevalence of sports/war rhetoric in politics and political assessment and the effects of such rhetoric, namely, the propensity to see one another as competitors, not as equals working toward a common goal.

This competitive framework was particularly common in right-wing Christian politics after 9/11, and scholars have argued that conservative Christians rely on embattlement and persecution rhetoric to rally support for political and military actions.[12] Elizabeth Castelli has pointed out, "The rhetoric of 'the war on Christians' operates outside of the empirical field, creating a self-referential and self-generating logic that begins from the premise that Christians are by definition perennially locked in battle with 'the enemy' in a cosmic war without end."[13] Castelli's analysis emphasizes that for evangelical Christians, there is no outside to spiritual warfare. Like Agamben's concept of the normative state of exception, many evangelicals perceive their world as constantly under urgent threat and can narrate every aspect of their lives as part of the ongoing battle between Satan and believers.

Due to its prevalence in conservative Christian political rhetoric, spiritual warfare was not out of place in sports ministry. Although the language of spiritual warfare achieved greater resonance after 9/11 because of concurrent political rhetoric, spiritual warfare in sports ministry almost never focused on politics. Though the political resonance with this presentation of spiritual warfare is important, it bears noting that very little of spiritual warfare in sports ministry was framed in political terms. For the Christian athletes I met, the more pressing battle was not political but athletic, and spiritual warfare was not politically enacted but fought through their bodies on the playing field.

Embodying Spiritual Warfare at Camp

Very early in the camp experience, campers recognized and elaborated on conflict as a central component of evangelical identity. Using materials included in *God's Game Plan* (the Bible provided to all campers), campers and huddle leaders discussed sport as spiritual warfare. For example, one Bible study question read, "In order to be victorious, we need to have a victory over something or someone. What is the battle we are in? Who or what is your opponent?"[14] Campers listed "battles" with the world, within themselves, and with Satan. In the huddle I observed, campers named things like self-doubt, physical insecurity, pride, and overinvestment in social standards.[15] The Bible study guide emphasized that doubt, especially doubt about their physical abilities, comes from Satan: "One of the greatest victories the enemy can have is creating unbelief. If we never recognize that Satan exists, then we will think that we don't have an opponent, and then we won't think that we are in a competition. At that point, he has won."[16] In this context, doubting the existence of Satan is part of spiritual warfare. Taking this seriously means treating spiritual warfare as all-encompassing.

On the second day of camp, the morning's speaker emphasized urgency and importance:

> Not if, it *is* coming. The enemy will attack. We're here to play sports, but sport is also the ground of spiritual warfare. The enemy works in three ways to attack you through sport: to make you behave in an un-Christian way, to exploit your weaknesses and flaws through self-doubt, and to distract your focus as an athlete. You will see it this week. The enemy will attack. But, I want you to know that you can have great joy, because we have the ultimate weapon against the enemy [holds up Bible]: the truth will help you fight.

The "attack" on Christian athletes was an embodied one. The speaker presented physical sensations like exhaustion as weapons in a war fought on the terrain of their bodies. Camp leaders instructed campers to see themselves as fighting against self-doubt and distraction, narrated as weapons of the devil, and therefore to see the opposite sensations, confidence and concentration, as gifts from God. Using this framework, Christian athletes could interpret all their sensory impressions as part of a powerful conflict between superhuman forces.

The camp curriculum dedicated a day's worth of study to the following Bible verses:

> This is why you must take up the full armor of God, so that you may be able to resist in the evil day, and having prepared everything, take your stand. Stand, therefore, with truth like a belt around your waist, righteousness like the armor on your chest, and your feet sandaled with readiness for the gospel of peace. In every situation take the shield of faith, and with it you will be able to extinguish the flaming arrows of the evil one. Take the helmet of salvation, and the sword of the Spirit, which is God's word. (Eph. 6:13–17 HCSB)

The curriculum broke this passage down into distinct elements; each part of the armor held a specific meaning that was integral to participation in spiritual warfare. For example, camp teachings connected sandals to the "gospel of peace." According to the instruction, this was a directive to share the gospel with others; the sandals represented a reminder that believers have to go to others, not expect others to come to them. Additionally, campers learned that the "peace" attached to the gospel stood for a proper sense of balance and a readiness for battle; even words like "peace" fell under the umbrella of spiritual warfare. A second part of the armor that bears mention here is the "sword of the Spirit," which camp leaders interpreted as the Bible. In this understanding, the Bible was an aggressive tool not only for defeating Satan but also for evangelizing to others. As one camp speaker put it, "Imagine this [camp] is a locker room. It's scary out there. The enemy works to marginalize Jesus Christ. Turn to your teammate right now and say, 'I'm prepared.' Your opponent is ready to rumble, but he can't match up to the word of God." For campers, the Bible was a weapon that could be used for athletic and spiritual victory.

According to the FCA camp curriculum, Satan attacks at the level of the body. Defending against this requires Christlikeness, connecting to Christ's power through meaningful suffering. Campers' athletic suffering then, like playing with pain or pushing through fatigue and soreness, could take on religious significance and affirm the reality of spiritual warfare. A final example from FCA camp may help demonstrate this.

On the final morning, campers gathered in the gym to complete a grueling twenty-five minutes of taxing drills called "Gut Check." As the culmination of FCA camp, Gut Check reflected the emphasis on spiritual warfare by creating a situation for campers to call on God as they pushed their bodies physically. The gym contained a series of twenty-five stations, each representing an exercise—push-ups, wall sits, calf raises, lunges, high knees, and so on. Campers and their huddle leaders spent one minute at each station and then moved on to the next in a grueling rotation around the gym. There was a station for prayer, but as one camp leader reminded everyone, "Prayer is not a station for rest. Prayer is a station to ask for help." Gut Check enacted an important distinction between Christian athletes and the sporting world at large; the exercises were the same as those that athletes would encounter at secular training camps, but at FCA camp, calling on God in moments of physical exhaustion was a practical tool for completing these exercises.

The atmosphere before Gut Check was tense. All week, the campers had been talking nervously about the event. In the previous evening's huddle meeting, Becky told the girls, "It's okay to be scared. I was terrified for my first Gut Check. The name itself is scary enough." Before the event, I overheard two campers talking about how they were going to be "faithful teammates" and not let anyone fall behind. They sounded nervous.

The challenge of Gut Check was twofold—to complete the exercises, but also to do so as a team. Despite the growing tension, the camp director reminded me that Gut Check is not about failure: "Anyone can go through Gut Check, you could go through Gut Check right now. You can do four push-ups in a minute and go through Gut Check." Because completion was the measure of success for Gut Check, everyone who completed it was equally accomplished. Even the children's huddle participated in Gut Check. No one counted how many push-ups a person did or ranked the teams at the end, and because everyone finished at the same time, all having endured the twenty-five stations, each athlete could feel proud of his or her performance without measuring it against anyone else's.

Even though campers would be able to go through Gut Check at a leisurely pace and technically complete the series of exercises, members of the huddles pushed each other to their limits. At the edge of what campers thought they could accomplish, huddle leaders encouraged them to call on God and continue on, modeling a combination of athleticism and religious devotion. As the volleyball huddle began a minute of wall jumps (jumping up and down while facing a wall, reaching to touch the highest possible point), they joined together singing a song that the worship band had played the night before. "Yes, Lord. Yes, Lord. Yes, yes, Lord," they sang over and over again, keeping the rhythm of jumping up and down together. Gut Check embodied the lesson that calling on God can help players succeed athletically. These campers learned that their limits were beyond what they had thought, and that they were capable of accomplishing things that had seemed terrifying and intimidating. Just as FCA taught campers that doubt and weakness are tools of Satan, Gut Check reinforced the idea that strength and perseverance come from God.

As the culmination of the FCA camp experience, Gut Check combined embodied, mental, and community action to support belief in the reality and power of God. Religious studies scholar Catherine Bell has argued that the purpose of ritualized events (like Gut Check) is the "production of ritualized agents, persons who have an instinctive knowledge of these schemes embedded in their bodies, in their sense of reality, and in their understanding of how to act in ways that both maintain and qualify the complex microrelations of power."[17] By narrating their lives as a battle, evangelical athletes elevated the importance of sport and combined embodied knowledge with religious certainty. For many of these campers, all of life, including athletics, was part of a spiritual battle. While they engaged the sporting world by playing on secular teams, they sought to remain distinctive by framing sporting participation as part of an eternal battle against Satan. As such, sports ministry produces a particular kind of ritualized agent who can use his or her embodied athletic experiences to do the religious work of confirming belief, identity, and community.

The Struggle for Christlikeness on AIA's Traveling Basketball Team

The FCA camp was for high school athletes. These young athletes interacted with college athletes and coaches and were generally willing to employ the language of spiritual warfare to narrate their physical experiences. However, this phenomenon is not limited to high school athletes. College and postcollege Christian athletes also employ the language of spiritual warfare to understand their sporting experiences. As noted in the previous chapter, Christian athletes describe athletic pleasure as a sign of God's approval and love. When they experience what Wes Neal called a "Total Release Performance" and M.J. described as "joy inexpressible," this motivates them to resist negative reactions to athletic hardship. They narrate this experience and its resultant power as "Christlikeness," and Christian athletes rely on their affinity with Christ to resist Satan's attempts to undermine their playing ability. During the several weeks that I traveled with Athletes in Action's women's basketball team, a group composed of ten college and postcollege players and a staff of six women, the team and staff frequently invoked spiritual warfare and Christlikeness. These discourses hold sway for older Christian athletes and continue to be prominent explanations for team struggles and team victories beyond high school sports or a weeklong camp experience.

Tina, an AIA staff member whose primary role was religious education but who had previously coached college basketball, explained it this way: "Christlikeness to me is a process. The opportunities to be Christlike normally come at the moments when, in our human-ness, we least want to think about being Christlike!" Tina experienced this in her struggle to give up cursing. Language is a very important part of Christian witnessing, not only because storytelling is integral to evangelism but also because evangelicals are aware that outsiders judge a Christian's dedication based on self-presentation. A coach who curses constantly but professes Christianity will not be taken as seriously as a Christian coach with clean language. Likewise, a player who curses on the court will lose credibility as a Christian witness. However, for many Christian athletes, including Tina, this was not an easy habit to change. She described her experience as follows:

> Believe it or not, I used to cuss like a longshoreman! At some point in reading the Bible, I began to notice a lot of verses having to do with the tongue or with our mouths and what types of things come out of it. I got pretty convicted about it and started working on it. It took a while for it to change, and at some point I no longer thought about it, it was just dif-

ferent. I remember noticing the change one day when I hit my head on the corner of a cabinet. Old Tina would've let out the F-bomb before she could even think about what she was saying. But I think I said something like, "Man, that hurts!!" And later it dawned on me that something had changed within.

Tina narrated this as an internal change, brought about by her increased attention to sacred texts and Christian practices. When her actions became habitual, rather than forced, she became fully integrated with the practice. In this way, she did not think of herself as imitating Christ; instead, her desire to become Christlike influenced her behavior in a way that she understood as closeness to Christ.[18] "It gets to the point where you don't have to stop and think about your behavioral choice. You just do the Christlike thing because it has become your nature." Cursing, especially on the court, could cause others to question a Christian athlete's sincerity, and that would undermine the goal of demonstrating Christlike behavior. If Christian athletes or coaches are able to alter behaviors like cursing, they are likely to attribute this change to God working in their lives, reinforcing their certainty of God's power.

Becoming Christlike has pragmatic effects for many Christian athletes. They count on Christlikeness to give them the ability to play through exhaustion, remain composed under pressure, deal with loss and injuries, and cultivate a perspective where their athletic performance does not determine their self-worth. During one halftime locker-room discussion, a player named Stacey told the other players, "Honestly, girls, call on him. I'm running. I'm tired. And that's when I know I can't do it alone. That's when you just have to ask, and he will surprise you." During the second half of that game, Stacey lifted her eyes to the ceiling in moments of extreme exhaustion. Then, she would keep going.

Simply understanding that Christlikeness was possible did not immediately lead to it. During one halftime, when the team was losing, I mentioned to an AIA staffer that the players seemed tired and depressed. She responded, "Yeah, most people don't understand that it's more than just basketball. God is working in their lives, and that can take a lot out of you." The AIA fall tour had a rigorous traveling schedule, and players never had the luxury of a home court. They played nine games in fifteen days, spending only one week together to train before touring. The team traveled from Ohio, through Canada, and across the Northeast and the Southeast, competing against Division I college teams. The travel and the intensity of their religious goals made for an exhausting combination. As players sought to experience Christlikeness on the court, some of them grew discouraged if they couldn't pinpoint results. Athletes in Action attempted to create a situation where becoming Christlike was possible, but it was by no means inevitable.

A few players expressed concern and frustration that they weren't playing basketball as intensely on the AIA team as they had on other teams. On a van ride to one game, the starting point guard said, "I was really at peace, but then I was confused because I wasn't playing as hard or as competitively. And it was nice not to have that pressure. Not to feel like, 'Oh, we lost. We're gonna have to run tomorrow.' Or, 'We gotta watch tape and look at our mistakes.' No, it's like, 'Hey, we got another game tomorrow.'"

Tina responded, "Yeah, all the things that used to motivate you are not there, so you have to rethink what motivates you. It's like we were talking yesterday with [the assistant coach] that when you start trying to implement this stuff, there's an initial decline in performance. And it will go up. It will go up better than you were before. And you don't decline because suddenly you're playing for God. You decline because you're trying to figure it out."

In this response, Tina presented both decline and improvement as integral to becoming Christlike. Tina recognized that changing the way you played sports was work, and this effort could negatively impact athletic performance. However, similar to Wes Neal's sense of maximizing athletic potential through Christian dedication, Tina saw the time spent figuring out how to play for God as a period of temporary decline leading to future athletic improvement.[19]

Within the framework of understanding athletic experiences as religiously meaningful, even injuries could represent opportunities for religious growth. For example, one player, Jenna, suffered a knee injury and told the team, "If I can't play, then I'm just dead weight and I should go home." Stacey responded, "You are here for a reason. We are all here for a reason. God brought this group together for this tour, and it's no accident that we are all together right now." Stacey understood injury as part of God's plan, and Jenna's injury fit her understanding. Because pain is an inevitable component of AIA's rigorous fall tour training and game schedule, Stacey understood this pain as evidence of God's involvement and used Jenna's knee injury to affirm God's existence and divine intentions. Stacey saw the purpose of AIA's fall tour as more than playing basketball games. If the team's purpose was simply to win games, then Jenna was right; her knee injury was grounds to send her home. But for Stacey and Christian athletes like her, an injured player was valuable because that player's presence must be part of God's plan for the team. Emphasizing that "we are all here for a reason" gave Jenna's injury religious significance.

The second-to-last game of the tour was a tough loss. I sat on the bench with the team and watched as Stacey cheered for the team despite the ongoing defeat. She would yell, "De-fense!" and clap twice, gesturing for everyone else to join in. At one point, Maria came off the court looking exhausted, and she sat down saying, "This sucks." Stacey gave her an intense glare and cheered louder.

In the locker room after the game, the players scattered on benches eating sandwiches and drinking Gatorade. Stacey had taken a bad knock to the face during the game and was nursing a cut lip. She misspoke about something and then joked to the trainer, "I think I have a concussion." Everyone laughed and went on eating. About fifteen minutes later, Laura knelt by Stacey's chair and saw that Stacey looked noticeably paler. Laura called for the trainer, who took Stacey out to the hallway to get some air. In the locker room, the atmosphere was tense—players looked at their half-eaten sandwiches, not knowing whether to keep eating or follow Stacey to the hallway. The trainer appeared in the doorway and motioned the team to come out to the hall.

Maria was already in the hallway, praying for Stacey, with her hands on her. The other players reached out to Stacey and touched her on her head and shoulders, with Maria saying, "Please, heal Stacey, God. We know that you are Lord and that you can heal her. You say it in your word. You are not man that you can lie, you can heal her and we know this." The other players responded with "Amen" and "Yes, Lord." After a short while, the trainer sent the team back into the locker room. Everyone sat down with their sandwiches again, but Maria said, "Can we just pray for her? I mean, we can eat later." The women formed a circle in the locker room, and each one prayed for Stacey. By the time everyone had contributed, an ambulance had arrived.

When the team filed back out into the hallway, Stacey was lying on the floor, and the attending EMT was asking her questions. She responded clearly, and her pulse and blood pressure were normal. The EMT said that she had experienced an anxiety attack. Back in the locker room, Abby laughingly said, "We prayed the devil right out of her." Stacey said she didn't know what had happened.

Stacey's episode is one example of how a physical, embodied event can support religious knowledge. Though Abby laughed when she attributed Stacey's physical state to the devil and identified the team's prayer as the mechanism for defeating the devil, her statement was not out of line in this context. Maria clearly saw prayer as an activity that could help Stacey. She prayed in the hallway while in direct contact with Stacey's body and then initiated a group prayer in the locker room to continue to ask God to heal Stacey. Stacey's recovery then became a sign of God's power, confirming prayer as a powerful Christian practice. Maria's words were not about belief but about knowledge. She declared to God that they as a team knew God's power and abilities. Stacey's subsequent recovery without medical assistance confirmed Maria's stated knowledge. As such, injuries posed an opportunity for the team to identify God working through their bodies.

Not every episode of praying over injuries on the AIA team had the same outcome. At the end of one practice, the team encircled several injured players and prayed over them, laying on hands. During a moment of tension the next day, one of the injured players, Tanya, told another teammate, "You all laid on your hands like you got the healing power of Jesus, but I'm still hurt, so don't be acting like you healed me." Compared with the other players, Tanya was less invested in AIA's evangelistic project. She would roll her eyes at the constant use of Christian language and distanced herself from her more devout teammates. Though Stacey or Maria might have interpreted Tanya's injury as God attempting to show the team something, Tanya did not talk about her injury in terms of religious significance. In contrast to the dominant Christian athletic paradigm, Tanya was openly skeptical of treating all aspects of her athletic life as part of God's plan or as part of spiritual warfare.

Tina, on the other hand, was fully invested in a worldview of spiritual warfare and described team tensions as a trial that God intended them to overcome. For example, early in the tour, it became evident that there was tension between the players and the coaches. After one practice, Tina spoke to the whole team about their relationship with the head coach. "All right, you all need to have a discussion right now about what's going on, because there is some serious tension that needs to be dealt with. Talk it out, then choose two players to go and talk to coach."

The conversation became heated almost before Tina left the room. Jenna spoke up, "I am feeling disrespected. I feel like all that we did at training camp, where we're all equal, is out. . . . I feel like the other day when I was like, 'I just need to step away,' and coach was like, 'We have to pray for you then,' made me feel like I was doing something wrong. And I hate that."

Jenna wasn't the only one who was feeling disrespected, but Stacey tried to reframe the situation as part of God's plan for the team. "Whenever there's animosity, it's always a little bit you and a little bit the other person. There is spiritual warfare, and we have to be aware of how the devil will come between us. We're all here for the same reason."

Tanya mumbled something from behind an ice pack on her lip. "I got something to say." Everyone turned to listen. "Are we playing to win? Or are we playing for God? Because I feel like we're playing to win. Because if we're playing for God, how come she didn't get in the game?" she asked, pointing to Laura, who didn't play the night before. "I mean, we were up by ten points, fifteen points. If we're playing for God, we all gotta feel that godly love, you know what I'm saying? I mean, it's confusing."

Abby responded, "Part of playing for God *is* playing to win."

Abby's statement was more complicated than it might seem. She could have meant that *winning* was important because it demonstrated to others that Christianity does not diminish one's athletic ability and would allow the team to gain a larger audience for witnessing. She could also have meant that *trying to win* was important because it is within this competitive struggle that one is most likely to call on God and experience Christlikeness. It is likely that she meant both of these things.

A number of other players weighed in on the issue of playing to win, and the consensus was that playing to win is important, playing as a team is important, and balancing those two things is difficult. Laura was in an especially difficult situation because she hadn't played in any of the games at that point, and everyone else had. "Of course, I want to play," Laura told me later that day. "I came here to play. But if coach doesn't have a place for me on the floor, then I have to deal with that. And of course it brings up my own insecurities. Like, I'm gonna think I suck or that I'm not good enough, but those are my insecurities, and I have to deal with them." Laura's language did not invoke a struggle toward Christlikeness but a struggle with herself. If Christlikeness is most often experienced during intense athletic competition, then lack of playing time may affect one's desire for Christlikeness. And, if confirmation of the possibility of Christlikeness serves to solidify religious knowledge, athletes who do not experience this confirmation may be less likely to invest in the evangelistic project of AIA. This was true on the fall tour, where the two players with the least amount of playing time, Laura and Tanya, were the most likely to criticize AIA and to resist framing their participation in religious terms.

The next night, the team had an exciting come-from-behind victory at the University of Massachusetts. Down 41–27 at the half, the team rallied and won 94–83 in overtime. Throughout the second half, Tina and Stacey would yell things like, "What was that? That was the Holy Spirit!" after a successful basket or "Who do you play for?!" to keep the team energized. After the win, Abby clapped me on the shoulder, saying, "You just witnessed a miracle." Abby and others understood the team's victory as a religious event that affirmed the power of God. The team's sportswriter wrote on their blog, "The incredible thing about this win is that the girls knew that it was Jesus who carried them, made their shots fall in the second half (they scored 27 in the whole first half and 17 alone in OT), gave them extra energy to persevere and ultimately win the game. Even more exciting than their win is that they seemed to get that realization at the end."[20] Athletes in Action staff attributed the win to Christ working through the bodies of these athletes.

The team was elated—except Laura, who didn't play. While the team was milling about in the lobby, laughing and joking with the other team after the game, a teary-eyed Laura ducked into a utility closet. I followed her in, and she said to me, "I don't want to be sad. I don't want to cry about it. If it weren't just me, if there were other players sitting on the bench too. . . . But, it's just me. And I feel really isolated." For

Laura, as an athlete traveling with a Christian team but not an athlete who competed, narrating the win in religious terms did not help her feelings of self-doubt and exclusion. The staff and players like Abby and Stacey framed the win as divine intervention, as evidence both of God's power and of the athletes' ability to experience this power through the activity of sport. But for second-string players like Laura, lack of access to competition undermined her religious knowledge and made her feel isolated and alone.

Tanya left the tour the next day. She felt that the enterprise of AIA was hypocritical. "When we won [against UMass], it was all about God's power, but the night before, when we lost, no one said a word about Jesus." Tanya and I left Boston on the same day, and when I rejoined the team in Virginia a few days later, no one mentioned her. I had expected some discussion of Tanya's decision to leave. In particular, I had expected that the team would be interested in conveying to me, the note-taking anthropologist, some sort of justification for why Tanya would leave. Instead, the main focus remained firmly on upcoming games and on the spiritual education of those present. Tanya was neither demonized nor explained away—she was simply absent.

During the last ten minutes of a losing game in Virginia, the coach sent Laura in from the bench. The team began to cheer for her, and when she made a three-point shot, everyone on the bench rose to their feet, exploding in cheers. After the game, Stacey asked Laura, "How did it feel when you made that shot?" Laura responded, "It felt normal. Like if I would have made that on my team, no one would have cared. But everyone was really excited because I don't play that much. That's the difference. Everyone went nuts for me." Laura noticed that her teammates paid special attention to her playing time because it had been a point of contention with the coach and the team had previously discussed it as a disruption of team unity. She felt uncomfortable with the extra attention and sought to normalize her sporting performance rather than elevate it as a religious experience. Tanya's departure and Laura's discomfort fall outside the narrative of becoming Christlike, and the rest of the team and the coaches largely overlooked these exceptions.

The related discourses of spiritual warfare and Christlikeness reflect a strong matrix of physiological, psychological, and social understandings. Athletes like Laura or Tanya who were resistant to or excluded from one or more aspects of this matrix were less likely to fully embrace the worldview of sport as an embodied battle between forces of evil and Christlike believers. While sports ministers argue that one can experience sensations of Christlikeness during practice or on the bench, as well as in games, in my experience the heightened intensity of game competition or a singular challenge like FCA's Gut Check provided the settings most conducive to this sort of interpretation.

The goal of experiencing Christlikeness has done much to offset the problem of winning discussed in chapters 1 and 2, but positioning Christlikeness as athletically embodied represents another disconnect between evangelical Christianity and the world of sports. In competitive sports, not every athlete is equally valuable or receives equal playing time. While FCA camp constructed the experience of Gut Check to be accessible to all Christian athletes regardless of ability or rank, in most athletic situations Christian athletes do not experience competition uniformly. As the disparities between active and benched players on AIA's team show, the tendency to employ the framework of Christlikeness and spiritual warfare may be directly related to the athlete's competitive experience. In this case, less time involved in intense competitive struggle translated into a tendency to undermine or reject the sports ministry framework of Christlikeness and spiritual warfare.

Making individual athletic experiences the most important aspect of sports ministry has had the unintended consequence of privileging athletes who get more playing time. While Wes Neal's theological innovations shifted sports ministry away from celebrity athletes, they did not entirely do away with hierarchy. In fact, it may be impossible to develop an egalitarian theology for sports ministry when sport itself relies on hierarchy. Abby's earlier statement, "Part of playing for God *is* playing to win," skims over the deep complexity of trying to align these two goals. For athletes like Abby, spiritual warfare can function as a closed system in which instances of athletic hardship are part of God's plan, distractions by Satan, opportunities to pursue Christlikeness, or all three. However, this paradigm does not hold perfectly. Christian athletes like Laura and Tanya resisted framing their lives as spiritual warfare and criticized AIA's practices. Their experiences demonstrate that Christian athleticism is not a unified whole but a work in progress, spearheaded by those with a vision of using athletics as an avenue to embody Christlikeness.

Conclusion

Early in my time traveling with the AIA team, they spent an evening volunteering with a Boys and Girls Club. We got very lost on our way, and by the time the players walked into the gym, they had only fifteen minutes to spend with the group of ten or so ten-year-old girls. The players quickly organized games and drills for the kids, trying to make the most of the time remaining. For the last few minutes, the kids sat on the floor, and the team stood in a row in front of them with Tina slightly out in front.

"We are a basketball team called Athletes in Action," Tina told the kids. "All these girls played college basketball at different schools around the country." She paused for the players to introduce themselves and hand out programs for the upcoming game. Then she asked, "Do you know the one thing that we all have in common?"

"You all play basketball?" one girl guessed.

Tina smiled, and said, "Well, the two things we all have in common?"

"You're on the same team?"

"You're all champions?"

"You're best friends?" someone guessed.

Eventually Tina said, "The most important thing that we have in common is that we're all Christians."

"Me too. I'm a Christian," piped up one of the girls, and some others agreed.

"What does it mean to be a Christian?" Tina asked.

One girl answered, "It means you go to church, read the Bible, pray . . ."

Tina responded, "*That's* what it means to be a Christian?"

Another girl tried to answer, "It means you are nice to everyone."

Tina looked at the kids, "Really? *That's* what it means to be a Christian?"

Finally, the answer came that she had been looking for. One girl quietly said, "You have to open your heart."

"There we go. Tell everybody what you said," Tina told her.

"You have to open your heart," she said a little louder.

"That's right. You have to open your heart. Does anyone know what a sin is?" Tina asked.

All the kids said yes.

"Give me an example of a sin."

"Being rude to someone."

"She does that 24/7," another girl said, pointing to the girl sitting next to her.

Tina smiled and said, "Being rude to someone. Has anyone ever done that?" The kids all raised their hands. "Has anyone ever done something you wish you hadn't?" Tina continued, and the kids raised their hands again. "Does anyone know about Jesus?" The kids said yes. "Well, when you open your heart to Jesus, all your sins get washed away. It's the easiest thing in the world. You only have to mean it. Doesn't that sound easy?"

"Yes," the kids responded, using a tone that reminded me of the way children respond to their teachers.

"Anyone want to do it?" Tina asked.

"Yes," they answered again. Tina asked the kids to stand, and the team encircled the group, holding hands. Tina led them in a prayer, and the kids repeated every word she said. So did Stacey and some of the other players. After the prayer, some of the kids were waiting to meet their parents. A few of them stood by Tina. She put an arm around one little girl, asking, "Did you accept Jesus into your heart today?" The girl nodded. "I'm so proud of you," Tina told her.

This instance demonstrates the ease with which evangelicals like Tina view conversion. It's as easy as a repeated prayer. But within evangelicalism, this prayer is framed as a moment with eternal consequences. FCA camp programming constantly reminded campers that their identity as Christians made them targets for the devil, and that Satan would use the activity most important to them, sport, to challenge their faith. This made sport part of spiritual warfare, an understanding reflected in AIA activities as well. What Tina did not tell those ten-year-old girls, but what perhaps she thought they might experience later, was that being a Christian athlete is a constant struggle to unite two identities: Christian and athlete. She also did not tell them that being on a Christian team does not prevent common sport struggles like injury, exclusion, or loss. And she did not tell them that Christian athletes disagree with each other about what it means to be a Christian athlete.

All that information could arrive with Christian athletic training at an older age. Many children who play sports in the United States are introduced very early to the idea that they can combine sport with Christianity.[21] As they reach high school age, and perhaps attend one of FCA's hundreds of summer camps, they may be taught lessons like the one Becky tried to teach her campers in her sprinted demand—"Beat me!"—or the one enacted through Gut Check: you can go further than you thought possible, and calling on God is what gives you this ability. Perhaps some of those high school students will become college athletes and get involved with a campus ministry like AIA, perhaps even volunteering to travel with a team to demonstrate their ability to be both a Christian and an athlete. But, throughout all of that, it will never be as easy as that prayer that Tina led for the children in that gym. Perhaps, like Laura or Tanya, the identities of Christian and athlete will not hold together, and what they will learn instead is that playing to win, even if it is playing for God, still entails inequality, struggle, and pain. But perhaps, like Stacey or Tina, those struggles will form the basis for religious knowledge of a powerful and present God.

PART II

Effects

4

Wearing Our Shorts a Little Longer

Testing the Boundaries of Evangelical Femininity

"I mean, I'm six foot two. I'm tall and strong. I'm the loudest, meanest player on the field. And that's just not allowed for women in the church. It's just not allowed," Nora, a player on the Charlotte Lady Eagles, told me. "It's not that anyone tells you explicitly how you're supposed to be. But there's a lot of covert messages—this is what a woman looks like, this is what her goals are. That's just not what I am. And I have that fight in my mind every day when I'm walking into a church or into campus ministry."

Nora experienced pressure from her religious community to comport herself in feminine ways. The covert messages she identified told her that her height, strength, behaviors, and priorities were out of line with the larger evangelical community. Sports ministry was a way for Nora to feel a sense of belonging to evangelicalism without modifying her appearance or sacrificing her goals. "With the Eagles," she continued, "there's twenty-six of us on the roster. And they get that we are all different. We can wear our shorts a little longer here. We can push harder, and it's not weird." In the context of the Charlotte Lady Eagles, Nora could wear longer shorts (in the style of male athletes) without experiencing anxiety that her religious community would interpret this negatively. Pushing hard on the soccer field was an activity that she enjoyed, and she liked that her tall, strong body made her valuable for her team. Being in an evangelical environment that valued her height and strength provided an alternative to church and campus ministry settings where she often felt out of place.

In part I of this book, I explored how evangelicals used sports to achieve their goals of witnessing and experiencing a sense of closeness with God. These goals are part of evangelical culture and are shared between men and women. Evangelical men and women also share another set of goals regarding their relationship to each other. Evangelical Christianity promotes marriage between a man and a woman as God's plan for every believer, and part of that marriage ideal includes bearing and raising children. When Nora said, "That's just not what I am," she meant not only that her appearance set her apart but also that her goal of being an elite soccer player was difficult to mesh with the evangelical priorities of marriage and motherhood.

Evangelicals have long connected women's bodies to sexual temptation and sinfulness. Because of this, evangelical women often feel pressure to appear and behave in ways that offset these dangers. As historian William Hoverd notes, Christianity's theological association of women with sin and bodily temptation has manifested in modern gym culture through increased pressure on women to vigorously pursue practices that project a sense of purity (like fasting and chastity) to overcome their bodily associations (like lust, greed, and gluttony). He argues that this Christian influence on American culture has led to the formation and success of the beauty industry, which offers products aimed at redeeming the always imperfect (and originally fallen) woman. Of course, this redemption is necessarily temporary to ensure women's continued reliance on beauty products.[1] The impossibility of and demand for perfection are not unique to evangelical women or even just to women, but evangelicalism's emphasis on sexual purity, marriage roles, and producing children makes this pressure to project femininity a very real part of female Christian athletes' lives.

Given evangelicalism's tendency to police women's bodies, women in sports ministry are in a unique position within evangelical culture. Sports ministry emphasizes that their athletic bodies are valuable for the religious projects of witnessing and maintaining a personal relationship with God. Yet, evangelical tradition emphasizes that women's bodies are most valuable for motherhood (to be attained within the confines of heterosexual marriage). Because of this conflict in priorities between sports ministry and evangelical tradition, participating in sports ministry has opened a space for evangelical female athletes to reflect on this conflict and to modify the evangelical demands on their bodies. I have identified three related sites where this reflection, negotiation, and modification have taken place for women in sports ministry: femininity, sexuality, and marriage. This part of this book includes a chapter on each of these related ideas and shows that sports ministry has provided female Christian athletes with ways to use their experiences as athletes to reassess their obligations as evangelical women.

Both sport and evangelical Christianity rely heavily on gender segregation and promote the idea of inherent differences between men and women. Through illuminating the gendered ideals within evangelicalism and within sport, this chapter shows that female Christian athletes are savvy negotiators of gender performance. They understand that evangelicalism demands traditional femininity and that playing sports can seem contradictory to that femininity. So, they have developed tools to understand and interpret their sporting experiences as compatible with their religious tradition's assumptions regarding godly femininity.

Evangelical female athletes tend to move between three different settings, each of which entails slightly different gendered expectations. They are members of a conservative Christian church community and, like Nora, are aware of this community's expectation that they will behave in traditionally feminine ways and marry a man. They are also members of sports ministry communities that provide tools for uniting evangelical Christianity and sport as shown in part I of this book. Often, they are also members of secular sports teams in which religious tolerance is the norm. On these teams, the athletes they practice and play with may or may not share the Christian athletic goal of experiencing God's pleasure or the goal of being in a straight relationship, but they do share the sporting goal of winning. These three worlds have spaces of overlap and spaces of disconnect, and the evangelical female athletes I studied demonstrated adept code-switching practices to negotiate these different demands on their bodies and behaviors.

Female Christian athletes' ability to recognize and engage with performances of femininity reveals that femininity is just that—a performance. Despite evangelicalism's claims that men and women are inherently different and that this difference manifests in femininity and masculinity, women in sports ministry tend to treat gender signifiers as malleable; they conscientiously modify their appearance, practices, and behaviors. At the same time, they work very hard to maintain a sense of essential gender differences between men and women. This can be confusing and difficult, but like other long-standing contradictions in sports ministry such as the problem of winning, negotiating gender has increased religious self-reflexivity and provided tools for reevaluating religious practice.

Sex and Gender

I am using the terms "sex," "gender," and "sexuality" to designate different yet related aspects of a person. Sex is a person's biological designation as male or female. Gender (masculinity and femininity) refers to the social expectations of behavior and self-presentation that accompany a person's sex. American culture has historically treated masculinity and femininity as a binary, with masculinity composed of traits like active, rational, intellectual, independent, public, and hard (both physically and emotionally), and femininity composed of the opposite set of traits— passive, emotional, embodied, dependent, domestic, and soft (both physically and emotionally). For the most part, our culture tends to assume that being male and acting masculine go together and that being female and acting feminine go together. The fact that these things do often go together is called a cultural construction; humans experience cultural expectations and often unknowingly adjust their behaviors, thoughts, and desires to reflect these expectations. Rather than thinking of gender as something connected to biology, it is helpful to think of it as an outcome of social relationships.

Our society tends to affiliate the expected gender expression of one's biology (women acting feminine and men acting masculine) with heterosexuality. Boys who are "sissies" or girls who are "tomboys" contradict gender expectations and can arouse suspicions of sexual deviance. Women in a masculine realm like elite sports experience cultural scrutiny regarding their gender and sexuality. The more masculine the sport (higher-contact sports that showcase a muscular body), the higher the level of scrutiny, but women in sports of all kinds experience gender scrutiny far more than men in sports.[2] There are exceptions to this; women in cheerleading or gymnastics, for example, are subject to much less gender scrutiny than women in higher-contact sports. Likewise, men in cheerleading or gymnastics are likely to experience higher levels of gender scrutiny than men in sports that are treated as unquestionably masculine like football.[3]

Gender studies scholars have recognized that gendered practices tend to reiterate normativity, but gender can also be a site of potential innovation. Most notably, Judith Butler has used the term "performance" to try to get at this tension between the normative and innovative elements of gender.[4] According to Butler, "In the first instance, performativity must be understood not as a singular or deliberate 'act,' but rather, as the reiterative and citational practice by which discourse produces the effects that it names."[5] Butler rejects the idea of performance as an individually driven enterprise (performance as choice) and turns to an understanding of performance that reflects cultural norms (performance as obligation). Performing gender, the ways that a person acts masculine or feminine, pulls from existing cultural ideas about masculinity and femininity. These cultural ideas allow people to evaluate each other's masculinity and femininity, to assess how closely aligned the person's behaviors and self-presentation are with cultural expectations.

For example, a man wearing makeup or a woman with a buzzed haircut would counter American expectations of gender performance and might raise suspicions of sexual deviance. These appearance choices seem out of place because we have learned existing social expectations such as that women should be concerned with appearing beautiful and men should not. Gender theorists argue that concerns about beauty are not biological (they do not come from your DNA or sex organs) but social (they are learned through human interaction). When Butler uses the phrase "reiterative and citational," she means that choices like makeup and hairstyle repeat (reiterate) and rely on (cite) existing social ideas. Performing gender does not mean that you make it up as you go along; it means you are working with a script.

Playing with gender is dangerous work. The moment we are born and the doctor announces, "It's a girl!" or "It's a boy!" we enter a world that holds different expectations for girls and boys. Conforming to or resisting these expectations gives us a sense of identity—I know I am a girl because girls like dolls and I like dolls. In general, girls have more leeway to act like boys than boys do to act like girls. Being a tomboy can be cool; being a sissy rarely is. Female athletes know that sports are consistently aligned with masculinity, making them acutely aware that playing sports can breach gender expectations.

Evangelical Christianity and Godly Femininity

Female Christian athletes pull from both evangelical Christianity and athletics to work out their identity. One player on the Charlotte Lady Eagles, Leslie, grew up with what she called "a poor definition of what it means to be feminine." For her, the world of sports compromised her femininity and led her to struggle with both her gender and her sexual identity. She said, "I think it's this way for lots of female athletes. They keep the tomboy label, they grow up receiving affirmation for playing sports, they play in college and after college. I think femininity means to have strength, beauty, tenderness, compassion, and to want to offer something, maybe even in a sacrificial way. Courage is a big part."

Leslie's language of sacrifice calls to mind Christ's crucifixion, and self-sacrifice is an important aspect of Christlikeness for athletes. Furthermore, she values female athleticism without rejecting the evangelical framework that encourages women to project femininity. Her definition of femininity combines traditionally masculine traits like strength and courage with traditionally feminine traits like tenderness and beauty. Defining femininity as both courageous and compassionate allows for the inclusion of traditionally masculine elements while still preserving traditional femininity; women can be feminine while running fast and playing hard (traditionally masculine traits like active and independent), but femininity remains connected to beauty and compassionate tenderness (traditionally feminine traits like embodied and emotional). Living this definition is incredibly difficult, but it is not without precedent in both evangelical Christianity and secular women's sports.

Public models of evangelical femininity are in themselves a challenge to traditional gender dichotomies because the public sphere is a traditionally masculine space (as opposed to the domestic sphere, a traditionally feminine space). Like evangelical women in sports, the public female voices of evangelical Christianity negotiate a tenuous balance between a traditionally masculine world and their religious community's expectation for women to prioritize domestic responsibilities. This may help explain why, when evangelical women engage the public sphere, they tend to explicitly support traditional gender roles.

While recent Republican politicians like Sarah Palin held more direct relevance for many of the Christian athletes I spoke with, Phyllis

Schlafly is perhaps the best example of an evangelical woman entering politics to promote traditional gender norms.[6] In the 1970s, feminists put women's rights on the national political agenda, resulting in legislation like Title IX and a Supreme Court ruling on *Roe v. Wade* that legalized access to abortion. Also on the table was an equal rights amendment (ERA) to the U.S. Constitution that would codify women and men as equal citizens with equal rights and responsibilities. The proposed amendment read, "Equality of rights under the law shall not be denied or abridged by the United States or by any state on account of sex." The story of how this amendment failed is in large part the story of evangelical women becoming active and outspoken proponents of traditional femininity.

Congress passed the ERA early in 1972, and the amendment required ratification by thirty-eight states before it could become part of the Constitution. Phyllis Schlafly published her article "What's Wrong with 'Equal Rights' for Women?" around the time of the congressional vote.[7] Her text was a direct critique of Betty Friedan's book *The Feminine Mystique*, which had grown in popularity since its publication in the mid-1960s.[8] Whereas Friedan challenged the notion that a woman's greatest happiness was found in her husband and children, Schlafly argued that the family was the highest achievement in the history of women's rights, and that bearing and raising a child was a woman's most precious right and responsibility. According to political scientist Donald Critchlow, "Specifically, [Schlafly] argued that the ERA would 'abolish a woman's right to child support and alimony,' and would 'absolutely and positively make women subject to the draft.'"[9] One month after Schlafly's article was published, Oklahoma voted against the ERA. After an initial wave of thirty state ratifications by mid-1973, ratification slowed with three ratifications in 1974, one in 1975, and one in 1977, bringing the total to thirty-five of the necessary thirty-eight, and the amendment failed.

Over the course of 1972, Phyllis Schlafly began to organize against the ERA and named her organization STOP (Stop Taking Our Privileges) ERA, holding her first conference in September 1972. At this time, five states had voted against the amendment (Oklahoma, Illinois, Ohio, Nevada, and Louisiana) but continued to bring it up for voting year after year. Both pro-ERA and anti-ERA activists were predominantly white, middle-class women. However, a significant demographic difference between these two groups was church affiliation; 98 percent of STOP ERA members were church members, whereas only 31 to 48 percent of pro-ERA activists were church members. STOP ERA appealed to a population that had not previously been involved in politics: younger, evangelical Christian women, many of whom were stay-at-home mothers. According to Critchlow, these new evangelical female activists "saw themselves as upholding the ideal of the two-parent family—a father, a mother working at home, and children—which they feared was being replaced in the 1970s by single-parent families and cohabitating couples, both heterosexual and homosexual."[10] Schlafly connected the ERA to other divisive issues like abortion and gay rights. She argued that the amendment was unnecessary given the existing Equal Pay Act (1963) and other legislation like Title IX (1972). Pro-ERA organizations were split on political strategies, with some like the National Organization for Women (NOW) preferring marches and rallies, and others like ERA-merica preferring lobbying the state legislature, but Schlafly successfully consolidated her constituency.

President Gerald Ford endorsed the ERA in 1974 when it seemed its passage was inevitable. By 1974, seventeen states had voted against the ERA, and full ratification required five more states to vote for the amendment. Schlafly's battle intensified. The biggest rally in opposition to the ERA was in 1975 in Springfield, Illinois. Eight thousand women from thirty states attended, and the Illinois state legislature ended up voting against the amendment. Within the Republican Party, the debate over the ERA was a significant challenge to Ford's nomination for the 1976 election. He won the nomination by a slim margin over the other contender, Ronald Reagan, but when Ford lost to Jimmy Carter in 1976, Reagan became central to the GOP, winning the presidential nomination in 1980.

Phyllis Schlafly and STOP ERA promoted an image of a female conservative Christian activist whose primary agenda was the preservation of traditional gender roles and gender differences. Schlafly continued to have an active career as an organizer and to promote this agenda. In a recent book coauthored with her niece Suzanne Venker, Schlafly portrayed feminism and the idea of gender equality as contrary both to nature and to women's best interests. Venker and Schlafly argue that feminists see no difference between men and women except their sex organs, and this contradicts their own viewpoint that gender differences are natural and important:

> The truth is that feminism has been the single worst thing that has happened to American women. It did not liberate women at all—it confused them. It made their lives harder. Women today are caught between man and nature. . . . Their female nature tells them sex requires love; marriage is important; children are a blessing; and men are necessary. The culture, meanwhile, tells them to sleep around and postpone family life because that will cost them their identity. And if their marriage doesn't work out, it's no big deal. They can always get divorced. Is it any wonder modern women are unhappy?[11]

Here, the authors affirm the evangelical narrative that marriage between a man and a woman is the natural state for humans and that any move to undermine this natural state will cause confusion and unhappiness. Venker and Schlafly argued that women's choices and behaviors (their gender) come from their innate "female nature," not from social conditioning. Furthermore, they present social conditioning as a challenge to essential femininity, arguing that contemporary American society expects women to be promiscuous and career driven. It is likely that contemporary American women (and men) experience contradictions in their gender conditioning, as Venker and Schlafly illustrate. However, this does not mean that one set of expectations is "natural" and the other is "cultural"; both are cultural, and presenting one as natural prevents any investigation into how and why women might learn this set of expectations and assumptions.[12]

Phyllis Schlafly's perspective and actions surrounding the ERA demonstrate some important cultural expectations for women. According to Venker and Schlafly's accounts of the failure of the ERA, the amendment lost popularity because Americans were confronted with two images of women: the STOP ERA women who promoted the values of domestic life and traditional marriage, and the pro-ERA activists who were unnatural both in their demands for equality and in their sexual orientation. For Venker and Schlafly, the choice was clear, and they describe how Americans rightfully opted for the former image of female activism:

Feminists cheered for ERA, and then rallied behind their other demands: taxpayer funding of abortions, the entire gay rights agenda, universal day care, and some 20 other feminist goals. After they released their balloons and pranced around with their placards, the whole country realized why they were pushing so hard for ERA—and what kind of women were pushing. The most popular buttons worn by delegates were, "A woman without a man is like a fish without a bicycle" and, "Mother Nature is a lesbian." At various booths, you could pick up booklets on "What Lesbians Do." The tremendous media coverage backfired, for it showed Americans what feminism is really about.[13]

In this excerpt, Venker and Schlafly never state outright that feminists are lesbians, but they insinuate that pro-ERA activism was dangerous because it undermined the correct relationship between men and women and that this inevitably undermined romantic and sexual norms like heterosexuality and marriage. By making this connection, Venker and Schlafly show their support of traditional gender roles and imply that failure to adhere to these gender standards constitutes a challenge to God's natural order.

Phyllis Schlafly and the fight to vote down the ERA set some important precedents for how evangelical women used their political voices. Schlafly and other conservative Christian women entered the public sphere to argue against equal rights for women because their religious beliefs could not support the idea that men and women were equal. These women believed that "gender roles are good and exist for a reason."[14] Because politics and the public sphere have traditionally been realms of masculinity, conservative Christian women treading in these domains developed ways of being present in public discourse without disrupting the gendered balance of power that they valued. If there was one important lesson from Schlafly's success, it was that conservative Christian women could and should be active in the public sphere, but that this action should always be done in a way that showcases and encourages traditional gender roles and gendered relationships.[15]

In a parallel masculine sphere, sports, female Christian athletes affirmed similar gender practices and sought to preserve and value gender differences. When I returned to Kansas City for my second visit to FCA headquarters in October 2006, I spent some time getting to know Katie, aged twenty-four and one of the editors of *Sharing the Victory*. Katie had been a college athlete and went to work for FCA right out of college. She had heard about the job opportunity from a college friend, Robbie, and the two began dating soon after her move to Kansas City. They had recently married. Because my trip to the FCA headquarters primarily consisted of digging through the archives and because Katie was my primary contact at *Sharing the Victory*, we interacted regularly during my visits. I would show her back issues that I thought were particularly provocative (like the "Sports and War" article mentioned in chapter 2) and talk with her about the current goals for *Sharing the Victory*. As an editor and author for the publication, Katie struggled with many of the issues raised in part I of this book. In a September 2010 sidebar titled "Competitive Balance: Can You Be Aggressive without Compromising Your Faith?," Katie explored the issue of playing dirty, coming to much the same conclusion as the Charlotte Lady Eagles. She wrote, "As Christian athletes, if we are playing with integrity, we won't feel like we are living two lives on and off the court. God has called us to use the gifts He's given us with excellence and to play all-out for His glory. Our bodies are His temples, and our sports can be acts of worship to Him." Although Katie's days as an elite athlete were behind her, it is clear that she was still very much in tune with the day-to-day struggles of being a Christian athlete.

She was also tuned into gender dynamics. When Katie joined the staff of *Sharing the Victory*, she was part of a major turnover in the publication's leadership. The previous editor had been a forty-year-old man with a middle-aged female assistant. By 2006, the magazine was staffed primarily by women in their twenties. This constituted a dramatic shift in the editorial board, and Katie was part of a push to include more magazine articles that related directly to women, covering topics like eating disorders or homosexuality. *Sharing the Victory* tended to focus on high-profile athletes (who are mostly male) but made an effort to profile elite female athletes in every issue. Like Phyllis Schlafly, the evangelical women featured in *Sharing the Victory* were treading in a male-dominated domain (sports), and they tended to promote traditional femininity and heterosexuality from within that domain.

Katie's sidebar on competitive balance accompanied an article profiling DeLisha Milton-Jones, Women's National Basketball Association

(WNBA) star from the Los Angeles Sparks. Milton-Jones described her struggle to play aggressively without compromising her Christian integrity. According to Milton-Jones, "I discovered that, through His Spirit, you can put a harness on the competitiveness and control it. You can go out there and push and shove with the best of them as long as it doesn't take you to the point of thinking or saying ungodly things and taking ungodly actions." Similar to the Christian athletes in chapter 1, Milton-Jones worked out a solution to the problem of how to play hard and preserve her Christian identity.

The article presented Milton-Jones's seven-year marriage as an example fulfilling God's plan of a spouse for every Christian. Milton-Jones said, "I feel totally blessed that God sent me my soul mate," placing her soundly within the bounds of evangelical stances on marriage. But the article also described aspects of Milton-Jones that challenged traditional femininity. In addition to chronicling her competitive drive and her desire to play aggressively with integrity, it quoted her as saying, "It's OK to stand up and be heard and not be shy about being a Christian."[16] Standing up and being heard reflect traditionally masculine qualities. Female Christian athletes are comfortable emphasizing these qualities if this is done for the purpose of preserving traditional gendered relationships like marriage. The title of the article, "D-Nasty Sunshine," encompasses the strange balancing act of the elite female Christian athlete. "D-Nasty" and "Sunshine" were two nicknames for Milton-Jones, and combining them for the title of her profile illustrates the dissonance of trying to be both aggressive (D-Nasty) and friendly/nurturing (Sunshine).

During one of my days digging in the FCA archives, Katie and I went out to lunch together. We talked about her recent marriage to Robbie and how they enjoyed working for the same organization. During that fall of 2006, during the second presidential term of George W. Bush, a number of Democratic politicians had begun to test the waters of presidential candidacy, including Barack Obama. Katie told me that she could never vote for Obama because she was a social issues voter. For many conservative Christians, the most pressing social issues in politics are abortion and gay rights. They see the Republican Party as aligned with their religious responses to these issues: abortion is wrong, and marriage is a heterosexual institution. However, Katie's husband, Robbie, was sympathetic toward Obama and thought he would be a better choice in terms of foreign policy. As an employee of a conservative Christian organization like FCA, Robbie felt compelled to keep his admiration of Obama a secret. Katie, on the other hand, could voice her support for the Republican Party because by doing so she was also implicitly supporting traditional gender understandings.

Similar to Phyllis Schlafly and WNBA player Milton-Jones, Katie was in a position of leadership (as an editor at *Sharing the Victory*) and used that position to affirm traditional gender values. However, these women's public confirmation of traditional gender norms, through either political activism, magazine interviews, or editorial choices, relied on expanding evangelicalism's definition of femininity to include aspects like those identified by Leslie: strength and courage. Phyllis Schlafly and other models of public and active conservative women have established a precedent: evangelical Christian women can and should use their strength and courage to affirm traditional gendered relationships.

Playing Like a Girl

In addition to evangelical female models in the public sphere, female Christian athletes also use the world of secular sports to discern how to combine sporting and religious obligations. A major milestone in women's sports in the United States was the passage of Title IX in 1972. In the 1960s and 1970s, the language of equal opportunity and equal rights, largely promoted by the black civil rights movement, the American Indian and Chicano movements, and the women's and gay liberation movements, became a pervasive way to discuss relationships between different groups in American society. Organized feminists were able to draw on this language to present disparities in athletic resources as an explicitly political problem.[17] Title IX was one result. The legislation guaranteed equal funds for men and women in all institutions that receive federal funding.[18]

At first, institutions were unsure whether Title IX applied to athletics, and following the compliance deadline in 1978, there were several legal clarifications on the exact meaning of the legislation. In 1984, the Supreme Court mandated a narrow interpretation of Title IX, which made it difficult to challenge sex discrimination in athletics. However, with the passage of the Civil Rights Restoration Act in 1988, legislative challenges to sex discrimination in sport increased dramatically. The 1990s ushered in a new era in women's sports. Enforcement of Title IX compliance grew due to a number of lawsuits against colleges and universities and the Clinton administration's focus on enforcing the policy.[19] When Title IX was first passed, only 1 in every 9 women participated in sports. By the early twenty-first century, this number was 1 in 2.5.[20] As the number of women playing sports increased, there were also more women pursuing athletic careers—as professional athletes, coaches, administrators, sportswriters, and newscasters.

The 1996 Olympics, dubbed by NBC "The Year of the Women," boasted a higher percentage of female athletes than ever before.[21] Partly due to the publicity and victory of the U.S. women's Olympic basketball team, the National Basketball Association (NBA) Board of Governors approved the concept of the WNBA, which began its first competitive season in 1997. Additionally, the women's U.S. national soccer team won the FIFA Women's World Cup in 1999, with perhaps the most memorable moment being Brandi Chastain's victory celebration after scoring the Cup-winning penalty shot against China. As male soccer players frequently do, she took off her jersey and waved it over her head, causing a scandal by revealing her sports bra and muscular torso. However, the resulting commotion was only possible because so many people were watching; Chastain's sports bra was broadcast to an estimated viewing audience of 40 million.[22] As sports scholars Leslie Heywood and Shari Dworkin wrote in 2003, "Female athletes were once oddities, goddesses, or monsters, exceptions to every social rule. Now the female athlete is an institution."[23]

Rising cultural acceptance of female athleticism had important implications for women not only in terms of increased sporting opportunities but also in terms of body image. As Yvonne Tasker noted in her book *Spectacular Bodies: Gender, Genre, and the Action Cinema*, the ideal body for women shifted from soft curves of the 1950s to hardened muscle tone of the 1980s and 1990s.[24] The hard female body became the elevated ideal in American culture, but this did not decrease the value of traditional femininity and family for conservative women or for the world of sport. While athletics for men has long functioned as a marker of traditional masculinity, women playing sports or pursuing a hard-bodied physique were flirting with gender deviance. Even with changing body ideals and increased sporting opportunities, female athletes, particularly at an elite level, felt pressure to demonstrate their femininity.

As women became publicly visible as professional athletes, particularly in high-contact sports and sports in which athletes' bodies are muscular and tall, such as basketball, female athletes developed practices that emphasized heterosexual femininity to offset any cultural suspicions that playing these kinds of sports made them mannish or gay. As Tiffany Muller notes in her study of the WNBA:

> WNBA athletes themselves often reinforce ideals of heterosexual femininity, whether consciously or unconsciously. It is not uncommon, for instance in postgame celebrations shown on screens inside the arena and to television audiences, to see WNBA players and female coaches with their children, which serves as a reminder of a woman's "primary" role as mother, and it is equally significant that this type of celebration is rarely seen or expected from male basketball players.[25]

These performances of traditional femininity serve to counter on-court performances of masculine behavior like rough play and physical prowess, as if to reassure the audience and the athletes themselves that women who are performing masculinity do so in a bounded and temporary way. Elite female athletes like these WNBA players demonstrate that they leave masculinity behind when the final buzzer sounds, a kind of balancing act practically unheard of for male athletes. Just as Phyllis Schlafly and STOP ERA encouraged conservative women to speak out publicly in favor of traditional gender roles, the world of sports, where a female athlete's success is contingent on pleasing her coach and her sponsors, also encourages public adherence to and support of traditional gender roles.

Women have made tremendous inroads into sporting culture, and one outcome of this is that female athletes now encounter the same dehumanizing situations that male athletes have long experienced. Elite sports is a world where winning is the most important goal, and this emphasis can negatively affect an athlete's sense of self-worth. Heywood and Dworkin write:

> While sports are indisputably a positive source of strength and self-development for girls, they can accomplish this only if the environment

in which female athletes throw their javelins, kick their soccer balls, and swim their fast and furious laps is an environment that respects girls and takes them seriously as athletes. . . . Over and over, women (and men, increasingly) say that a world in which an athlete is only as good as his or her latest win, a world where coaches invade personal boundaries, and where eating and sexuality are constantly monitored is destructive to self-esteem.[26]

A generation after Title IX, women in sport are taken seriously as athletes, but along with this comes the pressure to win at any cost that has consistently resulted in scandals in men's sports over cheating, drug use, and recruiting practices. Title IX made sport dramatically more accessible to women, but it did not change sport. The value of equal access that motivated Title IX is not the same as the values of competition and hierarchy that make sport what it is. There are more elite female athletes than ever, and some sports commentators have argued that women's teams demonstrate a different style of play then men's teams, but sporting culture in general has not changed, and the values of winning that so troubled Wes Neal and Gary Warner now trouble female Christian athletes, with the added complication that their participation in sport requires a constant monitoring of their femininity.

Sports Ministry and Female Athletes

In the mid-1990s, women began to outnumber men as participants in sports ministry. This demographic shift reflected a number of factors. First, women have long outnumbered men as churchgoers and as members of religious organizations.[27] Second, lawsuits over Title IX adherence resulted in institutions prioritizing athletic opportunities for women at every level, including youth and high school sports. At the same time that these early opportunities for sporting participation became more normative for girls, sports ministry organizations like FCA began to focus on youth and high school athletes as their primary demographic. This meant that young female athletes had access to sports ministry very early in their athletic careers and grew up, as many male athletes had, combining their athletic and religious identities. Third, by the 1990s, conservative Christian involvement in politics had publicly affiliated evangelicals with traditional gender roles and relationships. For women, membership in sports ministry groups aligned them with traditional femininity and heterosexuality. This could reduce anxiety for female athletes who consistently feel pressure to demonstrate their gender normativity.

Some female Christian athletes feel pressure to demonstrate traditional femininity more strongly than others. For example, in sports ministry settings where athletes from multiple sports are brought together, the women who play high-contact sports that showcase muscular bodies, such as soccer, basketball, and rugby, may feel set apart from women with leaner bodies. At the campus AIA meetings I attended in 2007, I was struck by the bodily differences between two groups of female athletes. One group of women were slender and of short to average height—they were on teams like the dance team or the cross-country team. The other group towered over the first. They were tall and muscular, and they certainly intimidated me. I remember having a conversation with one volleyball player who was a head taller than myself and thinking, it must be nice for these tall women to get together and be able to look in each other's eyes instead of having to look down at other women. Like Nora's self-awareness that her height and build made her stand out, athletic women whose muscular strength is evident in their bodies can develop a painful awareness of how their bodies contradict gendered expectations.

Resources for female Christian athletes include instructions for how to balance femininity and athleticism. One such text was *Experiencing God's Power for Female Athletes: How to Compete, Knowing and Doing the Will of God*, a collaboration by three female sports ministers. This book was published in the late 1990s and reflects many of the struggles that sports ministry organizations encountered as female participation dramatically increased. While the book itself did not circulate widely in the organizations I studied, the issues addressed and the tone of the work were prevalent in my fieldwork settings.

A central lesson of the book is that embracing femininity is an important part of fulfilling God's plan for the female athlete. The authors included an interview with Karen Drollinger, a former professional basketball player with a long history of involvement with Athletes in Action and Fellowship of Christian Athletes. Drollinger defined femininity as an inner confidence in one's gender and an ability to demonstrate that to others: "Femininity may not help a female athlete shoot free throws better, but accepting and fulfilling one's godly image gives her inner confidence to perform to the best of her ability. In other words, femininity is a necessity if women athletes are to be all that God created them to be."[28] Drollinger's statement is confusing because she began by stating that femininity is unlikely to improve athletic performance—it won't help you at the free throw line. Yet she followed this by arguing that embracing femininity is essential for maximizing athletic potential—so it might help with free throws after all. This sort of doublespeak appears throughout the text as the authors attempt to value femininity and athleticism at the same time. As with the earlier example of D-Nasty Sunshine, these seemingly contradictory values are difficult for sports ministers and female Christian athletes to balance.

The authors of *Experiencing God's Power for Female Athletes* demonstrate an appreciation of women's advancement in sport and emphasize that the benefits of sports ministry are not reserved for men. They especially emphasize this when describing Christlikeness. As the previous chapter has shown, Christian athletes narrate feelings of athletic pleasure as Christlikeness, a sensation of being connected to God. *Experiencing God's Power for Female Athletes* describes men and women as equally capable of Christlikeness. Retelling God's creation of humans in Genesis, the authors emphasize the creation of humankind rather than Eve's role in the fall from Eden:

> Genesis 1:27 states, *"God created man in his own image, in the image of God he created him; male and female he created them."* In the first part of the verse, "God created <u>man</u> in his [God's] own image," the word for man is *adam*, meaning humankind. This refers to all people. The expression "image of God" (*imago Dei*) refers to how God is reflected, or seen, in people. Males and females both reflect the image of God.[29]

While this interpretation of Genesis presents men and women as equal in the eyes of God, the authors are clear that this does not mean that men and women are the same: "God knew what gender you were going to be, and He is pleased that you are female! You are special because you were created female."[30] In this statement, as in Venker and Schlafly's work cited earlier, the authors conflate sex (biology) with gender (self-presentation and behavior). They imply that the biological des-ignation "female" is meaningful to God because it carries with it a set of behaviors and characteristics that God intended for women. They present women as having "a combination of masculine and feminine traits, but women have more emphasis on the feminine ones . . . [such as] soft, yielded, responsive, nurturing, and receptive."[31] According to *Experiencing God's Power for Female Athletes*, God intended women to complement men by embracing their feminine qualities. However, this can be challenging in the realm of sport, where these qualities do not often match the qualities that are necessary to win.

One method that female Christian athletes use to affirm traditional gender roles while actively participating in the masculine domain of sports is self-display.[32] The authors of *Experiencing God's Power for Female Athletes* argue that sport could compromise femininity if female athletes dress in masculine ways. They warn against hiding behind ath-letic clothing:

> It is possible that if sweatshirts and gym shorts are what you wear the ma-jority of the time, it may be more of a reflection about what you believe about yourself or how you want others to perceive you. . . . How do you feel when you wear dresses or clothing that is clearly feminine? Do you feel confident or uncomfortable?[33]

The authors emphasize that feminine appearance is important to inter-nal confidence in one's femininity, but at the same time, they caution against eating disorders and succumbing to cultural values of feminine beauty. "Magazine and television advertisements portray primarily thin, beautiful, smiling models . . . the problem is, this unrealistic message can lead to girls and young women believing that their happiness and popu-larity depend on achieving a certain dress size or weight."[34] The authors encourage the female Christian athlete to demonstrate her femininity to others through clothes and behaviors, yet she should also avoid anxi-ety stemming from an imperfect body image. Like Drollinger's earlier contradiction, this negotiation between feminine appearance and body anxiety demonstrates the deep difficulty of trying to value femininity and athletics at the same time. Readers are told, "[God] values you as a person, and part of who you are is your 'female-ness.' God values you as female!"[35] In connecting "female-ness" to feminine clothing, the authors equate feminine appearance with value to God.

One reason the authors of *Experiencing God's Power for Female Athletes* work so hard to value femininity and "female-ness" is because they see these things as natural extensions of heterosexuality. For these authors, femininity is not just God's intention for gendered behavior; it is intertwined with God's intention for sexual behavior, namely, heterosexual marriage: "Develop feminine qualities and characteristics in yourself that will show others that you are confident as a female both on and off the court. Examine the areas in your life to see what message you are sending to others in your dress, language (gossip, using profanity), relationships, etc."[36] In these examples, femininity is a quality that exists in its social display to others. Female Christian athletes may feel pressure to monitor their on- and off-field appearance to offset the masculine behaviors they demonstrate on the field, and actively trying to appear feminine entails paying attention to cultural standards of beauty. This is a difficult contradiction to reconcile, and the authors never fully address the challenges of demonstrating femininity through appearance without internalizing the negative impact of the commercialization of women's bodies.

Like the examples employed in *Experiencing God's Power for Female Athletes*, some women on the Charlotte Lady Eagles experienced a conflict between femininity and athleticism and turned to appearance as a way to negotiate these qualities. Some of the Lady Eagles were college athletes playing for the Eagles during the summer and returning to their Division I college teams in the fall. These players in particular experienced a stark contrast between playing for an evangelical team and playing for a secular team, and the differences between these two settings informed their self-display choices. For example, Andrea played at a large university in Texas that was Christian affiliated, but that, especially in terms of athletic recruitment, admitted many secular and non-evangelical students-athletes. This made Andrea's situation comparable to Nora's in that both their schools were Division I, and both athletic programs were secular. For Andrea, too, the length of shorts was an important marker of femininity, and she described how the team consciously used the length of their shorts to mitigate any suspicions that playing sports undermined their femininity. She told me:

I remember growing up and hearing comments like, "Whoa, you are such a beast," or "You are such an animal." I didn't like those comments. I like being athletic, and I didn't hide that, but I didn't like those comments. At [my college], I wouldn't mind going out to the cafeteria in my soccer clothes, but I would still try to look prettyish. Like, we would make our shorts a little shorter by rolling the waistbands. Not really short, just roll them one time in the waist. And my hair, I would wear a colorful headband. I was aware that we were going to be sweaty and could look gross and so I tried to address that a little bit.

Andrea's secular college team would roll their shorts a little shorter to mark themselves as feminine; Nora felt relieved to be able to wear longer shorts on an explicitly evangelical team. These different settings had a significant impact on athletes' self-display choices.

Shorts and the amount of leg they cover or reveal are important because of the power dynamics of gaze. In the mid-1970s, Laura Mulvey argued that filmmakers unintentionally privilege male ways of looking at women by using the camera to make the audience perspective one of a heterosexual man. She called this the "male gaze" and argued that this perspective has been so powerful that women also view images of women from a male, heterosexual perspective.[37] Whether or not men are actually looking, women look at other women as they imagine men would and so enforce a tenuous balance between modesty and exposure. Andrea's team's awareness that both men and women would be observing them in the cafeteria led to a reevaluation of their self-presentation and a desire to conform to the aesthetic values of the male heterosexual gaze.

Andrea's and Nora's language reveals an attention to display and a desire to appear feminine in situations where their femininity was important for social acceptance. From the college cafeteria to church to campus ministry meetings, female Christian athletes can feel a heightened obligation to project femininity because they are painfully aware that their identity as an athlete stands in tension with their identity as an evangelical woman. Given these sometimes uncomfortable negotiations of self-display, sports ministry serves an important role for these women. It can allow them to temporarily suspend their sense of obligatory feminine self-display; membership in sports ministry is a social indication that a woman is straight. Female Christian athletes may feel less pressure to perform feminine display on teams like the Charlotte Lady Eagles because these teams overtly identify as evangelical Christian.

Another player on the Charlotte Lady Eagles, Angie, recounted how her mother would police her wardrobe in middle school and high school to ensure that she was aware of the effects of her clothing choices. Angie told me:

> I grew up with three older brothers. Both my mom and my dad played sports in college. We are a very athletic family. I can remember being young, in middle school and even in high school, I was never allowed to wear soccer clothes to school. There was a time when Umbros were popular, but I wasn't allowed to wear them because they were soccer clothes. I got that from my mom, from her being in the world of sports and wanting to make sure I remained feminine. And it would've been seen differently—if another girl was wearing shorts and then headed off to her ballet class, [she would still be seen as feminine]. I was always more muscular than most of the other girls. It would have been taken differently if I wore gym shorts.

Angie's mother encouraged her to think about her femininity and policed Angie's wardrobe so that Angie would be forced to think about the repercussions of the way she presented herself. One outcome of this was that Angie habitualized markers of femininity and came to see these markers as important for her identity. She continued:

> I wear eye makeup when I play. I just put it on the morning; it's a habit. I wear the same makeup all the time no matter what I'm doing. I remember my mom not really pressuring me about it, but she did say, you might want to think about it. I mean, why act different just because I'm playing a sport? I like makeup, I like getting dressed up, I'm a girly girl. That doesn't need to change just because I'm working out or practicing.

Through her thoughtfulness about feminine self-presentation, Angie developed preferences and habits that she identified as "girly." She wanted to feel and appear girly while practicing or working out and used feminine markers like eye makeup to achieve this.

Jewelry is also an important marker of femininity. Another player, Lex, joined the coaching staff at a secular college in Charlotte after leaving the Eagles. In her new role as second assistant coach, she thought about her appearance more often than she had when she played for the Eagles. She recalled:

> In my early recruiting trips for [my school], I would wear earrings. I would do some trainings wearing earrings. When I was with the Eagles, I would never think about whether to wear earrings or not. But I really thought about it in this situation. I've always been an athlete. I've always walked around wearing stinking workout clothes. As a coach, I can wear earrings.

When playing for the Eagles, wearing earrings was not on Lex's mind, but in a secular sporting environment, wearing earrings became a practice that could communicate femininity. Display choices like shorter shorts, makeup, or jewelry confirm the power of the male gaze, and these practices affirm heterosexuality. As will be addressed further in the next chapter, coaches may overtly project femininity during recruiting in order to assure athletes and their parents that the team does not contain or encourage lesbianism. Like Nora's relief at being able to wear longer shorts without concern, Lex's inattention to jewelry while playing for the Lady Eagles demonstrates that a sports ministry environment, where heterosexuality is assumed, can relax the cultural pressure to mark oneself as feminine.

While the authors of *Experiencing God's Power for Female Athletes* presented feminine appearance as God's intention for female athletes, a way to increase internal confidence in one's gender, and even a method to improve athletically, evangelical women who compete in elite sporting environments are much more likely to live in the gray areas and contradictions evident in the text than in these stated certainties. One reason *Experiencing God's Power for Female Athletes* was unable to resolve the tension of simultaneously valuing femininity and athleticism is that sport was and remains culturally associated with masculinity, and succeeding on the playing field requires women to embrace traditionally masculine qualities like power, strength, action, and even violence. Participating in sports ministry does not resolve this tension, but it can provide an environment where the assumption of shared values creates a haven from the work of constructing a feminine appearance.

Conclusion

Female Christian athletes have access to a variety of environments, including evangelical churches, sports ministry groups, and secular sports teams. Some evangelical settings can function similarly to sports ministry settings and relax the expectation of traditionally feminine self-presentation. For example, several players and coaches from the Charlotte Lady Eagles went on to coach at a large conservative Christian university with a residential enrollment of around 12,000. This school was explicitly conservative, required regular worship attendance, and enforced a moral code of behavior for students (much of which policed physical interaction between men and women). One of the Charlotte Lady Eagles who joined the coaching staff at this school, Ellie, noted, "I'm bigger than most girls, but in Christian settings, I'm with people who are all in the same boat. In a Christian setting, everyone assumes you're straight. At [the Christian college where I coach], the female athletes are cool and guys like the girls, but in secular settings, that can be different." Ellie was aware that female athletes have muscular bodies and can stand out. In secular settings, that standing out can appear unfeminine and, by extension, not straight. However, because Ellie's school took a public stand against same-sex relationships, the overriding assumption was that students attending the school were straight. For muscular female athletes, this assumption of heterosexuality could be a reprieve, and as Ellie noted, the male students at the school liked the female athletes and saw them as cool.

Before Ellie and other Charlotte Lady Eagles players and coaches joined the staff at this particular school, I had visited it while traveling with the AIA women's basketball team in 2007. Most of the teams that AIA competed with were public school teams, and this was the only team that they played that was from an explicitly conservative Christian school. Another difference was that the AIA team had lunch with their opponents on the day of the game, whereas usually they would not interact socially with the opposing team until after the game. Tina opened the meal with a blessing. Then she noted that it was strange to meet the opposing team before the game, "but since we are all brothers and sisters in Christ, it shouldn't be weird." Because the opposing team was also explicitly Christian, the lunch was an opportunity for AIA to recruit players for the next year's tour, and Abby spoke to the group about the mission of AIA. One striking thing about the opposing team was the presence of three white, ponytailed identical triplets who were six feet tall.[38] These young women had considered attending the Christian college that Abby had attended, and Abby made some jokes about how she had tried to recruit them and now would be playing against them.

Because the teams had such friendly interactions before the game, it was surprising to see the behavior of the student body during the game that evening. It was the largest crowd for any of the games on tour, and the students were enthusiastic. Many fans had painted faces and home-made costumes, and they cheered loudly for their team. They also booed the AIA players and yelled "Airball!" when an AIA player lined up a free throw shot. Maria turned to me, saying, "This is a Christian school?" implying that she thought the fans' behaviors were out of line.

It was the final game of the tour, and the locker-room energy at half-time was positive. Abby reminded the team, "We can't forget who we play for or it will all go downhill." Despite this admonition, the team ran out of energy during the second half and lost the game. I watched as the triplets on the opposing team played systematically, consistently stealing the ball and making baskets. I could not help but think that this must be the stuff of basketball nightmares. Every direction you pivot, you see the same very tall, very talented, ponytailed player ready to take the ball away from you.

What Ellie said seemed to be true; the college respected and supported its female athletes. Women's college basketball does not traditionally draw a big audience, and preseason exhibition games like those that AIA played usually had sparse attendance. This game, however, was crowded with energetic and enthusiastic fans. Watching the triplets play, I thought about the confluence of evangelical femininity and female athletic excellence. They did not hold back; their tall bodies dominated the court. But they also demonstrated outward signs of traditional femininity through their self-presentation and comportment. Their long hair was tied back, and they wore brightly colored headbands. They were receptive and quiet players. When their male coach gave them a direction, they would calmly put his plays into action. They actively respected the referees. They reflected many of the attributes that the authors of *Experiencing God's Power for Female Athletes* identified as feminine—yielding, responsive, and receptive.

Christian sports settings like this particular college and the Charlotte Lady Eagles team can provide an opportunity for female Christian athletes to redefine femininity, but these opportunities do not diminish the theological importance of gender differences in evangelical Christianity at large. Women in sports ministry have developed a range of responses to the pressure to balance femininity and athleticism. Many of these responses rely on monitoring one's self-presentation. Their attention to clothing, makeup, jewelry, and hairstyles shows that female Christian athletes are adept negotiators of the signals of femininity, and they may use these practices to emphasize heterosexuality. In some instances, such as on the Charlotte Lady Eagles, where heterosexuality was assumed, athletes like Nora felt free to relax these practices, but, as the example of the AIA game at the conservative Christian school shows, sometimes the assumption of heterosexuality still carries with it the pressure to actively demonstrate traditional femininity through both behavior and appearance.

The relationship between femininity and heterosexuality for women often goes without saying in the worlds of evangelical Christianity, elite sports, and sports ministry. But this assumption masks a much more complicated reality. As the next chapter shows, there are women on Christian teams who experience same-sex attraction and struggle with how to understand their sexual desires in the context of sports ministry.

5

Challenging the Call

Sexual Desire and Sexual Deviance

"I want to go back to church, but can't find the guts to go. I know Jesus loves me. It's all the other assholes I'm worried about," Amy wrote in her blog three years after leaving the Charlotte Lady Eagles. When I knew her in the summer of 2008, Amy was married with a two-year-old daughter. When we reconnected in 2011, she was an out lesbian with a live-in female partner helping her raise her little girl. Amy and I had corresponded off and on after I spent a summer season with the Lady Eagles. Soon after the season ended, she told me that she disagreed with a number of evangelical teachings. "I get excited when the church is challenged. . . . Yes, I am a Christian, which makes it difficult to speak up about my concerns and disapproval." Later on, I asked if she would be going back to play for the Lady Eagles, and she responded, "I had a little falling-out with the Eagles, unfortunately. I think about them often, and have some great friendships with several of them, but because of certain life choices that do not coincide with the Eagles' beliefs, I am not welcome back." The life choices she referred to were her divorce and subsequent relationship with Rosa, a soccer player she had met while playing for a professional team. While Amy was clear with me that there was much she valued about being part of the Lady Eagles, she was also clear that the team would only accept her if she demonstrated substantial effort to live a straight lifestyle. "The common belief is that you can't be gay and Christian," she told me. "But I love Jesus. And I love her."

Over the past few decades, opposition to gay marriage has emerged as a defining feature of American evangelical politics. Many evangelical spokespeople argue that sexual relationships between persons of the same sex are contrary to God's will. For them, marriage is a sacred bond that connects believers to each other in divinely approved intimacy. Because, in this worldview, same-sex intimacy can never have God's approval, gay marriage is a contradiction in terms. Evangelicalism's fear and rejection of homosexuality are deeply interwoven with the gender logic of evangelical Christianity that posits different roles and behaviors for men and women.

Amy's experience of frustration and exclusion is not limited to Christian settings but can occur in secular settings as well.[1] As shown in the previous chapter, female athletes in traditionally male sports verge on gender transgression simply by excelling in a realm connected to masculinity. This can increase the likelihood that they will appear sexually deviant.[2] Accusations of homosexuality can be devastating to a female athlete's playing and coaching career in both secular and Christian settings. On some teams, the mere inference of lesbianism is enough to ostracize a player, to bench her, or to drop her from the team. Rumors circulate about lists of lesbian coaches provided to parents of recruits and spies posted at lesbian bars to out closeted coaches and players. Colleges and universities use negative recruiting to scare potential recruits and their parents, assuring them that there are no lesbians on their team but that there certainly are on rival teams.[3] This sort of negative recruiting is accomplished rhetorically, emphasizing the "family values" of one's own team and the "unhealthy environment" of the other teams.[4] Because of pressure to demonstrate their femininity and heterosexuality, secular female athletes have employed a range of publicity devices, from photo shoots with husbands and children to modeling for *Playboy*.[5] These practices have forced female athletes, straight or not, to emphasize and overemphasize heterosexual identity and traditional femininity.[6]

In Christian athletic settings, evangelicals make a distinction between lesbian desire and lesbian behavior. As they see it, lesbian desires are contrary to God's will but can be overcome through faith; lesbian behavior is sinful and must be confessed, forgiven, and prevented from recurring. For Amy and for other women on the Charlotte Lady Eagles who experienced desire for a same-sex romantic relationship, the organization expected them to change their desires through faith.

Though evangelical spokespeople continue to treat same-sex sexual behaviors as sinful and same-sex sexual desires as dangerous and contrary to God's will, my research shows that participants in sports ministry have a much wider spectrum of reactions to this issue. Like some evangelical youth, some sports ministry participants are part of a generational shift toward greater acceptance of homosexuality.[7] Some women on the Charlotte Lady Eagles thought of same-sex physical intimacy as a sin but related it to sins in their own lives like envy or pride, and some were deeply ambivalent about whether homosexuality was a sin at all. For those who experienced same-sex attraction, responses also varied. Some aligned with evangelical spokespeople and called on God to help them suppress their desires with the hope that these desires would change and that they could experience opposite-sex attraction and pursue a romantic relationship with a man. Some were ambivalent about the sinfulness of their desires or behaviors and remained closeted to avoid drawing attention to themselves. And some, like Amy, left sports ministry because they were unable to reconcile their life experience with the evangelical mainstay that homosexuality was wrong.

This variety of responses reveals that evangelical understandings of homosexuality (at least for women in sports ministry) are in flux. Many of the women I talked to were conflicted about homosexuality—they had a desire to support their tradition's biblical interpretation that homosexuality was contrary to God's will, but they also voiced a desire to respect and support their lesbian teammates. In general, the female Christian athletes I talked to were apprehensive about fully agreeing with this biblical interpretation and saw homosexuality as either forgivable, changeable through faith, or a gray area where they could not make a firm judgment. While this does not constitute a radical challenge to evangelical orthodoxy, it does show that participants in sports ministry may harbor strong differences of opinion from the leaders of their organizations and the spokespeople for their tradition. Like the opportunity to rethink and redefine femininity, participating in sports ministry has given some evangelical women the means to reflect on evangelical condemnation of homosexuality from the point of view of athletes.

Female Christian athletes encounter a significant theological struggle when trying to understand lesbianism. On the one hand, their religious tradition teaches that God has the power to enact significant changes in believers' lives, and some have even experienced changes in their own lives. On the other hand, they compete with and against out lesbians and have developed respect for these women. Ambivalence is the feeling of being pulled in contradictory directions simultaneously—it is an extremely difficult feeling to experience because the directions are equally compelling but cannot coexist. Either God intends humans to be heterosexual and has the power to intervene even at the level of sexual desire, God intentionally created a variety of sexualities, or God does not have the power to change a person's sexual desires. Americans' increasing acceptance of homosexuality has put considerable stress on evangelicalism because of this theological conundrum. Studying female Christian athletes' reactions to lesbians and to same-sex attraction can shed light on evangelicalism under stress. Though the founders of sports ministry never could have anticipated sports ministry becoming a venue to work out stances on sexuality, contemporary sports ministry organizations have had to address this highly charged issue.

Sexual Desire versus Sexual Behavior

Midafternoon on the first day of the Charlotte Lady Eagles' team retreat, Steph, the team captain, gathered the group for a lesson. She opened with a prayer: "Lord, every time we open your word, show us what's true in the world, so that we will be able to tell what's true and what's not true, so that we will be able to follow what's true and what is from you." This statement was a signal that Steph was about to address something controversial, something that God knows the truth about but that people often get wrong.

She talked about desire, specifically about the desire to be loved. "Everyone in the world desires to be loved and to love," she told the group.

> We search for it our whole lives. Little girls play wedding, dreaming of finding that love. But there is a difference between love and desire on earth and the love that God has for us. This is something our minds can't really understand, because his love is unconditional. We're not created like that, and it's hard for us to love someone we don't like. But, once you receive Christ, the Holy Spirit now dwells in your heart and lives on the inside of you. This changes your heart and changes your desires.

For Steph and for evangelicals like her, God has the power to guide human desire.

Steph was addressing desire as something that can affect sportsmanship (the desire to win), but she was also talking about sexual desire. She started with a sporting example:

I was in Brazil about six or seven years ago. Brazil has some dirty, feisty players. During one game, I made a good tackle, and the girl turned and punched me in the face. I was a little dazed, but I just turned and ran and got in position. After the game, though, the other players on that team, and to this day, they say to me, "Hey, remember when you got punched in the face and just walked away?" They remember that, and they were more open to me because of it. I grew up a fighter, I would never have walked away from that punch. But God does change the desires of your heart. I did not have a desire to retaliate. And others are more likely to listen when we demonstrate an action that's not a normal reaction.

Another example is this time I was marking this player called Angr, and she was *angry*! She fouled me a lot. And one time, I was taking a chest ball down and she full-on karate kicked me from the side with both legs. She knocked me down. I couldn't breathe. But, I just got up and continued to play. I knew then that God can change the desires of my heart. He was showing me the power that he gave to me. And, I felt bad for her, thinking, why would you intentionally want to hurt someone? And that was a total 180 for me.

Steph's examples of remaining unprovoked in violent sporting situations resonated with the gathered soccer players. Many of them were familiar with fighting back and had become elite soccer players because they played hard and refused to be pushed around on the field. As discussed in chapter 3, the Charlotte Lady Eagles valued a different vision of soccer, one in which their behaviors on the field reflected their Christian beliefs. Steph's story of no longer experiencing the desire to retaliate was a story of witnessing without words, and she credited God with changing this desire.

She concluded her message to the group by expanding her discussion of desire to desires beyond sports. "Whatever it is that you struggle with," she said, "whatever desire you have that maybe doesn't make God smile—you could be a liar, a murderer, maybe you like to date girls instead of guys, maybe you have pride—God really does change it when you ask him to. And that's the love that we can't understand." In her example, Steph equated lying, murdering, homosexuality, and pride and addressed these as human desires that God can change. She noted changes in her own athletic engagement; she is no longer "a fighter" and feels sorry for those who are. For Steph and for Christian athletes like her, changes in sporting behavior are evidence for the human capacity to change through faith, and she and other sports ministry leaders consistently pointed to homosexuality as an example of a desire that God wants to change.

The Charlotte Lady Eagles were explicitly evangelical; they played in a secular league and were the only team in that league with a stated religious affiliation. The women who played for the Lady Eagles had all played Division I college soccer, and a number of them played professionally or for the U.S. national team, coached college or club teams, and thought of soccer as their primary career. Because these women played soccer in both Christian and secular environments, they encountered more out lesbians and interacted with out lesbians in a more physical way than a nonathletic evangelical Christian would in his or her religious life. One player told me that every secular team she had played on was about one-third lesbians. As Nora put it, "Whether you know it or not, you have played with gay teammates." Because of this increased interaction with lesbians in their sporting lives and because of the attention to homosexuality as a sin in their religious lives, these female athletes thought about homosexuality a great deal.

As Steph's lesson shows, Christian athletes are likely to treat homosexuality as a form of desire.[8] Chapter 3 addressed the desire to be Christlike during athletic engagement, and the Christian athletes I studied understood some practices as blockages to being Christlike even though these practices were normative in the sports world—like cursing, intentional fouling, or stalling tactics. These behaviors, according to Christian athletes like Steph, stem from desires that are counter to Christ's intentions and may be the result of Satan's influence. Being Christlike in an athletic setting does not simply entail altering one's behavior; it requires reprogramming the desires of one's heart so that detrimental behaviors become not only inappropriate but unthinkable. On the field, in athletes' split-second responses to competitive situations, there is very little distinction between desire and behavior. Wanting something turns into doing something immediately and seemingly unconsciously. As such, Christian athletes are often more attuned to their desires than nonathletic evangelical Christians and are painfully aware of the close connection between desire and behavior.

Steph's speech treated homosexuality much the same as the sporting desire for retaliation; commitment to Jesus Christ can change one's innermost desires. To think of homosexuality as an unchangeable part of a person, like eye color or height, is not compatible with this understanding of homosexuality as desire. This helps explain why lessons like Steph's that address same-sex attraction are just as concerned with desire as with behavior. Especially for those who believe commitment to Christianity can change their desires, continuing to experience same-sex attraction can feel like a failure of faith. Confessing the ongoing experience of same-sex attraction can open one to scrutiny regarding religious sincerity: if God can change the desires of willing believers, then unchanging desire points to unwillingness to change. This has often made it very difficult for gays and lesbians to feel comfortable in conservative Christian communities.[9]

Policing sexual behavior is normative in evangelical settings. Conservative Christian colleges often police their students' sexual behavior, and probation or expulsion is compulsory for students who engage in premarital or extramarital sexual activity.[10] However, sports ministry makes a distinction between sexual behavior and sexual desire. While the majority of sports ministry participants see homosexual *behavior* as sinful, they tend to posit that homosexual *desire* is a human failing that can be changed with God's help. It was this distinction between desire and behavior that allowed for the variety of responses to lesbianism on the Charlotte Lady Eagles; when I raised questions regarding homosexuality, the women on the team often didn't know how to respond. Some supported the evangelical mainstay that the behavior was sinful but the person was redeemable ("Love the sinner, hate the sin"),[11] but others were less clear on the inherent sinfulness of this behavior, a view in tension with evangelical orthodoxy.

Ellie, the starting goalkeeper for the Lady Eagles, tried out for the U.S. women's professional league after the 2008 season and, after not making a team, joined the coaching staff at the well-known conservative Christian college discussed in the previous chapter. The school's women's soccer coaching staff was predominantly composed of former Lady Eagles players and coaches. When I asked her for her take on homosexuality, Ellie told me, "There's a different mind-set between Christians and non-Christians. If you are Christian and homosexual, there is guilt that they feel the way they are. But I think there doesn't have to be an antagonistic relationship between gays and Christians. It's not either-or. I think scripture is clear that it's wrong to be gay, but it's not like God hates you for being gay. Some people might believe that, but I don't. I've known players on the Eagles who God redeemed from homosexuality. Every person is different."

She went on to say that because of the conservative nature of the college where she coaches, she thought players on her team would not approach her if they were concerned about their sexuality. I asked her what she would tell a player if someone did approach her. "I guess if one of the players on my team was gay I would say, 'Do you believe that it is wrong, and that it's a sin? And do you want to overcome?' To some people it's a struggle, and to some people it's just the way they are."

"What would you say to someone who says, it's just the way I am?" I asked her.

She responded, "I would say, if you don't think it's a sin . . ." She sighed, then said, "I think scripture says that it is obviously wrong and a sin, but I deal with things that are on the same level. They might say that they don't think it's wrong to avoid feeling guilt. Maybe they've been lying to themselves so long that they think it's true. In a struggle, you have to be willing to give up yourself. God can help with that. But if someone's acting on it, they probably won't be willing to listen."

Ellie avoided my question. For Ellie and for conservative Christians like her, homosexuality is an obvious sin, and someone who did not see it as a sin was wrong. But Ellie was also clear that this sin, like every sin in her world, was not unforgivable; it required confession to God and a concerted effort to allow God to change the desire. Ellie offered a number of reasons why a person might be reluctant to treat homosexuality as a sin—maybe she is avoiding guilt, maybe she believes the lie that she has been telling herself that it is not a sin, maybe she is unwilling to listen. None of these options allow for sexual desire to be an unchangeable part of a person.

Another player, Tess, told me:

I don't know what the answer is. I don't think we serve a God who could be that cruel, to make someone that way and then tell them that it is wrong. I don't know if God sends gay people to hell. I wrestle with that all the time. It's hard for me. I've seen good friends live that lifestyle for years and then—I had a friend, she challenged God. She said, if you say this is wrong, prove it, change me. And he changed her radically.

While Tess was conflicted about condemnation of homosexuality, she was sure that God could change someone who desired to be changed.

Ellie was a certain that homosexuality was sinful, Tess was ambivalent, and Angie provided another take on the issue. She told me, "I've been around a lot of lesbians. And they've been some of my best friends in soccer and in life. The only solid answer that I have as a Christian is that I am supposed to love people. Until I live a sin-free day, which will never happen, then I should never judge or withhold love from someone."[12]

I pushed Angie on the idea of homosexuality as a sin, asking if it was possible to be both Christian and gay. She answered:

The short answer is yes. I believe in my understanding that the definition of a Christian is a Christ follower. The definition isn't someone perfect. It's someone who has the desire to be like Christ. I can be prideful and be a Christian—hopefully I will address that in my heart, but I can have pride and be a Christian. It's possible because I still have the desire in my heart to be Christlike without being perfect. I would hate for someone to miss out on the joy I experience because they think their sexuality keeps them separated from the Lord. He does love us. He knows we are not perfect.

For Angie, homosexuality was an imperfection like pride that does not prevent one from experiencing God's love but does entail work to "address that in my heart." Just as we were discussing the implications of this, Angie had to leave for soccer practice. Clearly the issue was weighing on her mind because she called me back a few days later to clarify her position:

I've been thinking about what you asked me about homosexuality and how I said, I can't cast the first stone. And I just want to say, I don't know if homosexuality is a sin. I just don't know. What I meant was, until I'm perfect, I can't tell anyone how to live. I don't know and I don't want to tell people if it is or isn't a sin. I just know I'm supposed to love people, and that's what I try to do.

It was very important to Angie that I understood that this particular issue was unclear for her.

This range of responses demonstrates a deep uncertainty regarding homosexuality. Angie and Tess were ambivalent about judging their friends and teammates, while Ellie remained certain that homosexuality was sinful though not unforgivable. This uncertainty and ambivalence may have emerged from the contradiction between evangelical presentations of homosexuality as changeable through confession and redemption and the testimonies of many gays and lesbians who say that their sexuality is an unchangeable and essential part of themselves. For evangelicals, God has the power to change the desires of any willing believer. Therefore, questioning whether sexual desire is changeable challenges the power of God. If God is unable to change a person's sexual desires, then God is limited and not all-powerful. It also raises questions regarding God's intentions for humans: if sexual desires are unchangeable, does this mean that God intentionally created humans to have a variety of sexualities? The idea that God may have intentionally created multiple sexualities contradicts evangelical teachings that heterosexual marriage is part of God's plan for every believer. The issue of whether sexual desire is changeable can cause intense struggle for believers because it calls into question foundational theological understandings of God's power and plan.

Treating Homosexuality

I asked Ellie what advice she would give to a Christian who experienced same-sex attraction but did not want to be gay, someone who thought of it as a struggle rather than his or her identity. Ellie said that she could share some stories of how God has radically changed people as examples of God's power to change willing believers. She was not sure if this was enough and said that she would ultimately refer the person to Christian resources that dealt directly with homosexuality like Exodus

International, a ministry dedicated to "freedom from homosexuality through Jesus Christ."[13]

Exodus International dissolved in 2013, but before its dissolution, it was highly influential in sports ministry and in larger evangelical culture. The organization relied on culturally established ideas of masculinity and femininity to educate wayward Christians on expected gendered behaviors. For example, it recommended a friendly football game to connect men to masculinity or a makeover party to connect women to femininity. Because "sports are just a natural way for guys to connect," and because women struggling with lesbianism "will stay away from skirts, makeup, and jewelry," these tactics taught participants that they were not different from average men and women and should embrace their gender roles. According to the Exodus International website, "It's not really about the points at the end of the game or the style of a person's hair; the goal is to change our distorted perceptions of ourselves and heal inner wounds."[14] For Exodus, homosexuality was an affliction that could be healed through Christianity, and that healing could be put into effect by conforming to traditional gender norms.[15]

The president of Exodus visited the conservative Christian college where Ellie was coaching. "One of the things he said that really stuck with me was that the opposite of homosexuality is not heterosexuality, its holiness. To not be gay, you don't have to be straight—it's not like you have to break up with your girlfriend and then find a boyfriend tomorrow. You just can't act on your feelings." While this may seem to contradict sports ministry's concern with same-sex desire as well as behavior, in fact it shows the relationship between desire and behavior. For evangelicals like Ellie, changing desire and changing behavior are mutually reinforcing. The idea is that not acting on same-sex attraction would open a person to God's help in changing those desires.

Celibacy, then, was one option for gay and lesbian Christians who were attempting to change their desires. According to Leonard LeSourd, a Christian author of a number of books on Christianity and gender:

> Christian homosexuals have two positive avenues to pursue. First, they can seek a complete inner healing and change of lifestyle from homo- to heterosexual orientation. Or, second, they can follow a path of lifelong celibacy. Any gay man [or woman] who makes an all-out commitment to

Jesus will be given the grace and strength and persistence to adhere successfully to one of these two routes.[16]

LeSourd's understanding exemplifies the dominant approach to homosexuality within the sports ministry community; homosexuality is a condition that one could suppress and eventually change through Christian commitment. From this perspective, same-sex physical intimacy is a clear sin, and the first steps in preventing this sin from occurring are suppressing the desire for same-sex intimacy and calling on God to change that desire.

Exodus's message appeared in *Experiencing God's Power for Female Athletes*, the sports ministry resource analyzed in chapter 4. The text included a fictional narrative about Jill and Becky, two college athletes who spent increasing amounts of time together, laughed at inside jokes, and made others uncomfortable by "hugging each other for long periods of time. It wasn't long before rumors started on the team that Jill and Becky were in a lesbian relationship." The authors warn, "What happened in Jill and Becky's relationship is not that uncommon. What started out as a positive friendship turned into an emotionally dependent relationship, . . . [crossing] physical boundaries and [leading] into a homosexual relationship."[17] For these authors, even rumors of homosexual behavior were a bad thing. From the story of Jill and Becky, it is unclear whether these rumors were grounded in reality or if the rumors themselves contributed to Jill and Becky's relationship. Since the 1980s, Exodus has used the phrase "emotional dependency" to describe homosexuality, most prevalently in the pamphlet *Emotional Dependency and How to Keep Your Friendships Healthy*,[18] which included multiple fictional accounts of how "emotionally dependent" relationships develop (similar to the story of Jill and Becky). These texts and other evangelical materials frequently describe homosexuality in negative terms and present dedication to Christ as a way to avoid falling into what they saw as inherently negative relationships. Homosexuality appears in these texts as a disease in need of healing.

Exodus, some ministry organizations, and some evangelical spokespeople have recently begun to rethink their strategies for dealing with gays and lesbians. Jeanette Howard, author of conservative Christian books for lesbians, thought when she wrote *Out of Egypt: Leaving Lesbi-*

anism Behind in 1991 that she too would experience heterosexual marriage and children,[19] but thirteen years later when she wrote her second book, *Into the Promised Land: Beyond the Lesbian Struggle*, she offered a different perspective on her situation:

> Despite all my efforts, prayer, application and service, I had to admit that I had not traveled along a continuum and entered the world of heterosexuality. Although my identity was not found in lesbianism, and I no longer felt compelled to engage in lesbian sexual behavior, there appeared to be no further movement. Despite joining a Christian dating agency and opening myself up to many avenues of experience, I could not honestly see myself ever committing to a man.[20]

In this publication, Howard describes a life of godly celibacy as her solution for being unable to enter a heterosexual relationship. She also points to Christian organizations like Courage in the United Kingdom that originally formed to help Christians overcome same-sex attraction but eventually accepted monogamous same-sex relationships as godly.[21] Although Howard could not condone this, she was willing to recognize that "certainties that I held back in the late 1980s, regarding sexual 'healing' have become less certain and less static in nature."[22]

In June 2013, the president of Exodus International, Alan Chambers, issued an apology to gays and lesbians who had experienced hurt or shame at the hands of the organization. Chambers and the board announced the dissolution of Exodus after thirty-seven years of pursuing a mission of sexual reorientation. Chambers's apology reflects much of the same ambivalence present in the Lady Eagles' reactions to homosexuality. He apologized for stigmatizing parents, causing heartbreak, and heaping shame and guilt on persons who continued to experience same-sex attraction, including himself. "[My ongoing same-sex attractions] brought me tremendous shame and I hid them in the hopes they would go away. Looking back, it seems so odd that I thought I could do something to make them stop. Today, however, I accept these feelings as parts of my life that will likely always be there." Though he announced his acceptance of same-sex attraction in himself and in others, Chambers equivocated with statements that affirmed traditional, conservative stances. He said, "Our journey hasn't been about denying the power of

Christ to do anything—obviously he is God and can do anything. . . . I cannot apologize for my deeply held biblical beliefs about the boundaries I see in scripture surrounding sex."[23] These statements reiterate evangelical mainstays that God's power is unquestionable and that the Bible condemns gay sexual practices.

Exodus may have closed its doors, but Chambers and others formed a new organization called Speak. Love. with a mission of promoting supportive dialogue regarding sexuality.[24] Christian lesbians like Candace Chellew-Hodge remained skeptical of this move. She voiced concerns that the new organization's emphasis on the prodigal son parable would only reinforce the idea that one must give up homosexual relationships in order to be accepted. "I hope my reservations are unfounded, because so much is at stake in this move. If time reveals this new organization to be nothing more than a shuffling of the Titanic's deck chairs then it will only reinforce the LGBT belief that the church is the very last place they can turn to for support."[25] In this statement, Chellew-Hodge echoed Amy's assertion that the church has often been unwelcoming toward gays and lesbians.

Sports ministry resources for men rarely address same-sex attraction as an issue for athletes. This stems from the gender assumptions addressed in the previous chapter: because Americans see sport as a masculine domain, men who play sports are confirming their masculinity and by extension their straightness. Recent events like the coming-out of NBA player Jason Collins and the NFL drafting openly gay Michael Sam may push sports ministry to address men's sexuality. If sports ministry does take on the issue of male same-sex attraction, it is likely to be just as complex and confusing as female same-sex attraction. The problem remains that any understanding of sexual desire as unchangeable contradicts evangelical orthodoxy on God's power and plan.

Struggling with Lesbianism on the Charlotte Lady Eagles

The leaders of the Charlotte Lady Eagles treated homosexual behaviors as sinful and promoted the idea that heartfelt faith could help one repress and eventually change homosexual desires. On the team, a handful of players experienced same-sex attraction, and they employed different strategies for dealing with it. Amy and Leslie were two Charlotte

Lady Eagles players who came to different understandings of how to process and react to their desires and behaviors. As noted earlier in this chapter, Amy left sports ministry to live as an out lesbian. Leslie, in contrast, became a full-time staff member for the Lady Eagles and fully embraced the idea that homosexual desire can be repressed and changed. She married a man and pursued a degree in Christian counseling to help Christian women like herself deal with sexual sins. Their story is an example of sports ministry participants' range of responses to homosexuality.

Amy grew up a believer in Christianity. "I've always been a believer. I've always sensed that there is something bigger out there. But I wasn't a churchgoer, and I didn't read the Bible." This is a common narrative in evangelical Christianity. Many participants in sports ministry begin their testimonies in a similar format, stating that they have long believed in God, but it was through evangelical Christianity that they came to understand their faith differently and first declared their commitment to pursue a personal relationship with Jesus Christ. Amy's story has another dimension: a lesbian past.

> I came out in college. That was the first time I acted on my attraction. I've had the attraction since age nine, but I'd only heard negative things about gays. I had a lot of pressure from my family to like boys, like family members asking, "Who's your boyfriend? What boy do you like?" And I would think, I like Stephanie. So I experienced a lot of shame for my attraction, but not from the church. It was more socially. It was very confusing.

As for many people who experience same-sex attraction, Amy's feelings carried shame, and she kept them a secret while she was growing up.

When Amy attended a public university and played on its Division I soccer team, she met some out lesbians, who accepted her into their community. One of her coaches bought her a Bible and wanted to talk with her about Christianity, but Amy felt she had to reject Christianity in order to be gay:

> He was open to questions. But I never asked those questions [about homosexuality], because I knew what the church thought. And I couldn't

argue with scripture. I didn't feel like I would belong in a religious community, but I've always had a strong desire for church community. I didn't go to church—I mean, I was out and people knew it, so I avoided that. I had a lot of support from my friends and family. My family didn't know any gay people. They were shocked [when I came out]. They saw homosexuality as unnatural. But they would say, "We love you no matter what."

Amy's certainty about how the church would react to her sexuality came from cultural sources. Because many evangelical spokespeople had openly condemned gays and lesbians and actively campaigned against gay marriage, Amy saw it as common knowledge that evangelicals opposed homosexuality.[26]

Amy's family treated her lesbian identity as a phase. Her father in particular thought of it as unnatural, and her family gave her books about female athletes developing unhealthy attachments to teammates. Like the narrative from *Experiencing God's Power for Female Athletes*, these books presented same-sex attraction as something to be wary of. Amy read that desires for a person of the same sex were an unhealthy state that could be treated with faith in God. She recalled:

About that time, I met Carl. Carl is a great guy, we were really good friends. I decided to date Carl, and that made my dad really happy. He would always ask, "How's Carl?" I was getting the message that this guy was better for me. And guys had told me, you just haven't met the right guy. And so I thought, maybe they're right—maybe I haven't met the right guy. Everyone wants a label from you: are you a lesbian? Are you bisexual? I was just trying to figure myself out.

Six months into her relationship with Carl, Amy became pregnant. Under pressure from their families, they were married three months later and had a daughter, Allie. At the time, Amy was twenty-one, and Carl was twenty. For Amy, soccer was her life's goal. She had trained with the U.S. national team and didn't want her pregnancy or parenting to prevent her from continuing to play soccer. At Carl's suggestion she contacted a number of teams, and the Charlotte Lady Eagles invited her to try out. She told me:

I got this e-mail to bring my testimony to tryouts—it's just part of tryouts. Like, bring your medical history, your insurance information, and your testimony. I had always been a believer, and I had a desire to learn. I was their new agenda, and I had no idea. That summer, I did get baptized. It was so easy to fall in and conform. It was comforting to be just like them. And there was a lot of love, a lot of genuine love—and some not so genuine love, contingent love. I read the Bible—Steph would teach us. And I thought, this is what I need to be a good mother. That was the first year.

That year, 2007, Amy walked around scared that her teammates would discover her premarital pregnancy or her lesbian past and would condemn her for it. That summer, she told no one about her history with women. "No. No way. No one knew that I had dated girls. I was already the girl who came in and didn't know anything about Jesus and didn't have a Bible." Though Amy was a believer, she did not grow up in the sort of evangelical community that some of the Charlotte Lady Eagles did. The Eagles organization recruited a number of Christians like Amy, familiar with yet peripheral to evangelicalism, and some of these athletes fully integrated with sports ministry despite their limited or negative experiences with evangelicals while growing up.

Amy eventually told the team about her premarital sex, and the team accepted her. When she returned to play for the Lady Eagles the following summer, she used her story to encourage new players to confide in the team about their struggles. On the first evening of the team retreat, when everyone gathered around the campfire and M.J. opened the evening's conversation with the story of her father's infidelity, there was a long, uncomfortable silence. It was Amy who spoke first:

Last year, when I joined this team, I expected to hate it and to hate everyone here. I just wanted to play soccer, and I thought Christians were pushy and close-minded. I didn't even have a Bible, that's how clueless I was. I walked around every day waiting for them to condemn me. I was defensive and guarded, because I felt like I was masquerading and that any day someone was going to call me out on it and condemn me. Then, last year, at team retreat, I couldn't handle it anymore. I broke down and confessed all of this sin that I had been carrying. When I got married, I was three months pregnant with Allie. I mean, that's a really evident sin.

But no one judged me or condemned me. And . . . I got saved last year here at team retreat. So, if you are carrying anything, you should know that this is a safe place and that you can trust us.

Amy's description of the team's acceptance of her "evident sin" of premarital sex left out that she continued to hide her lesbian past. She was more comfortable disclosing the taboo sexual behavior of premarital sex, perhaps because this was straight sex and therefore a more relatable sin for most of her teammates or perhaps because her subsequent marriage to Carl had eliminated the possibility of repeating this sin.

Throughout her marriage with Carl, Amy was conflicted. "I struggled with the feeling of being a lesbian married to a man. Carl knew my past—he thought it was a phase also. And being straight was so much easier. It really was. But I started to feel that attraction, and I missed the emotional connection with women. It is different [than being with a man], at least for me." For Amy, and for many gay Christians, homosexuality caused misery and guilt. She felt that it would be impossible to reconcile being gay with her Christian beliefs. Chellew-Hodge writes of similar feelings in her book *Bulletproof Faith*: "I spent years listening to a religion that told me the authentic self I sensed underneath the dogma and doctrine was an abomination. I spent years believing that my authentic self was something hated by God—something that needed to be changed."[27] And for Amy, marrying Carl was a way to enact that change, to turn from gay to straight, and sports ministry was a way to learn about parenting and to maintain her shift in sexuality that she believed was necessary for being a Christian.

After the campfire at team retreat, another player, Leslie, walked with Amy back to the cabins. They were having a good conversation, so Leslie suggested that they sleep apart from the other players so that they could keep talking. They talked late into the night and fell asleep. As Amy described it:

In the morning, Leslie got really strange. The night before, she had told me that she struggled with attraction to females. I'm not sure why she told me. I told her that I used to date women and she said to me, "God forgives you." Leslie never acted on it. She resisted friends that tried to date her. I was relieved that we understood each other, and we talked about other stuff. I thought it was awkward in the morning just because we had shared so much.

For the next few days, Amy struggled. She had started to feel an emotional connection with Leslie, and she wanted to be around her. As she explained:

> I felt so guilty. I was married and I wanted to be near another person. I prayed that it would be taken away. Leslie would ignore me at practice—she drove me crazy—then she would text me after practice to get coffee and talk about our struggle. For me, attraction to women was emotional. But Leslie told me that she liked female touch. Like snuggling with her mom or her sister. And the more we talked, I said that maybe we could get to that point where we could comfort each other. But it was like, if we were enjoying ourselves too much, she would sort of push me away—start quoting the Bible or put on Christian music. And I was really battling inside, thinking: this is cheating. I'm emotionally giving myself to someone else. I felt horrible, but I kept seeing where it went.

The team traveled to many away games that season. The staff assigned roommates at random, and at one of the away games early in the season, Amy, Leslie, and Tara shared a room. The room had two beds near each other and a third bed set apart, around a corner. Tara took the third bed, leaving Amy and Leslie the other two. Even the idea of sleeping so close caused tension between the two women. According to Amy:

> At dinner, Leslie completely ignored me. After Tara had gone to sleep and we were in our beds, I told her she was hurting my feelings, like I was a secret friend that she was ashamed of. She started crying, saying, "I just like you so much." Then she rolled over, like she was going to sleep. And I said, "Well, do you want to come and hold me?" And she did, she came to my bed. And we just held each other. It was very intense. In the morning, she wouldn't look at me and wouldn't talk to me. At chapel, before the game, I was just bawling—everyone thought I was just moody. When we were driving back, she told me, "I feel like you took advantage of me." And yes, I invited her, but she came to my bed.

The next week was my absolute worst week. I kept thinking, did I take advantage of her? Is she the one who's really seeking Christ? We barely talked. After practice, she would say things like, "I'm praying for you." And I went and bought the smallest journal I could find and wrote in it—oh so tiny—just to get my feelings out. I was just struggling. I felt like I needed to tell Carl, I felt like I needed a divorce. I could tell I was hurting him. And it wasn't Leslie, I just wasn't going to last in my marriage.

Amy and Leslie's attraction to each other threw them into emotional turmoil. They were in an environment that explicitly named same-sex attraction as an ungodly desire and same-sex intimacy (even cuddling) as a sin that must be confessed and addressed.

Because Leslie was single, her feelings were not about cheating. She saw her attraction to Amy as a sin, but she was afraid to confess it. She said, "I don't know if others would've been mature enough to handle our sin. That's the scariest thing in the world, when you don't know if others are going to be mature enough to handle it." The Charlotte Lady Eagles promoted the idea that willing believers can turn to God for assistance in overcoming negative human desires like vengeance, jealousy, and pride. Steph and other team leaders put same-sex attraction in this same category. Given this logic, a believer who continued to experience same-sex attraction needed to increase her willingness to change. Leslie feared that if she confessed her feelings of same-sex attraction, her teammates would doubt her faith or her willingness to let God change her.

In sports ministry, interventions at the level of homosexual desire often involve Christian counseling to determine the root of same-sex attraction, which Christian counselors tend to locate in past abuse or failed relationships with parents. According to Lori Rentzel's pamphlet *Emotional Dependency*, "Anyone can fall into a dependent relationship given the right pressures and circumstances. Those who come from dysfunctional families in which there was alcoholism or abuse, for instance, are especially vulnerable. . . . The compulsion to form emotionally dependent relationships is a symptom of deeper spiritual and emotional problems that need to be faced and resolved."[28] This trajectory made sense to Leslie as she tried to understand what had led her to seek emotional and physical comfort with Amy. She saw Amy and Carl's marital problems as a major factor:

Amy and Carl had some problems. She needed a lot. Carl was not ful-filling his husbandly role. I could see that she needed someone, and I thought that was me. I had started counseling for previous sexual abuse. And when you have two people in a place of need, they can develop an unhealthy dependent relationship. I know we are both sorry about that. It ruined our friendship.

Leslie's description is similar to the fictional narrative of Jill and Becky included in *Experiencing God's Power for Female Athletes*. Leslie saw her relationship with Amy as a result of dependency and unhealthy self-understanding.

For some evangelicals who experienced same-sex attraction, a care-ful examination of their past along with Christian counseling has led to a heterosexual lifestyle. *Sharing the Victory* has published multiple articles chronicling women who have rejected their lesbian past. One such woman wrote, "Since the major root of lesbianism is broken rela-tionships with parents and peers of the same sex, we as Christians have a responsibility to step out of our comfort zones and to establish healthy friendships with those involved in homosexual lifestyles." The author credited one such friendship with allowing her to eventually marry a man and have children.[29] In stories like this one, marriage and children are evidence that one has completely turned from gay to straight.

Once Leslie confessed her struggle with same-sex attraction to the team leaders, they required Amy and Leslie to see a Christian counselor to address their sexual desires. Amy saw it as an attempt to "pray my gay away," and it made her angry, but Leslie found the experience help-ful. According to Leslie, "In Christian counseling, you are treated with dignity and it's, like, let's look at the whole picture. In Genesis, humans are a combination of dignity and depravity. And counseling helped me be honest before the Lord in that tension." Leslie believed that homo-sexuality could be traced to past abuse or to failed parenting. She had a leadership role in the Lady Eagles ministry and was staying in Char-lotte after the season as a member of the Eagles' staff. She embraced the central tenets of sports ministry, including the theological understand-ing that God grants humans the strength and power to overcome and change their desires. When Leslie had first tried out for the Lady Eagles, she didn't make the team. "I had my first long bout with depression," she told me. "I was drawn to Christianity. It was uplifting, and I wanted that." For Leslie, belonging to the Eagles' community brought her out of her depression, and continuing to belong to the organization was important to her. Additionally, Leslie had a history of negative relationships with men and was already seeing a Christian counselor. All of these factors contributed to Leslie's openness to the project of Christian therapy that was meant to alter her sexual desires.

Amy, in contrast, was offended by the Eagles' approach to the situation:

> They set up marriage counseling, and the counselor asked about my family. I told her I was closer to my stepmom than my mom, and she said that I didn't get enough emotional attention from my mother. Basically, we tried to pray away my gay. Everything was focused more on taking away my gay than on my relationship with Carl.

Whereas Leslie had accepted the explanation that her same-sex attraction was the result of her past, Amy rejected the idea that her relationship with her mother was the root of her homosexuality. Many narratives of evangelical women experiencing same-sex attraction conclude with marriage and children as evidence that the believer has fully transformed into a straight person. However, Amy already was married with a child, and so she may have been less likely to accept this narrative of sexual transformation through marriage. Leslie was single and was fully immersed in a culture that presented heterosexual marriage as God's plan for every believer. This too may have contributed to her understanding of Christian therapy as helpful, even necessary, for aligning herself with God's plan.

Other players on the Charlotte Lady Eagles demonstrated a range of responses to homosexuality. One player, Andrea, told me:

> I live in a condo, and my neighbors are gay men. I'm trying to see for myself. I was taught that it's wrong, but I don't know. What I've come to is that it is a sin. It says it in Romans 1. But when I'm around gay and lesbian people, it's not the first thing I think. Especially my teammates. It's the last thing I think of. I don't see them as "that sinner," just as a person.[30]

For Andrea, increased contact with gays and lesbians caused her to temper the Christian teachings she had grown up with. While still certain that homosexuality was a sin, Andrea said, "All I have to do is think about myself. Jealousy. Even stealing a paper clip. It's all sin. Homosexuality is not any worse." As other players had told me, homosexuality was a sin comparable to sins in their own lives, and in their day-to-day interactions with gays and lesbians, they were relatively unconcerned with others' relationships and sexual choices.

However, Amy's experience on the Charlotte Lady Eagles did not reflect this claim that homosexuality was a sin comparable to stealing a paper clip. Amy felt strongly that "there is a ranking of sins," which was why she felt more comfortable telling the team about her premarital pregnancy than about her lesbian past. And the organization did respond very differently to Leslie and Amy's mutual attraction than they did to Amy's confession of premarital sex. While evangelical teachings are clear that premarital sex is a sin, Amy was not required to seek counseling for this behavior.

Amy explained that she did not like the idea of labeling homosexuality a sin:

> Leslie would say, it is a sin. But I couldn't say it. I knew there were two other girls on the team who were secretly dating each other and one girl who had a girlfriend in another city. One of the girls who was secretly dating revealed that to me. One day, we were told to pray for each other. There was something about the way she worded her struggle—I just told her that I used to date girls. She told me everything. After that we would share Bible verses, but we never talked about it again.

I was with the team over the course of that season for practice, for games, for sports ministry training, for devotionals, for small-group Bible studies, and for social events, and I had no idea that any of the players were closeted lesbians. In fact, I had no idea of what was happening between Amy and Leslie that summer. It wasn't until my follow-up research years later that they told me this story.

For Christian lesbians like Amy and those players in secret relationships, the closet was a way to have a lesbian relationship and still maintain their full participation on the team.[31] Amy worried that her position as a starter was in jeopardy, and she went to the Christian therapy sessions hoping to maintain her team position. Her playing time was not affected, but the organization did put together programming on homo-sexuality for the whole team. According to Amy:

> At the end of the season, during playoffs, there was a big team meeting. They had this handout on "peer intimacy." It was pretty intense. There were two girls they brought in to speak—one was a leader that didn't play soccer and one was an ex–Lady Eagle. They shared that they used to date women, then they became Christian. The way they put it, the power of the Holy Spirit had taken their gay away. I was pissed off. I just remember sitting in that circle pissed off. I was thinking I know her, her, and her, and I wonder, are there more?

Amy directed her anger toward the organization. She was offended by the idea that homosexuality was a desire that could be changed through the Holy Spirit. She also may have been angry at the closeted lesbians on the team. Their secrecy made Amy and Leslie stand out, but these were not the only two women on the team with lesbian desires. The organization's programming for the whole team showed that it probably realized that Amy and Leslie were not a unique case, but its presentation of homo-sexuality as treatable and changeable more than likely strengthened the appeal of the closet for those who hid their lesbian relationships

Conclusion

Sports ministry for women pays special attention to the issue of homo-sexuality. As Leslie noted, evangelicals (and Americans in general) tend to treat sexual deviance differently than nonsexual taboo behaviors:

> People don't want to talk about us being sexual creatures. There is a lot of shame. There is, like, a shame cloud over sexual identity. It's amazing that anyone can come out well in their sexuality. Women can't talk to their daughters, men can't talk to their sons—it's a real problem. I feel like sexuality is holy, meaning set apart. It makes our faces red, and we get all shifty. We should be able to talk about this without feeling shame.

The "shame cloud" over sexuality did make homosexuality a different kind of sin than anger or jealousy, despite players' claims to understand it similarly. Leslie's insight reveals that the link between desire and behavior was not the same for all kinds of desires and behaviors. Though a Christian athlete like Ellie might have experienced shame or regret when she felt envy or anger, both evangelical Christianity's outspoken opposition to gay marriage and the suspicions of lesbianism that pervade elite women's sport amplified the shame surrounding homosexuality.

Amy did not return to the Charlotte Lady Eagles the following season. She, like many of the other players on the team, tried out for the newly formed U.S. women's professional soccer league. A team accepted her, and she and Carl relocated so she could take the position. Many of her new teammates were familiar with the Charlotte Lady Eagles as an evangelical team and were curious about Amy and her experiences. Amy explained:

> After that summer in Charlotte, I just wanted to be real [on my professional team]. I met some great friends. The girls on the team would ask me questions about the Bible, and rather than answer those questions, I would say, we can look at it together. I feel like I became more genuine as a believer. I never claimed to know anything for certain. I don't want to use faith to oppress anyone else.

Amy felt that the Charlotte Lady Eagles had used faith to oppress her and the closeted lesbians on the team. She left sports ministry but did not abandon her faith. She, like other Christian athletes in secular settings, used her experiences in sports ministry to continue to explore her Christian faith and to have conversations with others about Christianity. She continued to wrestle with the idea of homosexuality as a sin and with her own confusion of feeling like a lesbian in a straight relationship.

Amy began to spend time with one of her teammates, Rosa, and they developed a close emotional connection. As with her experience with Leslie, she felt guilt about prioritizing this emotional relationship over her marriage to Carl. She told me:

> Rosa was in California training with a pro team. She said, "Do you want to meet me here? I'll buy the ticket. I just want to see you again." I went. I completely fell in love. When I came home, I told Carl. He left, he left Allie with me. My mind was made up, before even California. He called his parents. He said, Amy cheated on me, I'm coming home.

My parents got involved. It was hard on them. They were disappointed in me. It was, like, I was a cheater, my marriage is over, and now Allie has divorced parents. And I couldn't believe that I had cheated and lied and did so knowingly. I had so much guilt. It took a lot of therapy. I was worried that my relationship with Rosa could never be good because of how it started. It took a year to deal with it emotionally.

Amy turned to counseling to deal with her guilt, but unlike with the Christian counseling the Eagles had provided, her turn to therapy in this case allowed her to stay with Rosa.

After Amy left the Eagles to play professionally, Leslie called Amy as a staff person for the Charlotte Lady Eagles. She described their conversation:

I asked her if she would feel welcome to come back. She's a great player, I know we would love to have her back. We would want Carl and Allie to come too, but she had already filed for divorce, and said no, she wouldn't come back. She felt really condemned when she was leaving, but the leadership would have been happy to have her back.

The Eagles' acceptance of Amy's return to the team hinged on her reentering the team's recommended marriage counseling and sincerely attempting to live a heterosexual life.

Although this did not appeal to Amy, Leslie was very interested in pursuing a straight lifestyle. She set boundaries for herself with other women whom she found attractive and pursued a master's degree in counseling through a seminary in Charlotte. According to Leslie, staying in Charlotte allowed her to maintain her sense of belonging with the Eagles, and that made the difference for her in being able to have a straight relationship. Leslie told me:

Amy went back to an environment that communicated to her that she was a certain way. That's what she was hearing, all the voices in her life—it was like, oh, you like girls, you must be gay. When that happens, you don't really have a choice. Amy tried not to be gay—she read the Bible, she was praying, but she just gave up.

"Do you think that you had a choice?" I asked. Leslie responded:

> Choice is probably a bad word. There's so much stuff in your story by the time you're in your midtwenties. Unless you have someone to help you see differently, there is no choice. The voices of the world are about tolerance; you can be however you want to be. I don't think people choose homosexuality. That would be really hard.

Leslie didn't answer my question. In her worldview, God designs humans to be attracted to and partnered with the opposite sex. One could make a "choice" to disregard God's will, but for Leslie, that was not an imaginable option.

Choice is an important idea for evangelicals. Evangelicals treat salvation and belonging to an evangelical community as choices; both these things come from a conversion decision to commit to Jesus Christ. Evangelicals present their religious choices to others in hopes of influencing similar commitments. When Leslie said that Amy didn't have a choice, she invoked the ideology of evangelical outreach as a whole; Amy didn't have a choice because she was surrounded by worldly voices of tolerance instead of evangelical witnesses who could explain the option of evangelicalism clearly. However, many of the Christian athletes whom I met grew up in evangelical households, and some made their conversion decisions when they were only five years old. Their commitment to evangelicalism was not just a religious commitment; it was a family and community commitment. That is what I was trying to get at when I asked Leslie, "Do you think you had a choice?" She saw Amy as surrounded by influences that told her she was gay, but Leslie was uncomfortable seeing her own situation similarly, as surrounded by influences telling her she was straight.

On a Christian athletic team like the Charlotte Lady Eagles, the leadership, players, and audiences assumed the women were straight and, for some women, this lessened the pressure they felt to appear traditionally feminine. It also provided a strong closet for some lesbians who would rather keep their romantic lives secret. For these closeted women, a Christian team provided the opportunity to combine sport and evangelical Christianity, but they were not comfortable disclosing their sexual desires in that environment. As I have shown, heterosexuality was not universal even in a Christian sports environment that deeply valued heterosexual marriage as an important part of Christian living. Because evangelicals believe that heterosexual marriage is the only appropriate arena for sexual contact, they regard sexual desires or behaviors that occur outside of this relationship as sinful. For Amy and for other Christian lesbians, this attitude contributed to exclusion or closeting. For Leslie and for others like her who were interested in changing their sexual desires, evangelical Christianity provided tools for conforming to a straight lifestyle.

Whether to condone or condemn homosexuality cuts to the root of evangelical ideas about God's power, God's plan, and the obligations of believers in the world. For female Christian athletes with lesbian teammates, their respect for their teammates and their belief that God can change a person's desires have created deep ambivalence and confusion. If marriage is God's plan for every believer, then God must have the power to cultivate heterosexual desire. If God does not have this power or if marriage is not necessarily part of God's plan, then evangelicalism's theological foundations begin to crumble. The following chapter turns to how women in sports ministry maintain these theological foundations in their heterosexual dating and marriage relationships.

6

Faith Off the Field

Negotiating Gender at Home

Athletes in Action gathered for its weekly meeting on the campus of the University of North Carolina at Chapel Hill in the spring of 2007. The evening's speaker was on the coaching staff for the year's winning Super Bowl team. He addressed the group of about forty male and female college athletes, "The most important choice you make, other than knowing Christ, is marriage. Find a godly spouse." This perception of marriage as the second most important relationship in Christian life is common among evangelicals. Many evangelicals see a spouse as God's provision for personal happiness and for deepening faith and commitment to evangelical Christianity. "I can guarantee you that my wife is home on her knees right now praying for me," the guest speaker continued. "You know that many of your parents married someone who wasn't quite right, and that is hard, and there are a lot of divorces. A godly spouse is so important. Don't compromise. There will be a godly spouse provided for you. You just need to pray about it and follow God's plan."

A few weeks later, at another AIA meeting, Jada, an athlete who had recently graduated, brought up the pressure on young evangelicals to find a marriage partner. "I've been thinking about the future a lot, especially since graduating. I've been thinking about getting married and having kids. 'Bout that time—getting old." The students laughed at this, perhaps because they recognized the expectation of marriage as a very real pressure in evangelical communities.

"You know," Jada continued, "there's no guarantee that we'll even wake up tomorrow." Tom, the campus AIA director, had opened the night's meeting with a prayer for the families of the Virginia Tech shooting victims, and mortality was on the athletes' minds. "I've been trying to remember that I need to be thinking about the day I meet Christ, not the day I meet my husband." Jada mirrored the sentiments of the visiting football coach from weeks before—a spouse is second only to Christ. And, like the coach, she believed that God would provide her with a spouse. However, she used the idea of Christ's importance and God's will to deprioritize marriage. Her invocation of the "day I meet Christ" emphasized the impermanence of human life, and she implied that by keeping that impermanence in mind, she would be a better Christian. She fully expected that the future would hold a husband for her, and her confidence in this allowed her to focus more fully on what she understood as her religious rather than marriage obligations.

Marriage and family are extremely important in evangelicalism.[1] As Rebecca Davis points out in her examination of marriage in America, "Through the institution of marriage, Americans have idealized what being a man or a woman in this country signifies."[2] Davis's analysis of marriage counseling as a cultural trend in America shows that it "has had the ironic effect of making marriage seem simultaneously more flawed and more essential to the well-being of the individuals involved and the communities to which they belong."[3] Evangelicalism certainly fits this claim, as evangelicals have blamed flawed marriages for social ills as wide-ranging as drug abuse and crime to voter apathy, while at the same time promoting marriage as an integral part of Christian living, an experience that God desires for every Christian.[4]

In general, evangelical Christians believe that successful marriages depend on the correct differentiation of male and female roles. They often present men as rightful spiritual leaders and as God's chosen heads of households. According to Sally Gallagher's study of evangelical family life, "Questions about gender and authority take on symbolic significance as litmus tests of the acceptance of biblical authority overall."[5] Because evangelicals describe God as a father, God's authority is related to God's his gender. Therefore, to undermine the naturalness of gender hierarchy is to undermine God's authority.

Sports ministry organizations promote marriages as an important part of athletic and Christian life and are aware that these marriages confront different challenges than those of nonathlete couples. For example, FCA's president Les Steckel began a couples' retreat in 2002, specifically timed to take place between seasons for numerous sports so "coaching couples in particular can get reacquainted with one another before the season starts."[6] As FCA's *Sharing the Victory* writer Jill Ewert noted after interviewing University of Georgia head football coach Mark Richt and his wife, Katharyn Richt, "Today's world is tough on marriages. Statistics aren't good and in fact can be downright discouraging. Every once in a while, we all need to be reminded that God's plan for marriage and family does work. Yes, it takes effort and strategy, but it is, without a doubt, the highest and best way to go."[7] For Ewert and others in sports ministry, marriage is like the challenge of being a Christian athlete: the values of the world at large are temptations by the devil to undermine Christian living. In sports, these worldly values manifest in gamesmanship, selfishness, or retaliation. In marriage and dating, these worldly values could cause sexual impurity, marital discontent, or divorce.

Christian athletes spend a great deal of time thinking about how worldly desires (as opposed to Christlike desires) can affect their thoughts and actions. They are invested in using their religious beliefs to control their behaviors and desires; they are also firmly embedded in the world of sport, a world that is rife with sex, gambling, and drug and alcohol abuse. Like sportsmanship as an on-field demonstration of Christian values, marriage and dating are significant off-field practices that Christian athletes use to set themselves apart from the secular world.

Unlike earlier generations' explicit presentation of marriage as the ultimate fulfilling relationship for a woman, contemporary female Christian athletes are more likely to frame Jesus as the most important figure in their lives, allowing them to downplay urgency for marriage or childbearing.[8] Men in sports ministry frame marriage as a partnership with a teammate rather than a hierarchical situation of constant male leadership. Though both these presentations seem to undermine the conservative gender roles that evangelicalism espouses, the long-established emphasis on female submission and male headship has not disappeared entirely. Contemporary evangelicals are able to draw on both traditional and contemporary marriage depictions as resources for understanding their gender obligations.

In addition to their religious tradition, male and female Christian athletes have another set of tools at their disposal for understanding their gender: the world of sports. Access to a wide range of gender understandings has made male and female Christian athletes adept negotiators of gender obligations in their home life. For the women in this study, premarital independence (encouraged both in sports ministry and in sport generally) resulted in their delaying marriage longer than many of their nonathletic evangelical female counterparts. For men, redefining leadership as a form of service translated into ideas of wife-as-teammate rather than wife-as-cheerleader. For Christian athletic couples, these metaphors are powerful because both spouses have lived experiences of team participation. As such, male and female Christian athletes employ a wide range of self-understandings to redefine marriage theoretically and practically.

Conservative Gender Roles in Evangelical Marriage

On the first night of FCA summer camp, Mark, the evening's speaker, addressed the eighty or so male and female high school athletes who sat in the auditorium, women on one side and men on the other. "Listen to me, girls out there, don't settle. Guys, rise up and be men. Women are doing what men should be doing. God has called you guys to rise up and be leaders." I looked around and saw the high school girls near me nodding at this sentiment. The speaker, a former Harlem Globetrotter, was there to launch the camp theme—"Game Ready." For FCA, this theme encompassed athletic and personal preparation to live life and compete as evangelical Christians. The speaker continued, addressing the men's side of the room, "Men, don't be afraid to ask for help. Let your emotions out—be transparent and vulnerable this week."

I glanced behind me at Ross, who was one of the college athletes supervising the children's huddle and one of the only men sitting on the girls' side of the auditorium. He was nodding, though half distracted by the fidgeting children on either side of him. These were the children of the coaches and camp administrators, and three camp counselors cared for them during the day. Wherever the children's huddle went, Ross would instruct the boys to hold doors open for the girls, a chivalrous act that showcased male strength and female weakness. It is also significant that the children's huddle always sat on the women's side of the auditorium, implying that children are primarily women's responsibility. The other two counselors who supervised the children's huddle were women.

The speaker continued to address the men: "Pornography is killing young men. Our sisters are out there being raped and molested. These things hold us back from God. This week is about getting game ready, and I challenge you—you know, I have a meeting with four men once a month. It's an accountability group. Find yourself an accountability group."[9] He turned to address the women's side of the room: "And girls, you look good!" Everyone laughed. "Now, have some joy in your life. Get excited about your walk with God."

After the speaker concluded, the campers split into their huddle groups to discuss the camp lessons, and I joined the volleyball huddle for their meeting. As we walked to an open spot on the lawn, I thought about the speaker's differentiation of men and women and his tendency to treat men and women as fundamentally different, with distinct roles and obligations. He had emphasized over and over again that men are obligated to be leaders. But he had also told a story about being the parent who changed the most diapers—"My wife can't outserve me if I'm the leader." I had met the volleyball huddle earlier that day: a group of eight female high school athletes who not only were volleyball players but also served on student councils, organized mission work in prisons, and were presidents of their high school FCA chapters. I was sure that they would be offended that the speaker had called on men to be leaders and not acknowledged the capability of female leadership.

We sat down on the lawn, and one of the huddle leaders talked for a while about what it meant to be "game ready." The girls were clearly bored, picking at the grass and looking around. There was a lull, and I spoke up. "I'm curious. What did you girls find the most interesting about the talk tonight?"

Melissa responded quickly. She was a dominant figure in the group, going into her senior year of high school. "I was really impressed that Mark called on the guys to rise up and be leaders. I'm involved in a leadership group at my school, and, nationwide, leaders are six to one, girls to guys." She paused to let this statistic sink in. "I *wish* some guys would step up and get involved." I was about to follow up on this, when Becky, the other huddle leader, returned from picking up a late camper. After introducing the new camper, Becky told the girls, "Look, we're your huddle leaders. We're here for you. Anything you want to talk about is fair game." There was a pause. Becky continued, "I want to tell you again what Mark said in his talk—you are worth pursuing. You shouldn't be calling guys; they should be calling you. And if they aren't, they aren't the right guy. You don't have to settle—God is preparing a guy out there for you."

One of the other campers chimed in. "Yeah, it's like girls are like apples. The bad ones will fall to the ground and are easy to take, but it takes a real special and worthwhile guy to climb to the top of the tree to pick the best apple."

Melissa nodded and turned to Becky. "Do boys grow up when they get to college?" The campers looked at her expectantly.

"Well, it depends on the guy. If he has a good heart, he is worth waiting for him to mature. Girls mature faster than guys. It's a fact. So, know that a guy with a good heart is worth waiting for."

In this conversation, the FCA campers and leaders employed statistical, metaphorical, and biological evidence to support gender difference. Melissa's disappointment that men were the statistical minority in her leadership organization, the metaphorical comparison of girls to apples, and Becky's assertion that, biologically, men and women mature at different rates all worked together to form a picture of traditional gendered behavior—men as active and women as passive. Female Christian athletes like those in the FCA huddle demonstrated complicity with differentiating and hierarchically organizing gender. I had anticipated that these women, leaders and athletes as they were, would be hostile to a message that insinuated that they were doing men's work and that men could do it better. However, in the context of sport, with its institutionalized sex segregation, female athletes frequently hear this message. These high schoolers understood athletics as a realm of male superiority, and they saw men as athletically superior to women.[10]

The more time I spent with the FCA huddle and with female Christian athletes generally, the more I saw a consistent desire for male leadership and a tacit acknowledgment of male superiority. There was a sense that in a mixed-sex environment, like marriage or a female team with a male coach, men were naturally predisposed to leadership. However, in day-to-day living, the women I interacted with were not incapable or shy about assuming leadership roles in both mixed-sex and sex-segregated environments.

One site in evangelical culture that illustrates the intersection of marriage, sport, and evangelical Christian living is the men's ministry organization Promise Keepers. In the late 1980s, Bill McCartney, a Colorado football coach, envisioned America's stadiums full of men praising God together. He stuck to the vision, and at the height of the Promise Keepers movement in 1996, more than a million men attended stadium rallies nationwide.[11] Calling the group Promise Keepers based on seven promises of faith and fidelity,[12] McCartney and his followers engaged issues of modern masculinity: What does it mean to be a man? And what is the appropriate relationship between men and women? Religious studies scholar Becky Beal has called Promise Keepers an "essentialist retreat," meaning that the organization promotes essentialist definitions of gender roles and escaped to a sex-segregated space to reclaim these roles. Beal claimed that this sort of essentialist retreat parallels sport through a gender logic that positions men as essentially superior to women.[13]

Divorce, out-of-wedlock births, single-parent homes, and abortion were all on the rise in the 1980s and 1990s, and the Promise Keepers' leadership interpreted these trends as a crisis of the family. They claimed that family morality was declining because men had failed to uphold their responsibilities as husbands and fathers. Therefore, the crisis of the traditional family was men's fault and could be solved through men's actions. They argued that returning men to their rightful positions as leaders of their homes could reverse these trends and resolve the crisis.

According to John Bartkowski, a scholar of evangelical marriage, Promise Keepers' spokesman Edwin Louis Cole demonstrates the group's dominant discourse, what Bartkowski termed "instrumentalist masculinity": "The instrumentalist masculinity invoked by the likes of Cole is predicated on the notion of innate, categorical, and largely immutable gender differences (i.e. radical essentialism). According to purveyors of this radical essentialist discourse, manhood is characterized by aggression, strength, and rationality—qualities that are counterposed to 'feminine' responsiveness, sensitivity, and emotionalism."[14] Cole's discourse relied heavily on gender differentiation within marriage: husband headship and wifely submission.

However, Promise Keepers also employed a variant discourse calling for "servant leadership" on the part of husbands and "mutual submission" in a marriage. This is what the FCA speaker invoked when he stated, "My wife can't outserve me if I'm the leader." Bartkowski called this the new guard and noted, "New-guard advocates of patriarchy have sought to incorporate feminist critiques of male domination into their vision of marital relations while still envisioning the husband as the family's leader."[15] Evangelical marriage writers used the ideas of servant leadership and mutual submission to affirm the husband's role as primary leader. For example, Steve Farrar, author of *Point Man*, an evangelical marriage guide, attempted to explain this tension between male leadership and mutual submission via a football metaphor.[16] Bartkowski analyzed Farrar's approach:

> Farrar argues that although a quarterback and wide receiver share the "same objective" and must operate as an "effective unit" to achieve success, the quarterback "has the final say because he's the quarterback." According to Farrar's logic, the quarterback's position as play caller on the football field demands the exercise of authority that, while receptive to feedback from his subordinate teammates, must prevail in the face of disagreements or indecision.[17]

This metaphor of husband as team captain or as quarterback uses the hierarchical structures of sport leadership to naturalize male leadership in the home.

Scholars of sport and gender have noted that sport has a powerful role in maintaining cultural notions of male dominance. According to Susan Cahn:

> Through participation in a culturally masculine realm, men have strengthened their bodies and mastered physical force, acquiring both physical power and the permission to express it as masculine prowess. They have accumulated tools—physical strength, training in violence, and permission to use space and touch as they see fit—that have been used to assert male authority outside as well as inside the realm of sport.[18]

While it would be a mistake to assume that all men unilaterally have developed the tools that Cahn identifies here, her primary point is that it is culturally acceptable for men to behave in a dominant fashion, and that sport supports this behavior. Sport metaphors are appealing to evangelicals because both sport and evangelical marriage assume male dominance.

Resources for evangelical women have also turned to sports metaphors to differentiate gender roles. For much of sports ministry's history, wives of coaches and athletes were involved as supporters of their husbands' athletic careers—as cheerleaders for their husbands. In the early 1980s, for example, Athletes in Action's traveling wrestling team brought their wives along on tour, and "the four team wives formed a singing group and spoke or performed in sororities, churches, dorms, Bible studies, and everywhere their husbands competed."[19] From this perspective, wives were helpful supplements to traveling male groups; their contributions were valuable, but they were not integral.

In the 1970s, almost all women affiliated with sports ministry were wives of athletes or wives of coaches. There were female athletes and female coaches involved, but they were a minority and rarely appeared in sports ministry publications of the time. One of the few unmarried women to attend an FCA summer conference in 1970 was Catherine Lucas, a Roman Catholic nun. She was invited by her priest, who told her, if ministers could bring their wives, he could bring her. On the plane, she sat next to an NFL player, Jerry Stovall, who was also traveling to the FCA conference. When he found out she was going, "He wrinkled his nose and asked, 'What's a girl going to an FCA conference for?'"[20] While the men at the camp gathered in huddles, Lucas ran the "cuddle" group for wives. Throughout her story in *Christian Athlete*, Lucas professed an ignorance of the sports world and an active respect for male athletes. Like other women in sports ministry at the time, she promoted the idea that women should be supportive wives and mothers for the athletes in their families. Lucas's story demonstrates the assumption that the appropriate role for women in sports ministry was to support male athletes; it also underscores the comparative rarity of female participation in sports ministry before widespread implementation of Title IX.

The same year that *Christian Athlete* published Catherine Lucas's story, the magazine included results from a questionnaire distributed to coaches' wives at FCA conferences nationwide. Author Skip Stogsdill wanted to investigate what it was like to be a coach's wife, and his article described many struggles for these women, including lack of job security for their husbands, the time demands of a coaching career, and feeling neglected in favor of the team. Stogsdill presented these difficulties as "deep-rooted resentments" and quoted one wife as saying, "Often I'm so frustrated by the amount of time my husband spends coaching that I threaten to burn down the gym and plow up the playing field."[21] The questionnaire asked wives to give advice to a young woman considering marrying a coach. The first item on the list was, "Be as attractive and congenial as possible," followed closely by, "Be prepared to spend many hours and evenings alone."[22] Stogsdill concluded the article with a directive to the coach: "Coach, your wife dislikes plenty of things about your job, especially the hours and her subsequently having to wear two hats. Yet she believes the dividends far outweigh the drawbacks. Because she's a woman for all seasons, she loves you year-round for what you are. You belong to a breed of men most blessed."[23] Sports ministry in the 1970s offered limited roles for women; at the time, far more women were involved as wives than as athletes or coaches, and sports ministry encouraged these wives to be pleasant supporters of their husbands' endeavors.

By the 1990s, women had begun to outnumber men as sports ministry participants, but conservative ideas about gender roles in marriage continued. In 2006, FCA's *Sharing the Victory* launched a series of articles titled "Behind the Bench" that focused on wives of coaches, and the stories in these articles strongly resembled the lessons for coaches' wives that FCA promoted in the 1970s. Chris Steckel, wife of FCA president Les Steckel, spearheaded the series. The initial article included her story of meeting her future husband during a flag football match. She wrote that, after she made the game-winning touchdown, "a strong arm reached down and lifted me to my feet. 'Hey,' he said. 'What was your name again? And would you like to go out with me?' It was the beginning of a life together . . . 31 years of marriage and a lifetime of football."[24] Later in the article, she expressed sentiments similar to those of the coaches' wives surveyed in the 1970s:

> As a coach's wife, I knew the long hours of the season that took him away, the packing of boxes I'd unpacked too recently, and the effort of trying to ignore the criticism of the Monday morning quarterbacks who were calling for his job and our livelihood. But I knew, too, why God had called him to coach and called me to be a coach's wife. It was to influence young lives in a way unique to a coach and his family.[25]

"Behind the Bench" simultaneously elevated marriage as an important relationship and eclipsed female coaches altogether. Steckel's understanding that she was "called" to be coach's wife highlights a larger understanding within evangelical Christianity that marriage is divinely planned.

From presentations of coaches' wives in the 1970s, to Promise Keepers' descriptions of men's roles in the 1990s, to conversations at FCA camp in 2007, a consistent conservative gender ideology threads through sports ministry. Traditional gender roles undergird sports ministry and evangelical Christianity as a whole. Sports ministry is part of an evangelical project to educate young Christian men and women on correct relationships with each other. However, despite the ubiquity of conservative gender understandings in sports ministry, the changing world of sports offers another set of tools that Christian athletes use to understand gendered relationships.

Sport as a Challenge to Conservative Gender Roles

As noted earlier, evangelical marriage resources have used football metaphors for affirming male dominance within marriage. Farrar's husband-as-quarterback and sports ministry's long history of attention to athletes' and coaches' wives (with the assumption that these wives either were not athletic or were less athletically successful than their husbands) have promoted the idea that the husband is the more qualified decision maker of the couple. However, some evangelicals have used football to challenge this gender understanding and explore the ideas of mutual submission and primary dependence on God rather than on one's spouse.

In 2006, a church in Albany, Georgia, made a movie that became very popular with evangelical Christians—*Facing the Giants*, the story of a private Christian high school's football team and the married life of its coach.[26] According to the evangelical magazine *New Man*, associate pastor Alex Kendrick of Sherwood Baptist Church in Albany "began receiving visions of a story addressing the issues men face, such as facing fears, failure, hopelessness, addictions, and insecurities. It was during this time that Kendrick also felt inspired to grapple with those issues in the context of a football film."[27] *Facing the Giants* was the church's first feature-length film and recouped $10 million on Sherwood's original $10,000 investment.[28]

The movie follows the character of football coach Grant Taylor, paying particular attention to his marriage as he and his wife struggle to conceive a child. The film contains few examples of male household dominance. Instead, Taylor is frequently shown in tears, with his wife comforting him. According to one filmmaker, "We've seen men and women cry during screenings of this movie because I believe they see a part of themselves in Coach Taylor." Michael Catt, senior pastor, added, "These movies have given men in our church an opportunity to express their faith and it helped them see that church doesn't have to be feminized."[29] Despite Taylor's tears and mutual submission in his marriage, his role as a football coach assured audiences of his manliness. Coaching football closely associated him with a masculine institution, and therefore Taylor's tears did not undermine his masculinity. Arguably, this film would not have been as successful if it focused on a high school history teacher or a pediatrician. Taylor's affiliation with sport, particularly the unquestionably masculine sport of football, allowed the filmmakers to explore vulnerability in marriage without compromising the masculinity of their main character.

As Taylor's football team continued to lose, throwing his job and the financial well-being of his family into jeopardy, Taylor struggled with feeling powerless and weak in a situation seemingly beyond his control. The turning point of the film finds Taylor outside at sunrise, the natural beauty of the sun streaming through trees accompanying his confession of weakness before God and his request for God to take control of the situation. Following this revelatory moment, Taylor alters his coaching strategy to present football as a way to honor God rather than as an extracurricular pursuit separate from Christian life. The film presents this coaching method as successful not only in creating a winning football team (and saving Taylor's job) but also in healing players' family relationships and even contributing to the Taylor family conceiving a child against all odds.

Part I of this book showed that Christian athletes see their sporting activities as religiously meaningful, and *Facing the Giants* is one example of how marriage relationships are implicated in these practices. Contrary to the instrumentalist masculinity that Bartkowski saw as dominant in Promise Keepers, coach Taylor demonstrated the new guard philosophy of mutual submission in marriage. One lesson of this film is that male weakness in the home does not translate to wifely dominance but to a situation of mutual support. This is mirrored in Taylor's approach to his relationship with God—by confessing his own weakness, Taylor turned to God for strength and was able to accomplish football wins, job security, and marital happiness. This fictional account aimed to convince men that submission is divinely ordained and worldly beneficial. Especially for athletes (male and female) who have long been trained that submission to a coach's or a team captain's authority is central to winning games, mutual submission within a marriage may resonate with their sporting lives, and they can use their sporting lives as a resource for understanding their off-field gender obligations.

The female Christian athletes profiled in this book were aware of marriage as an evangelical expectation and of the effect that getting married may have on their athletic opportunities. For women in particular, the desire to play sports and the desire to pursue a godly marriage can be difficult to negotiate. Tina, the team chaplain for AIA's women's basketball 2007 fall tour, expressed anxiety about being away from her husband to travel with the team: "I don't want to miss any moment of tour, but it's also really early in my marriage, and I don't want to miss any of that either. I'm trying to just have these feelings and not feel guilty for them. It's hard, you know, it's not cut-and-dry. I don't want to say that God is complicated, but he is not as cut-and-dry as I expected." Tina was torn between two important religious experiences, sports ministry and marriage. She realized that it would be hard to do both at the same time and felt that she had suspended her marriage in order to go on fall tour. Her feelings of guilt confused her because she believed God intended her to do both these things, travel with the team and be a wife, and she struggled with how to do them simultaneously.

Participation in sports ministry poses a potential conflict with evangelical expectations for marriage. This conflict is more pronounced for women who, through their participation in sports ministry, felt less pressure to demonstrate traditional femininity. Nora, the six-foot-two forward for the Charlotte Lady Eagles, was well aware of the church's covert messages regarding what a woman should look like and what her goals should be. She told me:

It's a couples' world. That's not necessarily a Christian thing. Society is made for couples, and especially after a certain age, you feel like if you're not in a couple, well, what are you doing? I mean, I would love to get married at some point. I think there's a real fear within the team that because we are strong people and can deal with a lot, we are seen like we don't want to get married. And we definitely stay single longer. It's a fear that I have, tall and strong as I am, that guys are going to think, whoa, this lady's a handful [and be turned off].

Nora rightly observed that marriage is not an exclusively evangelical practice but a social pressure that exists in the United States as a whole. However, she also noted that within conservative Christianity a woman "tall and strong as I am" challenged the underlying gender logic lingering from the 1970s (and previously) that wives should be supportive cheerleaders.

Another player, Tess, had gone on to coach soccer at the same conservative Christian college as Ellie and described her experience with marriage pressure there:

I think there is pressure. I would get so disgusted at [this school]; the girls would tell me things their professors say to the students, encouraging them to get married. It was like a running joke. You had better find your husband here, or, what are you going to do? It made my skin crawl. These are just kids! And some of them would get married—they are nineteen years old and getting married! To each his own, but I think it's shocking. I believe the Lord loves a godly marriage, but in his own time. Marriage is a tremendous task. I'm thirty, and I'm happy I waited this long.

At Tess's college, there was a sense that beyond the walls of the institution students were less likely to meet a Christian partner. This culminated in pressure to marry early.

Ellie described the same college with an equally critical tone, "At [this college], there is a trend of 'ring before spring.' Everyone gets married right out of college. If I would've gotten married right out of school, I would've missed out on playing for the Eagles, going to Brazil, other things." Both these coaches saw marriage as an important part of Christian life, but they also understood marriage as something that could limit athletic opportunities for women and criticized rushing into a marriage commitment.

Ellie and Tess knew that evangelical marriage obligations could impinge on their athletic opportunities. As a female professional golfer writing for *Sharing the Victory* described it, "I felt like the Lord was telling me that Martin was the man I was going to marry. That was a point in my life where golf kind of stepped down on my priority list."[30] Although this golfer continued to play professionally, her marriage became an avenue to glorify God that was as important to her as the witnessing platform she had as a high-profile athlete. Her reprioritization reflects the lingering idea that a woman's commitment to her husband is primarily enacted through support and that her role as supporter is divinely ordained.

Since the 1970s, sports ministry resources have generally shifted away from presenting wives as supportive cheerleaders and turned toward describing spouses as teammates. This presentation of spouses as teammates mitigates the social division of wife as supporter and husband as doer, but behind the teammate label lingers the assumption that wifely support and husbandly action are essential for a healthy marriage. Ritchie McKay, the head basketball coach for the University of New Mexico, wrote an article for *Sharing the Victory*'s series "Behind the Bench" entitled "My Wife, My Teammate." In the article, McKay walks the reader through his revelation that his wife, Julie, is not just a supportive cheerleader; she is his teammate. His view of a teammate, however, still included the assumption that wives should be primarily supportive. He wrote that after hearing Promise Keepers founder Bill McCartney describe his wife as his teammate, "it really changed my view of who Julie is. It made me realize that she actually possesses things that have been given for my benefit. Genesis 2:18 (NIV) says, 'I will make a helper suitable for him.' God knew we, as men, would need help and vice versa. And in my case, a lot of help." Later in the article, McKay stated, "If I were to give advice to any woman—especially a coach's wife—on how she can help her husband, I would take a page out of Julie's book: find a way to praise him."[31] Even though the title of this article was "My Wife, My Teammate" and this metaphor puts husbands and wives on an equal plane, the article still reflects the idea that husbands should be like the team captain or Farrar's quarterback; the husband is the active decision maker, and the wife is a passive supporter.

Some female Christian athletes have embraced the rhetoric of teammates and used it to reevaluate their marriage roles. Elite runner Sara Hall wrote an article for *Sharing the Victory* about her life as an athlete and a Christian. She mentioned her husband, Ryan Hall:

> When I graduated [from Stanford], . . . God provided the greatest sup-
> porter of my faith in the form of my husband, Ryan. We know that God
> brought us together for a reason: to accomplish His Kingdom plans on
> earth. And I also believe God called me to be Ryan's helper—the best
> support person in his life and in his running career. That doesn't just
> mean being his cheerleader, but also having to say the things that aren't
> always easy.[32]

Hall described Ryan as her supporter, and herself as his. But, contrary
to descriptions of wives of athletes from the 1970s, this was not about
cheerleading but about saying "the things that aren't always easy," like a
teammate or even a coach would do. Perhaps contemporary evangelical
women's ability to act out this new definition of wife-as-teammate has
stemmed from the greater number of female athletes competing today.
As noted previously, only 1 in every 9 women participated in sports in
the 1970s, but by the early twenty-first century, the numbers were 1 in
2.5.[33] These athletic women have gained the knowledge and experience
of what it means to play on a team.

"One thing I learned from sport is that God made me a powerful
person on purpose," M.J. told me when I asked her about her married
life after leaving the Eagles. She emphasized that sport had instilled in
her a sense of confidence in her opinions and the ability to voice those
opinions within her marriage. However, she was also clear that her own
power and strength did not overturn traditional evangelical ideas about
marriage. "Our house would be categorized as the husband as head of
the household, and I'm his wife. I married him because I trust him—I
trust him with my life. So I trust him to make big decisions and with our
finances. And that's what it would look like from the outside." M.J. emphasized gender roles in order to distinguish her marriage from secular
marriages. Having a marriage that appears different from secular marriages is similar to the Charlotte Lady Eagles' desire to stand out from
secular soccer teams.

M.J. brought her experiences as an athlete to bear on her evangelical
marriage. Increased sporting opportunities for women of M.J.'s generation may have contributed to more complex understandings of gender
roles within marriage. M.J. offered a theory on generational differences
for evangelical women. She told me that many of the players on the

Charlotte Lady Eagles had mothers who hadn't attended college, and that many of the team's players had attended Christian colleges that gave them the opportunity to study the Bible. "This means that they had to work through and reexamine the things that people say, 'Well, this is what the Bible says.'" In particular, M.J. emphasized that these women had the opportunity to reexamine Bible verses that they may have heard used to discount or discourage female leadership. "A lot of women are victims of one verse being chucked at them. Like the verse in Ephesians that women need to submit. I grew up hearing that all the time, and I never heard the next verse about a husband who serves. I didn't see that until the Eagles."

M.J. was referring to Ephesians 5:24–25 (NIV): "Now as the church submits to Christ, so also wives should submit to their husbands in everything. Husbands, love your wives, just as Christ loved the church and gave himself up for her." Many of the Christian athletes I encountered chose to attend a Christian college so that they could have the experience of playing for an explicitly Christian team. For M.J. and other female Christian athletes, the ability to study the Bible in a sports ministry setting or at a Christian college allowed a more nuanced reading of Bible verses that defined gender roles within marriage. This ability to interpret the Bible, as well as the experience of playing on a team, may have contributed to female Christian athletes redefining and adjusting marriage roles.

Another couple featured in *Sharing the Victory* demonstrates both how contemporary female Christian athletes are likely to prioritize Jesus over their spouse or boyfriend and how being part of an athletic couple can strengthen the metaphor of the couple as a team. *Sharing the Victory* provided an example of Christian dating in the sports world in an article showcasing Landry Jones, quarterback for Oklahoma University, and Whitney Hand, shooting guard for Oklahoma's women's basketball team. The metaphor of teammates appeared throughout the article. For example, after Hand experienced a season-ending injury, Jones comforted his girlfriend with the assurance that her athletic career was not the most important thing to him or to Jesus. According to Hand, "It was like Jesus was teaming up with Landry to love on me." Though Hand described Jesus and her boyfriend as teammates, she clarified that Jesus was more important to her than Jones:

I want to be more in love with Christ than I am with Landry. If Landry and I were to break up, I wouldn't want my walk with Christ to disappear with him. Landry is not my walk with Christ, and I don't want to be in that position in his life either. I never want him to love me more than he loves Jesus.

The couple clarified that understanding each other as athletes made their relationship easier, but they prioritized their commitment to Jesus. As Hand put it:

It's something that we've struggled to learn, but we both have come to understand that no other person can completely fulfill you—only Jesus can do that. And until you know who you are in Christ and understand His love for you, it's going to be difficult for you to love another person correctly. You'll always be putting them in a position they weren't designed by God to hold in your life.[34]

The effect of this rhetoric was that Hand, the girlfriend, was not a cheerleader for her boyfriend but could see herself as, and be treated as, a teammate with primary loyalties not to her male partner but to Christ.

The female Christian athletes whom I spoke with were comfortable seeing men as household leaders, but they were also firmly invested in marriage not as a relationship of one-sided service but as an opportunity for both spouses to demonstrate submission and servant leadership. According to Andrea:

It's true. Marriage is a big deal in the Christian world. . . . I think it's a big deal because of the other beliefs that go with Christianity, like the countercultural idea not to have multiple partners. I do think marriage is the healthiest way. A main theme in the New Testament is serving each other, having subservient love and sacrificial love toward each other. And that's hard to do with boyfriend and girlfriend. In that, you're looking to please yourself. In marriage, that's not the case. It's a commitment to love sacrificially, how Jesus did.

For Andrea and for evangelicals like her, marriage is significantly different from dating because commitment to marriage allows the believer to deepen his or her commitment to Christ. In this understanding, marriage, like athletic pleasure and pain, is an opportunity to experience Christlikeness through self-sacrifice. Andrea shared this example:

> This guy at work, he said he wished he never got married. He asked me, "What's your favorite kind of cereal?" Then he said, "Imagine you have to eat that cereal every day for the rest of your life. You might see another cereal that you would like to try, but you can't because you've committed to this one kind of cereal." And I thought, well, that's hard to think about eating the same cereal every day. But he was thinking of it as fulfilling himself. The cereal doesn't get anything out of being eaten.

For Andrea, marriage entailed sacrifice and service; it was not about finding the perfect complementary person to complete you. For her, the cereal metaphor was flawed because only the eater was active; the cereal was just passively consumed. While this metaphor may have held some sway for a previous generation of evangelical women who understood their primary role as submission,[35] for this Christian athlete and others like her, marriage did not make sense as a relationship between an active man and a passive woman. Both participants in the marriage had a responsibility to not treat the other like cereal—to make sure their actions were not about self-fulfillment but were aimed at mutual fulfillment, striving for Christlikeness through self-sacrifice.

Tess mirrored this sentiment when she told me, "You can't go in [to a marriage] with the expectation that it will complete you or thinking about things you'll receive from it. Some people get married because it seems like the logical thing to do next, but there is a lot of sacrifice involved. If you really love someone, you want to serve your spouse." In negotiating marriage roles, contemporary evangelicals in sports ministry are likely to employ complex definitions of service and submission. They no longer see these activities as limited to wives but see them as a requirement for husbands as well. Though vestiges of wife-as-cheerleader remain in this emergent understanding of wife-as-teammate, the rhetoric of servant leadership and mutual submission has allowed evangelical women and men more flexibility in their marital roles.

Marriage and Gender Roles on the Field

Christian athletes live their lives trying to balance two identities—
"evangelical" and "athlete." For evangelical men these identities have
been easier to assimilate because the skills they learned in one realm
translated ideologically to the other. Especially in terms of evangelical
marriage logic, men could combine their sporting and religious lives
with limited contradiction because both emphasized power, leadership,
and strength. For female Christian athletes, however, the identities of
"evangelical woman" and "female athlete" constituted somewhat contradictory gender understandings. Though the emergent rhetoric of
evangelical couples as "teammates" has allowed some Christian athletes to reinterpret their marriage roles, the lingering assumptions of
wife as cheerleader (on the sidelines, in the background) informed their
understandings of the marriage team. Because for women, the gender
expectations of "evangelical" and "athlete" do not match up, they have
used tools from both of these realms to understand themselves and their
relationships.

A few of the women on the Charlotte Lady Eagles had young children under the age of three, and these women frequently brought their
children to practice. Sometimes a babysitter would come along too, but
usually the trainer, an injured player, or I would look after the children
while the team practiced. The first time this happened, I watched the
coach to see his reaction to bringing children to practice. He did not
seem to notice the children and did not comment on their presence.
I realized that the Lady Eagles had probably had mothers on the team
since their first season in 1998; bringing children to practice was normal
for this team. The children would often play on the edge of the field
with spare soccer balls. At one practice, I saw Amy's daughter, Allie, a
toddler who had just mastered walking, kicking a soccer ball in front of
her as she walked. The soccer ball came up to her chest, but she was un-
perturbed and quietly dribbled the ball in an arc at the edge of the field.
Skyler, Amanda's son, was about a year older and twice as big. He too
kicked a soccer ball in front of him wherever he walked. I couldn't help
but be amazed by the ease of these small children's interactions with soccer balls. I imagined how natural the game would seem to them as they
grew up. I also was very conscious of the fact that the team treated Allie

as just as likely to excel at soccer as Skyler. Often, the coach's daughter Andi would come to morning practice to warm up with the team and assist with drills. She played on her high school team, also coached by her father, and had every intention of playing for the Lady Eagles when she was older. Athletes and coaches encouraged and expected young women like Allie and Andi to excel as athletes.

However, the female athletes who encouraged these young women were also aware of and complicit in evangelicalism's overarching conservative gender paradigm. On occasion, the men's soccer team, the Charlotte Eagles, would practice directly after the women's practice, and I would stay to observe. I saw the male athletes' children playing on the edge of the field during practice, but these children's mothers supervised them, not members of the men's team. Even though the teams treated male and female children as just as likely to be athletically talented, their actions demonstrated an assumption that a man's athletic career required more attention. It went without saying that women would provide child care at the women's team's practices, and wives accompanied male athletes to provide child care at men's practices. While members of the women's team sometimes brought a babysitter, none of their husbands came to practice to watch children during any of the practices that I attended. (At games, however, child care was more evenly distributed between husbands and wives.)

Though female Christian athletes tended to accept gender difference and hierarchy, there was very little talk of sport as something that should belong entirely to men; the idea of a "female athlete" was not a contradiction in terms but a role that evangelical women could embrace. While the role of the female athlete presents a potential challenge to conservative gender ideology, it can also confirm this ideology through female athletes expressing a desire for male leadership or, as in the following example, by responding differently to male leaders.

The Charlotte Lady Eagles' assistant coach, Emily, had recently had foot surgery and sat with me on the sidelines during practices. For my first week or so with the team, Emily was my soccer teacher. I would arrive for the 6:00 a.m. practices with my thermos of coffee, in time for the opening devotional and group prayer. Then, as the team took to the field, Emily and I would sit in the pavilion just beyond the sidelines, and I would profess my ignorance of soccer—"Hey, Emily," I would ask, "how many players are on the field at once?" Or, "Um, what exactly is 'off sides' anyway?" Over the course of these general education conversations, I also gleaned information about gender roles on this evangelical team.

As noted, the head coach of the team was a man who also coached high school soccer in the area. A few days into my time with the team, he missed practice to celebrate his twenty-fifth wedding anniversary. Ordinarily in this situation, Emily would have led practice, shouting orders while standing on her crutches on the field. However, on this particular day, it was raining, and Emily couldn't be on the field with her cast. Jonathan, the team manager, led practice. Emily, Tess (who was injured), and I watched from our sideline bench. Emily and Tess were old friends, and they would often discuss mutual friends or past seasons. Emily turned to Tess, saying, "This is totally God. I was trying to think of a how to get Jonathan to coach practice. Because he's ready—he's just really conscious of the fact that he's coaching coaches, and that makes him nervous." A number of the players on the Charlotte Lady Eagles coached high school, club, or college teams during the school year.

We turned to watch Jonathan on the field leading a series of drills that the players readily performed. Emily would call him over for instructions periodically—"Let them stretch more. They're really sore." But, generally, she seemed proud of Jonathan and genuinely pleased that he was leading in her place. Emily leaned over to Tess and me to point out a "cute" nervous tic of Jonathan's; he would pop his wrist against his hip while walking among the players on the field. Emily smiled about it.

In this instance, it was clear to me that Emily was the authority in the situation. Jonathan took her advice without question, and she could see his coaching as "cute." However, in another instance, Emily told me rather bitterly that female athletes automatically respect a male coach but not a female coach. "If you're a man coaching women, you have to do something to lose their respect. But if you're a woman, you have to earn it," she explained. Another player, Lex, experienced this difference in her coaching career. According to Lex, the players she coached had different expectations for men and women:

> Being a female coach, we have to be fit. A male coach can be overweight and out of shape, but he'll still be respected because he is still stronger

than the girls. For us, we have to look like the players. We have to be fit. It's one of the only ways to get the respect that men automatically get.

As female coaches, Lex and Emily recognized that they had to work to gain the kind of respect that they saw male coaches receive with less effort.

As an example of this differing level of respect, Emily told me that one of the players had refused to take her advice to tape her ankle. Emily felt that she had to bring this refusal to the head coach's attention. When the athlete heard the same advice from him, she willingly wrapped her ankle. I asked Emily if she thought that this difference in respect level came from men's longer history in athletics. "Hmm, maybe," she responded. "But I also think there is something about men and women that makes men better leaders."

Her response referenced the evangelical mainstay on male headship. But Emily's critique was not actually about leadership. She clearly felt she was as good a leader as the head coach. After all, he repeated her advice on ankle taping, and her behavior on that rainy day demonstrated that she saw herself as a superior coach to Jonathan. Her critique was not that women could not lead but that women do not respond to female leadership in the same way that they respond to male leadership. She was not unhappy with female *leaders* but with female *followers*. Yet at the same time, she understood herself as a female follower both in her role as an assistant coach and in her religious identity as a follower of Christ. So, even though she was sometimes frustrated by players who did not routinely respect her coaching authority, she also expressed the same sentiments that led to this failure to respect female coaches—men are naturally better leaders.

Following this season with the Eagles, Emily took a job coaching women's soccer at a conservative Christian college. After a season there, she brought Jonathan and Ellie on as assistant coaches. Ellie described the coaching situation to me: "Well, my role is as the second assistant coach. Emily is the leader, and Jonathan is the assistant leader. My role is with the goalkeepers. . . . As a coach, then, no matter what, I am on Emily and Jonathan's side. They are pretty much mommy and daddy to those girls, and we all have to be on the same page." In this situation, Emily was the head coach, with Jonathan as her assistant. She was the leader. But Ellie still used a family/marriage metaphor to describe the way they handled the team. They functioned as parents. It is common in American sporting culture to portray male coaches as father figures, but in this situation Emily and Jonathan were parent figures with the primary decision-making authority invested in the female parent. As such, this description preserves the idea of marriage as an important human relationship but shifts the power dynamic, subtly challenging the evangelical mainstay of male headship.

These examples show that sports ministry has provided another set of tools for evangelical women to use to understand their gendered relationships. Though conservative ideas lingered, like the idea that women should provide child care during practices and that male coaches more easily commanded respect, new understandings emerged as well. To repeat M.J., she learned from sport that "God made me a powerful person on purpose." This identity as a powerful person, bolstered by sporting experiences, allowed women like Emily to feel comfortable as a head coach with a male assistant and allowed female Christian athletes like Tess, Andrea, and others to embrace the idea of service in a marriage as active and as required for men as well as women.

Conclusion

Much has changed since the 1970s depictions of Christian women in sports ministry as supportive cheerleader-wives to athletes and coaches. As more women joined the athletic ranks, this presentation declined but did not disappear. Robert Putnam and David Campbell's research on religion in America has shown that from 1973 to 2008, highly religious women and secular women entered the workforce in increasing numbers and at a virtually identical pace.[36] They also found that both for women who always attend church and for those who almost never attend, there was a decline in support of traditional gender roles across the board. Both of these groups of women are more likely to think it is okay for married women to work, that women do not have to put their husband's career before their own, and that a working mother is not detrimental for rearing children. Women who always attend church remain about 10 percent more likely to uphold conservative gender understandings, but in general, conservative gender understandings have decreased about 30 percent since the 1970s.[37] According to Putnam and Campbell,

"Deeply religious Americans are less traditionalist in their views about gender roles than their secular counterparts had been a generation earlier."[38] This decline in conservative gender understandings for women is evident in sports ministry, as the coaching relationship between Emily and Jonathan demonstrates. However, though female Christian athletes pursue and excel at sporting careers, as mothers they still feel obligated to provide child care even at practice, an expectation that was not present for their male counterparts.

Women and men in sports ministry have a variety of resources at their disposal for understanding their gender roles. Since the 1970s, these resources have expanded to include "servant leadership," "mutual submission," and "teammates." In putting these ideas into practice, both women and men have achieved more leeway in their gendered behaviors and relationships. However, this wiggle room continues to be constrained by vestiges of previous generations' ideas of marriage roles. Female Christian athletes in particular combine and negotiate between these sometimes contradictory resources, and sports ministry provides the context for their negotiation. A movement that began with the primary goal of promoting a masculine image of evangelical Christianity has had the unforeseen consequence of allowing both men and women more freedom in their gendered relationships. The concluding chapter summarizes this trajectory, tracing how sports ministry opened a site for religious self-reflexivity and expansion of orthodoxy.

Conclusion

A Tale of Unintended Consequences

Athletes know their bodies. One cannot become an elite athlete without subjecting one's body to arduous training, refining it to be efficient, powerful, and quick. It is because athletes demonstrate this mastery that they are admired and elevated in American culture. When sports ministry first emerged in the 1950s and 1960s, evangelicals sought to capitalize on Americans' admiration of elite athletes, showcasing Christian athletes as examples of the benefits of Christian life. This book has investigated the unintended consequences of that project.

Christian athletes confronted a number of challenges as they tried to combine evangelicalism and sport—how to witness, how to know if God was pleased, how to interpret athletic hardships like injury or loss—but the most significant challenges arose regarding evangelical mainstays on gender, sexuality, and relationships. Due to increased athletic opportunities for women and sports ministry's shift to valuing individual religious experience over traditional witnessing, women came to dominate sports ministry, and when they did, they used their religious embodied knowledge to rethink the evangelical demands on their bodies to be feminine and straight.

Sports ministry is a significant phenomenon in the United States. In 2013, FCA sponsored events on more than 9,000 junior high, high school, and college campuses, claiming to have spread its message to 450,000 students.[1] In the same year, AIA held meetings for student athletes on more than 200 campuses; provided chaplains for eleven NFL teams, four WNBA teams, and throughout Major League Soccer and the North American Soccer League; and sent hundreds of U.S. athletes on more than twenty international tours to compete against international teams and run sports clinics for local youth.[2] Since the 1950s and 1960s, when these two organizations emerged, more than 100 sports ministry organizations have formed to target athletes in every conceivable sport. Additionally, many megachurches have athletic staff and sports programming, Christian colleges offer opportunities to play on exclusively Christian teams, and online resources for Christian athletes offer Bible studies and team resources for use outside of sports ministry organizations. This network of sports ministry organizations and resources touches a significant swath of the American population, but, as this book has shown, evangelical engagement with popular culture has not been one-sided or simple. Through the process of working out the role of sports for evangelicalism, Christian athletes developed new understandings of their religion and their bodies.

Religious diversity in the United States has greatly increased since the 1950s. Until recently, sociologists of religion argued that religious diversity combined with a secular public sphere would ultimately result in a decline of religiosity. This was called the "secularization thesis."[3] However, as the twentieth century progressed, religiosity in America did not decline as predicted. Instead, a different trend emerged of some Americans becoming more religious and some Americans becoming less so, resulting in a polarization of the American religious landscape.[4] Like the conservative/liberal divide that infuses American politics, there does not seem to be a way of standing in the middle of the religious spectrum, of being moderately religious.

American evangelicalism is a theology that promotes polarization. Evangelicals tend to divide their environment into two categories: worldly and godly. Worldly elements are negative and represent both disconnection from God and the dangerous condition of human pridefulness. Godly elements are those activities and settings that draw believers closer to God and allow the believer to gain a sense of conforming to God's plan. What is most interesting about American evangelicalism is that in order for evangelicals to feel that they are doing godly work, they must engage worldly settings and activities. Many evangelicals take it as their mission to demonstrate godliness in "the world." This is what evangelicals mean when they employ the phrase "*in* but not *of* the world."[5]

And here things get complicated. Here is where sports ministry can help us to understand larger trends of religion in the United States. As evangelicals engaged cultural realms outside of traditionally religious spaces (business, education, and popular culture forms like music, film/television, and sports, to name a few), they encountered a wide range of persons, some religious and some not. One might expect that a doctrine of polarization would lend itself to intolerance and animosity, but as this book has shown, that was not the case for women in sports ministry. These women found themselves taking a more tolerant view on homosexuality than their religious tradition promoted. This is a case of pluralism becoming personal. Through sports ministry, Christian athletes formed meaningful relationships with teammates that they otherwise might have regarded as irretrievably damned.

The encounter between evangelical Christianity and sport shows that many of evangelicalism's self-understandings have more leeway, more room for negotiation, than many outsiders realize. The tenets that define evangelicalism and distinguish evangelicals from other Protestants show their flexibility when read against the story of evangelical involvement in sports. Evangelicals first imagined sport as a way to convert outsiders, but sport became a way for evangelicals to evaluate and modify their understandings of gender and sexuality. Examining their involvement in athletics shows how evangelical engagement with secular culture forced participants to develop a religious self-reflexivity that challenged some of their deeply held religious claims. In sports ministry, the body is the site where believers experience confirmations and challenges to their faith. The story of how the body came to occupy such a role reveals the unintended consequences of prioritizing the body and embodied religious experience.

Athletic Celebrity and the Beginnings of Sports Ministry

Early twentieth-century conservative Christians presented secular engagement as a contaminant that could corrupt Christian beliefs, but following World War II evangelicals engaged popular culture with explicitly secular audiences in mind. Unlike fundamentalists of a previous generation, postwar evangelicals rejected isolationism and embraced a strategy they called "engaged orthodoxy." Engaged orthodoxy meant employing all the cultural tools at their disposal to tell nonbelievers of salvation through Jesus Christ. When the National Association of Evangelicals formed in 1942 and established this new strategy, it formed a new identity for conservative Christians in the United States; evangelicals were Christians who engaged secular culture and turned to secular resources to accomplish religious goals.

Sport is part of this story. With the rise of televised sports in the 1950s, evangelicals began to see sport as a resource for evangelical outreach. Sports ministry founders imagined celebrity athletes as spokespeople with the potential to garner a large audience of nonbelievers. Sport's long affiliation with character building and moral education made athletes appealing as witnesses. American culture promoted athletes as morally virtuous, and athletes were key endorsers in the commercial sector; an athlete was an icon who could generate attention and revenue. By the late 1950s and 1960s, evangelical Christians began to see sport as a site with witnessing potential and began recruiting celebrity athletes who were Christian to vocalize their faith publicly and present evangelical Christianity as a strong, moral, and important life choice. By 1965, Oral Roberts was overt about promoting sports at his university in Tulsa, Oklahoma. He said, "Athletics is part of our Christian witness. . . . Nearly every man in America reads the sports pages, and a Christian school cannot ignore these people. . . . Sports are becoming the number one interest of people in America. For us to be relevant, we had to gain the attention of millions of people in a way that they could understand."[6] Evangelicals entered the sports world in droves, forming organizations that educated athletes on how to deliver their Christian testimony from the platform of sport. By the early 1970s, sports ministry organizations had formed to target all major professional sports, and private Christian colleges had begun to significantly invest in sports programming for their students.

However, sport proved difficult to marshal for evangelical witnessing purposes. Hierarchical organization of participants and competition are central features of sport. Teams are ranked, team members are ranked, leagues are ranked—sport seems to organize everything in its domain along hierarchical lines. This means that those at the top of the hierarchy are very valuable, both as athletes and as celebrity endorsers. The power of these celebrities inspired evangelicals to begin sports ministry, but evangelicals came to realize that the same logic that allowed sporting celebrities to wield significant cultural power also made them morally vulnerable. If one's power (both in the sports world and as an evangelist) depended on winning, then winning remained the central and unchallenged goal of sport.

The centrality of winning was difficult for some sports ministers to reconcile with their religious beliefs and sparked critique of the evangelical project. Gary Warner, editor of FCA's member publication *Christian Athlete* in the 1970s, began to openly criticize Christian involvement in sport and noted a lack of ethical attention to competition and other features of the sporting industry. From outside sports ministry, *Sports Illustrated* writer Frank Deford leveled his critique against what he called "Sportianity": "To put it bluntly, athletes are being used to sell religion. They endorse Jesus, much as they would a new sneaker or a graphite-shafted driver."[7] In the 1970s, when both these critiques appeared, ethical reevaluations of sport had become increasingly common. Christian athletic celebrities made for easy targets because critics assumed that Christian commitments should entail a moral obligation to improve sport. Yet, as Deford noted, "Sportianity does not question the casual brutality [of sports]. . . . It does not censure the intemperate behavior of coaches. . . . The fear of taking a stand on moral issues is acute."[8]

While evangelicals first saw sport as an ideal resource for using the power of athletic celebrities to attract cultural attention, when they began to engage the world of sport, they were confronted with a deficiency within their theology. Sport raised the question: Do the ends justify the means? Sporting celebrities could draw attention to Christianity, but if they also behaved in morally questionable ways on (or off) the field, was this attention achieving its goal? This is what I call the problem of winning. When sports ministers confronted the problem of winning, they found that sport could be a different sort of resource than they originally envisioned. Rather than a simple platform for voicing evangelical ideas on salvation, the embodied experiences of sport could provide a feeling of divine connection, a sensation of Christlikeness.

The Hidden Possibility of Sport: Embodying Christlikeness

Wes Neal is perhaps the most indicative character in the story of sport ministry's recognition of individual religious experience. As chronicled earlier, Neal was a weight lifter who traveled with Athletes in Action's weight-lifting team in the late 1960s. He and his fellow weight lifters demonstrated their physical strength to gain an audience for a gospel message. This celebrity evangelism strategy was fairly successful, but Neal found it unsatisfying. He wanted to be able to "lift weights God's way," instead of using celebrity recognition to evangelize. According to Neal,

"My team and I began to think about how to lift weights God's way. We turned to the motto of Campus Crusade, which is 'Witness in the Holy Spirit and leave the results to God.' But that didn't help us much because we still didn't know how to lift weights in the power of the Holy Spirit."

Resources from evangelical Christianity were insufficient to deal with the questions Neal encountered. He turned to his own athletic experiences to examine what it meant to be a Christian athlete. Neal reimagined Christian athletics on an individual level by exploring how an athletic performance could be a praise and worship experience. He came to the conclusion that athletes could use sport to physically affiliate themselves with Christ. He compared intense athletic dedication, especially pushing through pain, to Christ's physical sacrifice in his crucifixion, the event that is the cornerstone of evangelical theology.

For Neal, sport became an avenue to experience joy and divine connection. This caught on and was practically normative in sports ministry by the time I did my fieldwork. Jennie, a Christian soccer player on the Charlotte Lady Eagles, told me, "I've had the joy of soccer since I was a kid. But since then, I learned that this gift came from God and that I can glorify God by using my talents. When soccer became about something bigger than me, it became a bigger joy. Now, I can't *not* use this gift." Jennie is one of many contemporary Christian athletes who understand athletic pleasure as a gift from God. During my two years of fieldwork with sports ministry organizations, I encountered numerous references to athletic pleasure as godly joy. This is significantly different than understanding athletics as a platform for evangelizing because understanding athletic pleasure as godly joy positions sport as religiously important *in itself* rather than as a means to share the gospel. Christian athletes see their joy in sport as a message from God indicating that God is pleased, and the idea of athletic pleasure as divine connection is key to understanding contemporary sports ministry.

In the Christian athletic community, joy is not a simple emotion. For example, many Christian athletes believe that joy can be incomplete or false. They described joy without God as misleading and detrimental. Jennie told me, "When you're a soccer-head like I am, soccer can become an obsession. It can become selfish and prideful and that is unhealthy. It's selfish if it's for your own joy, but when it is about bringing joy to God, it can be for a greater purpose. That's one thing that is scary about not being close to God—you can't get to this kind of joy." For Christian athletes like Jennie, the only real source of joy for humans is a personal relationship with Jesus Christ, and this understanding of joy informed their athletic lives.

Christian athletes employ two related evangelical discourses to understand athletics as religious experience: Christlikeness and spiritual warfare. In these discourses, athletic embodied sensations like pain, exhilaration, soreness, muscle memory, fatigue, and mastery represent either sensations of close connection to Christ or the tactics of the devil trying to keep the believer from experiencing such a connection. As I described in chapter 3, Christian athletes called on Christ when they felt they were at their athletic limits. In their worldview, reaching one's limits could make one vulnerable to Satan's influence, a voice in the athlete's head saying, "You can't do it." Athletes like Stacey on the Athletes in Action women's basketball team saw fatigue as a moment to call on Christ. As she said, "That's when I know I can't do it alone. That's when you just have to ask, and he will surprise you." For Stacey and others like her, calling on Christ for athletic assistance is a pragmatic tool that helped her compete to the best of her ability. It was also a defense tactic in an ever-present battle with Satan, a force of evil whose primary motivation was to separate the believer from Christ.

Sport became a resource for evangelical Christians to understand their religious obligations differently. Rather than seeing their primary goal as witnessing to nonbelievers, Christian athletes came to see it as bonding with Christ in order to fight against the tactics of the devil. They saw this battle to be Christlike as a powerful form of witnessing, perhaps even more powerful then voicing one's testimony. Athletes and coaches called this "witnessing without words" and hoped that their intensity in competition would demonstrate Christlikeness and convince their audience of the reality of Christ. Christian athletes' battle to demonstrate Christlikeness occurs at the level of the body, making sport a different sort of resource than evangelicals first envisioned. Sports ministry's stated goal remains outreach to nonbelievers, but their strategy for achieving this goal changed. Rather than using sport to garner an audience for athletic celebrities, sport became a method for witnessing without words, for witnessing with one's body, and a means to connect with Christ and fend off the tactics of the devil.

Reevaluating Evangelical Politics of the Body

When I conducted my research, women had outnumbered male participants in sports ministry for about a decade. These women unintentionally challenged traditional gender understandings just by playing sports. While men who play sports tend to confirm gender expectations by demonstrating masculine traits—such as strength, precedence, agency, and leadership—women in sport demonstrate these same traits, challenging the idea that masculinity belongs solely to men. This is interesting in the context of evangelical Christianity because gender roles are central to evangelical marriage and family life.

Politically, conservative Christians have embraced issues of the family and have sought legislation that reflects their understandings of what a family should look like—marriage should be between a man and a woman, and within a marriage, the man is the head of household and primary decision maker.[9] As this book has shown, female Christian athletes have been able to mitigate this picture of the family by using their knowledge of sport to augment their understandings of femininity, homosexuality, and marriage. Women in sports ministry are powerful agents who operate within a constraining gender paradigm. When evangelicals took it as their mission to engage secular culture, they gained access to social spaces and structures that operated with different priorities. The spaces and structures of sport have enhanced evangelical women's agency by allowing them to creatively negotiate and combine varied gendered expectations.[10]

Evangelical theology tends to emphasize differences between men and women. These differences often imply gender hierarchy. For evangelicals like the authors of *Experiencing God's Power for Female Athletes*, men's masculinity and women's femininity are God-given traits. Particularly for evangelical female athletes, the directive to act feminine can conflict with their desire to compete at an elite level. When these women reflected on their femininity from the point of view of athletes, they developed two overlapping strategies for maintaining a sense of their own femininity and, by extension, a sense that their gendered behavior aligned them with God's plan. One strategy was to redefine femininity to include traditionally masculine elements like strength and leadership. Another strategy was to strictly monitor one's outward appearance, especially in secular or nonathletic evangelical settings, to demonstrate that athleticism could go hand in hand with femininity. Female Christian athletes used their hair, jewelry, and clothing to mark themselves as feminine in the masculine realm of sports.

Many of the female Christian athletes with whom I spoke had played with and competed against out lesbians. These women interacted with lesbians as teammates and thought of them as valuable contributors to their shared athletic enterprise. Many found that the evangelical mainstay that homosexuality is a sin was difficult to reconcile with their respect for lesbian athletes. For some, the solution was to withhold judgment on whether homosexuality is a sin. For others, homosexuality was a sin, but it was a sin like any other, including sins that all athletes could experience, like jealousy, retaliation, or pride. This lessened the importance of sexual orientation, despite the Christian Right's political emphasis on this issue.

Coaches, players, and fans tend to assume that Christian athletes are straight. As we have seen, this was not always the case, but the assumption of heterosexuality has allowed women who might come across as masculine, and therefore as potentially sexually deviant, relief from constantly monitoring their femininity. For female athletes like Leslie and Amy on the Charlotte Lady Eagles, experiencing same-sex attraction was confusing and deeply troubling. These two women demonstrated different trajectories—Amy left sports ministry to live as an out lesbian, and Leslie committed to sports ministry and pursued a straight lifestyle. Others on the Charlotte Lady Eagles remained closeted to more easily participate in sports ministry. These struggles and choices represent a range of reactions to the sensitive issues of sexual desire and behavior.

In evangelical Christianity, it is common for believers to talk about marriage as part of God's plan. Marriage represents a step in one's faith journey, and gender roles in marriage are one method that evangelical Christians use to distinguish themselves from secular couples. Sports ministry publications emphasized two metaphors to frame gendered relationships in marriages—wife-as-cheerleader and couple-as-teammates. These are somewhat chronological as the wife-as-cheerleader metaphor was more common in the 1970s and the wife-as-teammate metaphor came to the fore in the 1990s with the growth of Promise Keepers and other men's ministry organizations. However, the idea of wife-as-cheerleader did not entirely disappear and continues to undergird understandings of what kinds of teammates the spouses can be. (To reiterate Farrar's example, the husband is the quarterback; the wife is the wide receiver.)

Just as female Christian athletes interacted with more out lesbians than the average evangelical and developed ways to temper and reinterpret the evangelical mainstay on the sinfulness of homosexuality, female Christian athletes used their athletic experiences to understand and experience the metaphor of spouses as teammates. Promise Keepers and men's ministries of the 1990s emphasized servant leadership and mutual submission as correct marriage practices. For Christian athletes, these terms made sense because servant leadership and mutual submission were necessary in their sporting lives. While marriage remains an important part of evangelical life for Christian athletes (and marriage remains defined as between a man and a woman), the sports world helped Christian athletes, and women in particular, negotiate marriage and home-life roles from a wider perspective than is perhaps possible for the nonathletic evangelical Christian.

Unintended Consequences

Postwar evangelicals engaged secular culture, and they intended to use all resources at their disposal to evangelize non-Christians. Sport became one of those resources when evangelicals began sports ministry. Examining the relationship between sport and evangelicalism shows us the unintended consequences of employing secular resources for religious purposes. While in some ways sport was a good fit for evangelical purposes, it also opened up new possibilities for challenging evangelical theology and practice.

Consequences of cultural engagement are difficult to predict. Evangelical involvement in sport focused attention on the body and brought on a reevaluation of some of evangelical Christianity's most closely held political and social understandings, namely, those regarding gender and sexuality. While sport continued to function in sports ministry to affirm the power of God and humans' capacity to access that power, sport also provided a competing set of gender understandings. Sports ministry spurred female Christian athletes to think about their embodied religious sensations, and through this, they began to think differently about some of evangelicalism's most closely held theological convictions on femininity, homosexuality, and marriage. As Christian athletes turned to their own bodies to understand their religious identity, they opened up the possibility of reevaluating and renegotiating evangelical tenets on gender and sexuality. Challenges to conservative religious traditions can emerge in unlikely places; evangelical engagement with sport had the unintended consequence of producing subtle and complex shifts in religious beliefs and practices.

NOTES

INTRODUCTION

1. In this book, all informants have pseudonyms to preserve confidentiality. These pseudonyms are consistent throughout the text. I have identified some people by their generic position rather than a pseudonym when this was more effective for preserving confidentiality. Whenever I quote someone without a citation, this was an interaction that occurred during fieldwork, interview, or informal conversation.

2 Athletes in Action, http://www.athletesinaction.org/about/ (accessed July 30, 2011).

3. "Then Jesus came to them and said, 'All authority in heaven and on earth has been given to me. Therefore go and make disciples of all nations, baptizing them in the name of the Father and of the Son and of the Holy Spirit, and teaching them to obey everything I have commanded you. And surely I am with you always, to the very end of the age.'" Matthew 28:18–20 (NIV). For analysis of how understandings of the Great Commission shaped Campus Crusade for Christ, see John G. Turner, *Bill Bright and Campus Crusade for Christ: The Renewal of Evangelicalism in Postwar America* (Chapel Hill: University of North Carolina Press, 2008).

4. Fellowship of Christian Athletes, "Ignite the World of Sports for Jesus Christ: The Fellowship of Christian Athletes 2010 Ministry Report," http://www.fca.org/assets/2012/06/FCA-Ministry-Report-Lg-2010-B.pdf (accessed January 4, 2015); Athletes in Action, "Athletes in Action Annual Report: 2011," http://athletesinaction.org/Media/Default/About/annual-reports/2011-AIA%20AR.web.pdf (accessed January 4, 2015).

5. Fellowship of Christian Athletes, "2012 Ministry Report," http://www.fca.org/about-fellowship-of-christian-athletes/ministryreport/ (accessed January 4, 2015); FCA reported camp attendance in 2009 as 47,000 and in 2007 as 42,000. Fellowship of Christian Athletes, "FCA Ministry Annual Impact Report," http://www.fca.org/assets/2012/06/2009-Annual-Report-Final.pdf (accessed January 4, 2015); Fellowship of Christian Athletes, "2007 Annual Camp Report," http://www.fca.org/assets/2012/06/2007-Annual-Report.pdf (accessed January 4, 2015).

6. Fellowship of Christian Athletes, "2012 Ministry Report"; Athletes in Action, "Athletes in Action: Annual Report 2012," http://athletesinaction.org/Media/Default/About/annual-reports/Annual-Report-2012.pdf (accessed January 4, 2015).

7. On distinctions between evangelicalism of the 1940s and 1950s and fundamentalism of the 1920s, see George M. Marsden, *Understanding Fundamentalism and*

Evangelicalism (Grand Rapids, MI: Eerdmans, 1991); Mark A. Noll, *American Evangelical Christianity: An Introduction* (Malden, MA: Blackwell, 2001). Evangelicals like Billy Graham saw national politics as morally bereft, but unlike fundamentalist strategies of the 1920s and 1930s, evangelicals in the 1950s, 1960s, and 1970s engaged political leaders and raised political issues. See J. Brooks Flippen, *Jimmy Carter, the Politics of Family, and the Rise of the Religious Right* (Athens: University of Georgia Press, 2011); Steven P. Miller, *Billy Graham and the Rise of the Republican South* (Philadelphia: University of Pennsylvania Press, 2009); Daniel Williams, *God's Own Party: The Making of the Christian Right* (New York: Oxford University Press, 2010); Darren Dochuk, *From Bible Belt to Sunbelt: Plain-Folk Religion, Grassroots Politics, and the Rise of Evangelical Conservatism* (New York: Norton, 2010).

8. See Christian Smith, *American Evangelicalism: Embattled and Thriving* (Chicago: University of Chicago Press, 1998), especially chap. 4.

9. Much scholarship on American evangelicalism argues that evangelicalism is not as homogeneous or monolithic as evangelical spokespeople present it. This important insight has made it difficult to determine who belongs in the category "evangelical." Religious studies scholars tend to cluster and delineate evangelicals in America either through self-identification and measurable behavior or through historical identification of institutions. On self-identification and measurable behavior, see Christian Smith, "Appendix B: On Religious Identities," in *American Evangelicalism*, 233–247; and Robert Wuthnow, *The Restructuring of American Religion: Society and Faith since World War II* (Princeton, NJ: Princeton University Press, 1988).

10. Robert Putnam and David Campbell, *American Grace: How Religion Divides and Unites Us* (New York: Simon and Schuster, 2010), 104–105. Putnam and Campbell also note that at the same time that evangelicalism was experiencing a small swell and decline, the number of Americans who identified as not religious remained steady at 7 percent from 1973 to 1993, but by 2008 had grown considerably to 17 percent. For the authors, the increase in the number of people who declare no religious affiliation is a more important finding than the slight changes in evangelical congregational membership.

11. Michael Hout and Claude S. Fischer, "Why More Americans Have No Religious Preference: Politics and Generations," *American Sociological Review* 67 (2002): 165–190.

12. Scholars have explored the interactions between conservative Christians and American politics at length. For some representative works, see Jason Bivins, *The Fracture of Good Order: Christian Antiliberalism and the Challenge to American Politics* (Chapel Hill: University of North Carolina Press, 2002); Jeffrey W. Robbins and Neal Magee, eds., *The Sleeping Giant Has Awoken: The New Politics of Religion in the United States* (New York: Continuum, 2008); Daniel Williams, *God's Own Party: The Making of the Christian Right* (New York: Oxford University Press, 2010); David Harrington Watt, *Bible-Carrying Christians: Conservative Protestants and*

Social Power (New York: Oxford University Press, 2002); Randall Balmer, *The Making of Evangelicalism: From Revivalism to Politics and Beyond* (Baylor, TX: Baylor University Press, 2010); Peter Goodwin Heltzel, *Jesus and Justice: Evangelicals, Race, and American Politics* (New Haven, CT: Yale University Press, 2009).

13. Smith, *American Evangelicalism.*

14. For an exploration of conservative Christianity, see Andrew M. Greeley and Michael Hout, *The Truth about Conservative Christians: What They Think and What They Believe* (Chicago: University of Chicago Press, 2006).

15. The first book of the *Left Behind* series is a good demonstration of this. Tim LaHaye and Jerry B. Jenkins, *Left Behind: A Novel of the Earth's Last Days* (Carol Stream, IL: Tyndale, 1995). Scholars have explored evangelical use of popular culture at length. While the consumers of Christian media remained largely Christian, the ability to imagine such media as an evangelical tool informed production sensibilities and consumption practices. See, for example, Tona J. Hangen, *Redeeming the Dial: Radio, Religion, and Popular Culture in America* (Chapel Hill: University of North Carolina Press, 2001); Quentin J. Schultze and Robert Herbert Woods Jr., eds., *Understanding Evangelical Media: The Changing Face of Christian Communication* (Downers Grove, IL: InterVarsity Press, 2008); Crawford Gribben, *Writing the Rapture: Prophecy Fiction in Evangelical America* (New York: Oxford University Press, 2009); Jay R. Howard and John M. Streck, *Apostles of Rock: The Splintered World of Contemporary Christian Music* (Lexington: University Press of Kentucky, 2004); Robert Wuthnow, *All in Sync: How Music and Art Are Revitalizing American Religion* (Berkeley: University of California Press, 2006); William Romanowski, "Evangelicals and Popular Music: The Contemporary Christian Music Industry," in *Religion and Popular Culture in America*, ed. Bruce David Forbes and Jeffrey H. Mahan (Berkeley: University of California Press, 2005); David W. Stowe, *No Sympathy for the Devil: Christian Pop Music and the Transformation of American Evangelicalism* (Chapel Hill: University of North Carolina Press, 2011).

16. Quoted in William J. Baker, *Playing with God: Religion and Modern Sport* (Cambridge, MA: Harvard University Press, 2007), 194.

17. Quoted in James A. Mathisen, "Reviving 'Muscular Christianity': Gil Dodds and the Institutionalization of Sport Evangelism," *Sociological Focus* 23 (1990): 242.

18. "Baseball Chapel," http://www.baseballchapel.org/index.cfm?Fuseaction=MediaIn formation&CFID=3596105&CFTOKEN=81038206 (accessed July 29, 2013).

19. "PAO History," http://pao.org/who-we-are/history/ (accessed July 29, 2013).

20. Upward Sports, "History," http://www.upward.org/history/ (accessed July 29, 2013).

21. Much appreciation to my research assistant, Kendall Hughes, for amassing these data.

22. In 2012, Phoenix First in Phoenix, Arizona, had one full-time director, one part-time assistant, and several personal trainers who worked as independent contractors at the church's fitness facility. Second Baptist Church in Houston, Texas, had five campuses, two of which had significant athletic resources. Together,

the two campuses employed ten full-time directors and assistant directors, and more than twenty part-time and seasonal employees. Other megachurches like Prestonwood Baptist in Plano, Texas, had six full-time staff and four part-time staff and trainers, and Southeast Christian in Louisville, Kentucky, had seven full-time and five part-time athletic employees as well as two interns. As more and more megachurches adopt athletic programming, these numbers are likely to grow.

23. Association of Church Sports and Recreation Ministers, CSRM—Colleges, http://www.csrm.org/colleges.shtml (accessed February 5, 2012). Many of these institutions began offering courses in sports ministry in the 1990s, and some instituted a major over the following decade.

24. In 2011, Baptist Bible College in Clarks Summit, Pennsylvania, had an enrollment of fifteen sports ministry majors, and Kuyper College in Grand Rapids, Michigan, had ten to twelve. In 2014, Dallas Baptist University reported twenty-five majors in its Camp/Sports Ministry program, and Mississippi College in Clinton, Mississippi, reported six majors in sports ministry.

25. Moody Bible Institute, "Sports Ministry Optimal Schedule," http://www.moody.edu/uploadedFiles/Education/Undergraduate/Undergraduate_Programs/Sports_Ministry/Sports_Ministry_Major/sports_ministry_optimal_schedule.pdf (accessed May 1, 2012).

26. Other scholars of religion and sport have noted the role of embodiment in the confirmation of belief. For two examples, see Julie Byrne's exploration of female Catholic basketball players in midcentury Philadelphia in *O God of Players: The Story of the Immaculata Mighty Macs* (New York: Columbia University Press, 2003) and Joseph Alter's ethnography of Hindu wrestlers in contemporary India in *The Wrestler's Body: Identity and Ideology in North India* (Berkeley: University of California Press, 1992).

27. For example, R. Marie Griffith's work on Women's Aglow, an evangelical fellowship for women, demonstrated that evangelical women were aware of gender dynamics and employed the rhetoric of "submission" in ways that subverted traditional understandings of feminine submissiveness. See Griffith, *God's Daughters: Evangelical Women and the Power of Submission* (Berkeley: University of California Press, 2000).

28. See Christine J. Gardner, *Making Chastity Sexy: The Rhetoric of Evangelical Abstinence Campaigns* (Berkeley: University of California Press, 2011).

29. Ministry Athletes International, http://www.maisoccer.com/main/ (accessed July 30, 2011).

30. I am not alone in this notebook approach. For a full description, see Robert M. Emerson, Rachel I. Fretz, and Linda L. Shaw, *Writing Ethnographic Fieldnotes* (Chicago: University of Chicago Press, 2011); for application of this method, see Diane Nelson, *A Finger in the Wound: Body Politics in Quincentennial Guatemala* (Berkeley: University of California Press, 1999).

31. This insight has been the topic of much consternation in the field of anthropology. For investigations of anthropological credibility, see Anna Grimshaw, *The*

Ethnographer's Eye: Ways of Seeing in Anthropology (Cambridge: Cambridge University Press, 2001); Akhil Gupta and James Ferguson, eds., *Culture, Power, Place: Explorations in Critical Anthropology* (Durham, NC: Duke University Press, 1997); D. Soyini Madison, *Critical Ethnography: Method, Ethics, and Performance* (Los Angeles: Sage, 2011).

32. This has emerged as a conventional anthropological strategy for dealing with issues of credibility. For some representative works that employ this strategy in the anthropology of religion, see Susan Friend Harding, *The Book of Jerry Falwell: Fundamentalist Language and Politics* (Princeton, NJ: Princeton University Press, 2000); Karen McCarthy Brown, *Mama Lola: A Vodou Priestess in Brooklyn* (Berkeley: University of California Press, 1991); June McDaniel, *Offering Flowers, Feeding Skulls: Popular Goddess Worship in West Bengal* (New York: Oxford University Press, 2004).

33. Charles Lippy, *Being Religious, American-Style: A History of Popular Religiosity in the United States* (Westport, CT: Praeger, 1994); David Hall, ed., *Lived Religion in America: Toward a History of Practice* (Princeton, NJ: Princeton University Press, 1997); Nancy T. Ammerman, ed., *Everyday Religion: Observing Modern Religious Lives* (New York: Oxford University Press, 2006).

34. Harding, *Book of Jerry Falwell*, 60.

35. Thinking of knowledge as a process and of information as generated, rather than discovered, has shaped my investigation in this book. I am indebted to the field of science and technology studies (STS) for modeling this kind of epistemological investigation. As a field, STS investigates how scientific knowledge is pursued, declared, and solidified into fact. For some representative works, see Ludwik Fleck, *Genesis and Development of a Scientific Fact*, trans. Frederick Bradley (Chicago: University of Chicago Press, 1981); Thomas S. Kuhn, *The Structure of Scientific Revolutions, 3rd ed.* (Chicago: University of Chicago Press, 1996); Barbara Herrnstein Smith, *Scandalous Knowledge: Science, Truth, and the Human* (Durham, NC: Duke University Press, 2006); Bruno Latour, *Reassembling the Social: An Introduction to Actor-Network-Theory* (New York: Oxford University Press, 2007). Contemporary scholars have used these insights to investigate the production of knowledge about bodies. See, for example, Joseph Dumit, *Picturing Personhood: Brain Scans and Biomedical Identity* (Princeton, NJ: Princeton University Press, 2003).

36. Harding, *Book of Jerry Falwell*, 60.

37. For an excellent exploration of this tension in men's sports, see John Donald Gustav-Wrathall, *Take the Young Stranger by the Hand: Same-Sex Relations and the YMCA* (Chicago: University of Chicago Press, 1998).

CHAPTER 1

1. Greg Linville, "Recreation and Sports Ministry: An Evangelistic Approach," in *Recreation and Sports Ministry: Impacting Postmodern Culture*, ed. John Garner (Nashville, TN: Broadman and Holman, 2003), 155.

2. It is common in contemporary evangelical Christianity to emphasize leading by example. Evangelical Christians may see their behaviors, rather than their

declarations of faith, as setting them apart from nonbelievers. This has allowed evangelicals to embrace secular spheres like the business world as sites for evangelical leadership. See Monique El-Faisy, *God and Country: How Evangelicals Have Become America's New Mainstream* (New York: Bloomsbury, 2006), especially chap. 3; Michael Lindsay, *Faith in the Halls of Power: How Evangelicals Joined the American Elite* (New York: Oxford University Press, 2007).

3. Many sports ministry resources exist that promote ways to use athletics for evangelistic outreach. See, for example, Steve Connor, *Sports Outreach: Principles and Practice for Successful Sports Ministry* (London: Christian Focus, 2003); John White and Cindy White, *Game Day Glory: Life-Changing Principles for Sport* (Tallmadge, OH: SD Myers, 2006); Byron August and Krystal Ashe, *Touching Lives through Your Sports Program* (Broken Arrow, OK: Ready for the World Ministries, 2007).

4. Lowrie McCown and Valerie Gin, *Focus on Sport in Ministry* (Marietta, GA: 360 Sports, 2003), 83.

5. Ibid., 85.

6. Both ministry resources and scholarship on youth evangelism confirm Sean's claim that the altar call is less integral to religious practices of younger evangelicals. See Brett McCracken, *Hipster Christianity: When Church and Cool Collide* (Grand Rapids, MI: Baker Books, 2010); Putnam and Campbell, *American Grace.*

7. The literature on religion and embodiment is quite extensive. For some representative works, see Thomas J. Csordas, *Body/Meaning/Healing* (New York: Palgrave Macmillan, 2002); Robert R. Desjarlais, *Body and Emotion: The Aesthetics of Illness and Healing in the Nepal Himalayas* (Philadelphia: University of Pennsylvania Press, 1992); Elaine Scarry, *The Body in Pain: The Making and Unmaking of the World* (New York: Oxford University Press, 1987); David Morris, *The Culture of Pain* (Berkeley: University of California Press, 1991); Caroline Walker Bynum, *Resurrection of the Body in Western Christianity, 200–1336* (New York: Columbia University Press, 1995).

8. Émile Durkheim, *The Elementary Forms of Religious Life*, trans. Karen E. Fields (New York: Simon and Schuster, 1995), 386.

9. Catherine Bell, "Performance," in *Critical Terms for Religious Studies*, ed. Mark C. Taylor (Chicago: University of Chicago Press, 1998), 205.

10. Harding, *Book of Jerry Falwell*, 58.

11. Arguably, religious mass production began in earnest with the mass distribution of wallet-sized cards featuring Warner Sallman's Head of Christ on one side and the Lord's Prayer on the other. However scholars have noted that these cards reminded Christians of their existing beliefs and were not a witnessing strategy. See David Morgan, *Icons of American Protestantism: The Art of Warner Sallman* (New Haven, CT: Yale University Press, 1996). On the longer history of Protestant popular witnessing in the United States, see Nathan O. Hatch, *The Democratization of American Christianity* (New Haven, CT: Yale University Press, 1991); Mark Noll, *The Rise of Evangelicalism: The Age of Edwards, Whitefield and*

the Wesleys (Downers Grove, IL: IVP Academic, 2010); and Catherine Brekus, *Sarah Osborn's World: The Rise of Evangelical Christianity in Early America* (New Haven, CT: Yale University Press, 2012) on the Great Awakenings and Protestant revival.

12. Campus Crusade for Christ decided in 2011 to use the name Cru for its ministries in the United States and to maintain its original title for its international ministries. The U.S. leadership of the organization began reevaluating the name in 2009 and chose Cru after extensive research. Many chapters of Campus Crusade for Christ had been using the nickname "Cru" since the mid-1990s. Part of the decision to reevaluate the organization's U.S. name stemmed from a realization that Americans have a negative association with the word "crusade." Cru, "Frequently Asked Questions," http://www.cru.org/about-us/donor-relations/our-new-name/qanda.htm#1 (accessed August 2, 2013).

13. Richard Quebedeaux, *I Found It! The Story of Bill Bright and Campus Crusade* (San Francisco: Harper and Row, 1979), 93.

14. This economic strategy is called Fordism and is explored at length in David Harvey, *The Condition of Postmodernity: An Enquiry into the Origins of Cultural Change* (New York: Wiley-Blackwell, 1991). Harvey identifies the contemporary age as "post-Fordist," meaning that standardization has fallen out of vogue in favor of niche marketing and that mass production has been replaced by short-run production to meet consumer demand for higher turnover of commodities.

15. Michael Richardson, *Amazing Faith: The Authorized Biography of Bill Bright* (Colorado Springs, CO: Waterbook Press, 2000), 71–80.

16. Campus Crusade for Christ, "About Us," http://www.campuscrusadeforchrist.com/aboutus/history.htm (accessed January 22, 2011).

17. The prayer reads, "Lord Jesus, I need You. Thank You for dying on the cross for my sins. I open the door of my life and receive You as my Savior and Lord. Thank You for forgiving my sins and giving me eternal life. Take control of the throne of my life. Make me the kind of person You want me to be." Cru, "How to Know God Personally through Jesus Christ Right Now," http://www.cru.org/how-to-know-god/would-you-like-to-know-god-personally/index.htm (accessed April 17, 2013).

18. Quebedeaux, *I Found It!*, 97. For an exploration of how this was a departure from a traditional gospel message, see David Harrington Watt, *A Transforming Faith: Explorations of Twentieth-Century American Evangelicalism* (New Brunswick, NJ: Rutgers University Press, 1991), 22.

19. Watt, *A Transforming Faith*, 18.

20. John G. Turner, *Bill Bright and Campus Crusade for Christ: The Renewal of Evangelicalism in Postwar America* (Chapel Hill: University of North Carolina Press, 2008), 102.

21. Quoted in Wayne Atcheson, *Impact for Christ: How FCA Has Influenced the Sports World* (Grand Island, NE: Cross Training, 1994), 158.

22. Historically, Protestants have demonstrated periodic discomfort with combining sports and Christianity. Most famously, baseball player turned preacher Billy Sunday left professional sports because he could not reconcile the values of sport with his Christian beliefs. For discussion of this and other periods of discomfort, see Tony Ladd and James A. Mathisen, *Muscular Christianity: Evangelical Protestants and the Development of American Sport* (Grand Rapids, MI: Baker Books, 1999); and William Baker, *Playing with God: Religion and Modern Sport* (Cambridge, MA: Harvard University Press, 2007).

23. Muscular Christianity, a turn-of-the-century movement that emphasized strength and manliness as Christian obligations, set a precedent for sports ministry. Muscular Christianity emerged in Britain in the 1850s and spread to America after the American Civil War. The most crucial popular literature of muscular Christianity was Thomas Hughes's Tom Brown adventure stories. The most widely read of the series, *Tom Brown's School Days*, chronicles the coming of age of young Tom Brown, a rugby player at a private boarding school. Through physical education, Brown developed a fighting spirit that allowed him to defeat bullies and defend his friends. He was the fictional epitome of the muscular Christian ethos—the idea that boys turn into men through dedication to hard work and that Christian moral character can be cultivated through athletic training. Thomas Hughes, *Tom Brown's School Days* (Cambridge, MA: Macmillan, 1857). For analysis of muscular Christianity, see Clifford Putney, *Muscular Christianity: Manhood and Sports in Protestant America, 1880–1920* (Cambridge, MA: Harvard University Press, 2001). Historians have noted that the late nineteenth century and early twentieth century saw the rise of the use of the term "character building," which carried Protestant connotations. See David Macleod, *Building Character in the American Boy: The Boy Scouts, YMCA, and Their Forerunners, 1870–1920* (Madison: University of Wisconsin Press, 2004); Axel Bundgaard, *Muscle and Manliness: The Rise of Sport in American Boarding Schools* (Syracuse, NY: Syracuse University Press, 2005). A major muscular Christian institution was the Young Men's Christian Association. On the cultural context and effects of the YMCA's emphasis on physical education, see Gustav-Wrathall, *Take the Young Stranger by the Hand*; Nina Mjagkij and Margaret Spratt, *Men and Women Adrift: The YMCA and the YWCA in the City* (New York: NYU Press, 1997); and Thomas Winter, *Making Men, Making Class: The YMCA and Workingmen, 1877–1920* (Chicago: University of Chicago Press, 2002).

24. Joe Smalley, *More Than a Game* (San Bernardino, CA: Here's Life, 1981), 31, 26.

25. Pamela Odih, *Advertising in Modern and Postmodern Times* (Thousand Oaks, CA: Sage, 2007), 5.

26. Steven J. Jackson, David L. Andrews, and Jay Sherer, "Introduction," in *Sport, Culture and Advertising: Identities, Commodities and the Politics of Representation*, ed. Steven J. Jackson and David L. Andrews (New York: Routledge, 2005), 10.

27. Barry Smart, *The Sport Star: Modern Sport and the Cultural Economy of Sporting Celebrity* (Thousand Oaks, CA: Sage, 2005), 38.

28. Smalley, *More Than a Game*, 145.

29. This was a historical development. See J. A. Mangan, *"Manufactured" Masculinity: Making Imperial Manliness, Morality and Militarism* (New York: Routledge, 2011); Putney, *Muscular Christianity*.

30. James W. Keating, "Sportsmanship as a Moral Category," in *Philosophic Inquiry in Sport*, ed. William J. Morgan and Klaus V. Meier (Champaign, IL: Human Kinetics, 1995), 243. For an analysis of how sport in the United States uses religious metaphors to make moral claims, see Jeffrey Scholes and Raphael Sassower, *Religion and Sports in American Culture* (New York: Routledge, 2014).

31. Jay Coakley, *Sport in Society: Issues and Controversies* (Boston: McGraw Hill, 2001), 92 (emphasis in original).

32. Coakley is not the only scholar who recognizes the flaws in assuming that sport inherently builds character. A number of works argue that sport socialization has had the negative effects of promoting uncritical capitalism, homophobia, and an unhealthy obsession with body image. See Douglas Foley, *Learning Capitalist Culture: Deep in the Heart of Tejas* (Philadelphia: University of Pennsylvania Press, 1994); Dan Woog, *Jocks: True Stories of America's Gay Male Athletes* (Los Angeles: Alyson, 1998); Alan Klein, *Little Big Men: Bodybuilding Subculture and Gender Construction* (Albany: State University of New York Press, 1993).

33. Dave Hannah, "On the Move with Athletes in Action," *Athletes in Action Magazine*, Winter 1981, 20.

34. Dave Hannah, "Athletes in Action History," *Athletes in Action 1981–1982 Basketball Yearbook* (Memphis, TN: Athletes in Action Sports Information Department, 1981), 8.

35. Brent Dennis, "Confessions of a Pitbull," *Sharing the Victory*, September/October 1989, 18.

36. Quoted in Leilani Diane Corpus, "A Straight Arrow Who'll Straight-Arm You," *Sharing the Victory*, March/April 1989, 4.

37. Shirl Hoffman, *Good Game: Christianity and the Culture of Sports* (Waco, TX: Baylor University Press, 2010), 147.

38. Ibid., 149.

39. Ibid., 232.

40. Ibid., 234.

41. This sort of critique also appears in sports scholar Robert Higgs's analysis of sports ministry as Christian heresy; he agrees with Hoffman when he writes that "certain aspects of sport make them unsuitable for an alliance with religion." Robert J. Higgs, *God in the Stadium: Sports and Religion in America* (Lexington: University Press of Kentucky, 1995), 3.

42. Tom Krattenmaker, *Onward Christian Athletes: Turning Ballparks into Pulpits and Players into Preachers* (Lanham, MD: Rowman and Littlefield, 2010), 76.

43. The AIA sportswriter who accompanied the team attributed this quotation to Saint Francis of Assisi.

44. Brian Massumi, *Parables for the Virtual: Movement, Affect, Sensation* (Durham, NC: Duke University Press, 2002), 77.
45. Keating, "Sportsmanship as a Moral Category," 247.
46. Smith, *American Evangelicalism*, 131.

CHAPTER 2

1. Neil Wolkodoff, "Let's Redefine Winning," *Sharing the Victory*, January/February 1985, 16.
2. Hugh Hudson, dir. *Chariots of Fire* (Warner Brothers, 1981).
3. The title for this section is taken from a text by Wes Neal, *The Making of an Athlete of God* (San Bernardino, CA: Campus Crusade for Christ, 1972).
4. Wes Neal, *The Handbook on Athletic Perfection: A Training Manual for Christian Athletes* (Prescott, AZ: Institute for Athletic Perfection, 1975); Neal, *The Handbook on Coaching Perfection* (Los Angeles: Action House, 1976); White and White, *Game Day Glory*; Wes Neal and Gordon Thiessen, *Doing Sport God's Way*, DVD (Grand Island, NE: Cross Training, 2008).
5. Gary Warner, *Competition* (Elgin, IL: David C. Cook, 1979), 45.
6. Frank Deford, "Religion and Sport," *Sports Illustrated*, April 19, 1976, 88–102; Deford, "The Word According to Tom," *Sports Illustrated*, April 26, 1976, 54–69; Deford, "Reaching for the Stars," *Sports Illustrated*, May 3, 1976, 42–60.
7. Deford, "Religion and Sport," 100. This continues to be a major critique of sports ministry from within the Christian community. Shirl Hoffman critiqued sports ministry in the 1990s for the same reason. "When sport is harnessed to the evangelistic enterprise, evangelicals become as much endorsers of the myths reinforced by popular sports as they do of the Christian gospel." Shirl Hoffman, "Evangelicalism and the Revitalization of Religious Ritual in Sport," in *Sport and Religion*, ed. Shirl Hoffman (Champaign, IL: Human Kinetics, 1992), 121. According to a recent book by William Baker, "[Christian athletes] use sports as a means to the end of religious conversion. Gone, in the evangelical equation, are older concerns about the relation of sports to physical health or the moral lessons to be gained from athletic competition." William Baker, *Playing with God: Religion and Modern Sport* (Cambridge, MA: Harvard University Press, 2007), 217.
8. Deford, "Religion and Sport," 102.
9. Jerry Pile, "Sports and War," *Christian Athlete*, January 1972, 2–8. Sports historians have noted that the 1950s through the 1970s was a period of major change for American sports. For scholarship on sports and the Vietnam War, see David Zang, *Sports Wars: Athletes in the Age of Aquarius* (Fayetteville: University of Arkansas Press, 2001); Kathryn Jay, *More Than Just a Game: Sports in American Life since 1945* (New York: Columbia University Press, 2006). For changes in race relations, see Mike Marqusee, *Redemption Song: Muhammad Ali and the Spirit of the Sixties* (New York: Verso, 1999); Lane Demas, *Integrating the Gridiron: Black Civil Rights and American College Football* (Piscataway, NJ: Rutgers University Press, 2010); Charles Martin, *Benching Jim Crow: The Rise and Fall of the Color*

Line in Southern College Sports, 1890–1980 (Champaign: University of Illinois Press, 2010). For accounts of second-wave feminism and sport, see Susan Ware, *Game, Set, Match: Billie Jean King and the Revolution in Women's Sports* (Chapel Hill: University of North Carolina Press, 2011); Anne Flintoff and Sheila Scraton, eds., *Gender and Sport: A Reader* (New York: Routledge, 2002); and Nancy Hogshead-Makar and Andrew Zimbalist, eds., *Equal Play: Title IX and Social Change* (Philadelphia: Temple University Press, 2007).

10. Pile, "Sports and War," 2–8.
11. Deford, "Reaching for the Stars," 60.
12. Ibid.
13. Hoffman, "Evangelicalism and the Revitalization of Religious Ritual in Sport," 121.
14. Paul Hoch, *Rip Off the Big Game: The Exploitation of Sports by the Power Elite* (Garden City, NY: Anchor Books, 1972), 22.
15. Ibid., 82.
16. Deford, "Religion and Sport," 100.
17. Dave Meggyesy, *Out of Their League* (Berkeley, CA: Ramparts Press, 1970).
18. Warner, *Competition*, 11.
19. Smith, *American Evangelicalism*, 124.
20. See chapter 1 for an exploration of *Have You Heard the Four Spiritual Laws?*
21. According to Shirl Hoffman, "The most popular doctrine in locker room religion, bar none, is 'Total Release Performance,' promulgated through the evangelical network by The Institute for Athletic Perfection. By employing a slick bit of theological open-field running around the Pauline athletic metaphors and ethical exhortations contained in I Corinthians 10:31 and Colossians 3:23, the Institute has derived the teaching that God's acceptance of an athletic performance as a spiritual offering depends upon the athlete's love for Christ and the intensity with which the athletic performance is executed." "Evangelicalism and the Revitalization of Religious Ritual in Sport," 117.
22. Quoted in Neal, *Handbook on Athletic Perfection*, 67.
23. Ibid., 69–70.
24. Ibid., 43.
25. Ibid., 20.
26. Ibid.
27. Frank Zane, "Zane's Unit Training for Delts," *Muscle Builder and Power*, May 1975, 13.
28. Neal, *Handbook on Athletic Perfection*, 72.
29. This thought was prevalent in self-help literature at the time, including Norman Vincent Peale's immensely popular book *The Power of Positive Thinking* (New York: Simon and Schuster, 1952). R. Marie Griffith theorizes that Peale's success, combined with the historical remnants of New Thought and social pressures on appearance, led to multiple publications on Christian dieting advice. Griffith, *Born Again Bodies: Flesh and Spirit in American Christianity* (Berkeley: University of California Press, 2004), 160–205.

30. Maxwell Maltz, *Psycho-Cybernetics* (New York: Pocket Books, 1960), 39.

31. Bill Glass, "Obsessed!," *Christian Athlete*, January 1970, 14. Carol Flake focuses on Glass in her critique of evangelicalism and sports. Flake, *Redemptorama: Culture, Politics, and the New Evangelicalism* (New York: Anchor Press, 1984), 89–114.

32. While Santa Monica's "Muscle Beach" had been popular among athletes since the 1920s and 1930s, the use of weight-training equipment became central in the late 1940s. The gym industry exploded nationwide after World War II, leading to the development of weight machines like the Universal in the late 1950s. Marla Matzer Rose, *Muscle Beach* (New York: St. Martin's, 2001), 123.

33. George Butler and Robert Fiore, *Pumping Iron* (Cinema 5 Distributing, 1977).

34. Arnold Schwarzenegger, *The Encyclopedia of Modern Bodybuilding* (New York: Simon and Schuster, 1985).

35. Arnold Schwarzenegger with Douglas Kent Hall, *Arnold: The Education of a Bodybuilder* (New York: Simon and Schuster, 1977), 32.

36. Jim Murray, *Inside Bodybuilding* (Chicago: Contemporary Books, 1978), 18 (emphasis in original).

37. Schwarzenegger and Hall, *Arnold*, 88.

38. Neal, *Handbook on Athletic Perfection*, 11.

39. Ibid., 63.

40. Warner, *Competition*, 27–28.

41. Hoffman, "Evangelicalism and the Revitalization of Religious Ritual in Sport," 119.

42. Warner, *Competition*, 78.

43. Schwarzenegger and Hall, *Arnold*, 16.

44. Charles Gaines and George Butler, *Pumping Iron: The Art and Sport of Bodybuilding* (New York: Simon and Schuster, 1974), 48. In the 1977 documentary film by the same name, Schwarzenegger is even more explicit in equating the pump to an orgasm. "It's as satisfying to me as coming is, you know as having sex with a woman and coming. So, can you believe how much I am in heaven? I am getting the feeling of coming in the gym, I am getting the feeling of coming at home, I am getting the feeling of coming backstage when I pump up, when I pose out in front of 5,000 people, I get the same feeling. So, I am coming day and night. I mean, it's terrific, right. So, I mean, I am in heaven." When Butler made the documentary, he tried to re-create many of the quotations he had included in the book *Pumping Iron*. It is likely that Butler prompted Schwarzenegger to reiterate his description of the pump as orgasm, and Schwarzenegger likely exaggerated this connection for the camera.

45. See, for example, Serinity Young, *Courtesans and Tantric Consorts: Sexualities in Buddhist Narrative, Iconography, and Ritual* (New York: Routledge, 2004); Walter Stephens, *Demon Lovers: Witchcraft, Sex, and the Crisis of Belief* (Chicago: University of Chicago Press, 2002); Ioan P. Couliano, *Eros and Magic in the Renaissance* (Chicago: University of Chicago Press, 1987); David J. Hufford, *The Terror That Comes in the Night: An Experience-Centered Study of Supernatural Assault Traditions* (Philadelphia: University of Pennsylvania Press, 1982); Paul

Deane, *Sex and the Paranormal: Human Sexual Encounters with the Supernatural* (London: Vega, 2003); Jeffrey J. Kripal, *Roads of Excess, Palaces of Wisdom: Eroticism and Reflexivity in the Study of Mysticism* (Chicago: University of Chicago Press, 2001). Scholars have most often applied analysis of ecstatic religious experience to women, perhaps because of the long history of female mystics and saints describing religious encounters in sexual terms. Linda Hurcombe, ed., *Sex and God: Some Varieties of Women's Religious Experience* (New York: Routledge, 1987); Ioan M. Lewis, *Ecstatic Religion: An Anthropological Study of Spirit Possession and Shamanism* (London: Routledge, 1989). Peter Gardella has noted the sensual/sexual tones of religious rebirth narratives in nineteenth-century and early twentieth-century evangelicalism, focusing on women in these movements. Gardella, *Innocent Ecstasy: How Christianity Gave America an Ethic of Sexual Pleasure* (New York: Oxford University Press, 1985). In addition to the focus on female religious ecstasy, scholars have noted a tendency to conflate emotionalism and African American religious experiences. See, for example, Jerma Jackson, *Singing in My Soul: Black Gospel Music in a Secular Age* (Chapel Hill: University of North Carolina Press, 2004); Glenn Hinson, *Fire in My Bones: Transcendence and the Holy Spirit in African-American Gospel* (Philadelphia: University of Pennsylvania Press, 2000); Clarence Taylor, *The Black Churches of Brooklyn* (New York: Columbia University Press, 1994).

46. Angelika Malinar and Helene Basu, "Ecstasy," in *The Oxford Handbook of Religion and Emotion*, ed. John Corrigan (Oxford: Oxford University Press, 2008), 246.

47. Nils G. Holm, ed., *Religious Ecstasy* (Stockholm: Almquist and Wiksell, 1982).

48. Catherine of Siena, *Dialogue of the Soul*, excerpted in *Invitation to Christian Spirituality: An Ecumenical Anthology*, ed. John R. Tyson (New York: Oxford University Press, 1999), 183.

49. Saint Teresa of Avila, *The Interior Castle*, excerpted in *Introduction to Christian Spirituality*, 260.

50. Lynn Neal, *Romancing God: Evangelical Women and Inspirational Fiction* (Chapel Hill: University of North Carolina Press, 2006), 164.

51. Jeffrey J. Kripal, "Sexuality and the Erotic," in *The Oxford Handbook of Religion and Emotion*, ed. John Corrigan (Oxford: Oxford University Press, 2008), 172–173.

52. By describing this pain as masculine, I do not mean to imply that only men have access to these sensations. However, I do wish to argue that for men and women, sporting pain is a masculinizing experience. Scholarship on female bodybuilding explores the idea of women using weight training to access masculine pleasures that historically have been reserved for men. See Leslie Heywood, *Bodymakers: A Cultural Anatomy of Women's Bodybuilding* (New Brunswick, NJ: Rutgers University Press, 1998).

53. Neal, *Handbook on Athletic Perfection*, 88.

54. Ibid.

55. Ibid., 89.

56. Ibid., 32.

57. William Hoverd points out parallels between Christlike suffering and modern weight training in his book *Working Out My Salvation: The Contemporary Gym and the Promise of "Self" Transformation* (New York: Meyer and Meyer Sport, 2005), 101–102.

58. Michael Messner, *Taking the Field: Women, Men, and Sports* (Minneapolis: University of Minnesota Press, 2002), 120–121.

59. Leslie Heywood and Shari Dworkin, *Built to Win: The Female Athlete as Cultural Icon* (Minneapolis: University of Minnesota Press, 2003).

60. The Bible verse that M.J. referenced here was most likely 1 Peter 1:8 (NIV), which reads, "Though you have not seen him, you love him; and even though you do not see him now, you believe in him and are filled with an inexpressible and glorious joy."

61. William James, *The Varieties of Religious Experience* (New York: Image Books, 1978), 371.

CHAPTER 3

1. Marcel Mauss, "Techniques of the Body," in *Sociology and Psychology: Essays*, trans. Ben Brewster (London: Routledge, 1979), 95–123.

2. For some scholarship on the role of the devil in the history of evangelical Christianity, see Christine Leigh Heyrman, *Southern Cross: The Beginnings of the Bible Belt* (Chapel Hill: University of North Carolina Press, 1998); Bill Ellis, *Raising the Devil: Satanism, New Religions, and the Media* (Lexington: University Press of Kentucky, 2000).

3. Embodied suffering has a long history in the Christian tradition. Scholars have noted the primacy of suffering in the development of the early church. For two examples, see Elizabeth Castelli, *Martyrdom and Memory: Early Christian Culture Making* (New York: Columbia University Press, 2004); Judith Perkins, *The Suffering Self: Pain and Narrative Representation in the Early Christian Church* (New York: Routledge, 1995).

4. FCA and other sports ministry organizations have mined many Bible verses for their application to athletics. Subsequent FCA camp programming has used Philippians 3:13–14 ("Brothers, I do not consider myself to have taken hold of it. But one thing I do: forgetting what is behind and reaching to what is ahead, I pursue as my goal the prize promised by God's heavenly call in Christ Jesus" [HCSB]) for the 2008 theme "Get Focused"; Romans 12:2 ("Do not be con-formed to this age, but be transformed by the renewing of your mind, so that you may discern what is the good, pleasing, and perfect will of God" [HCSB]) for the 2009 theme "Inside Out"; Colossians 1:11 ("May you be strengthened with all power, according to His glorious might, for all endurance and patience, and with joy" [HCSB]) for the 2010 theme "Unleash the Power: Strengthen Your Core"; and Acts 2:36 ("Therefore let all the house of Israel know with certainty that God has made this Jesus, whom you crucified, both Lord and Messiah!" [HCSB]) for the 2011 theme "Game Changer: Make a Play." As noted in the

previous chapter, sports ministry resources often emphasize particular verses to create a vision of Christian athleticism. The Pauline Epistles feature prominently in this literature.

5. On embattlement as a central component of evangelical identity, see Smith, *American Evangelicalism.*

6. Giorgio Agamben, *State of Exception*, trans. Kevin Attell (Chicago: University of Chicago Press, 2005), 22. In a previous work, Agamben argued that modern politics "cannot be grasped if it is not understood as necessarily implying the difference between the two terms: the *police* now becomes *politics*, and the care of life coincides with the fight against the enemy." Agamben, *Homo Sacer: Sovereign Power and Bare Life*, trans. Daniel Heller-Roazan (Stanford, CA: Stanford University Press, 1998), 147.

7. Melissa Conroy, "An Army of One? Subject, Signifier, and the Symbolic," in *The Sleeping Giant Has Awoken: The New Politics of Religion in the United States*, ed. Jeffrey W. Robbins and Neal Magee (New York: Continuum Books, 2008), 184.

8. On this rhetoric and its implementation, see Donald E. Pease, *The New American Exceptionalism* (Minneapolis: University of Minnesota Press, 2009), especially chap. 5; John Robert Greene, "Crusade: The Rhetorical Presidency of George W. Bush," in *The Second Term of George W. Bush: Prospects and Perils,* ed. Robert Maranto, Douglas Brattebo, and Tom Lansford (New York: Palgrave Macmillan, 2006), 101–114.

9. David Harvey, *A Brief History of Neoliberalism* (Oxford: Oxford University Press, 2005), 197.

10. Clayton Crockett, "Jeb Stuart's Revenge: The Civil War, the Religious Right, and American Fascism," in *The Sleeping Giant Has Awoken: The New Politics of Religion in the United States*, ed. Jeffrey W. Robbins and Neal Magee (New York: Continuum Books, 2008), 93.

11. Jason Bivins, *Religion of Fear: The Politics of Horror in Conservative Evangelicalism* (New York: Oxford University Press, 2008), 230.

12. This was not the only time that conservative Christians used this sort of rhetoric. On competitive rhetoric in the fundamentalist/modernist controversy of the 1920s, see George Marsden, *Fundamentalism and American Culture* (New York: Oxford University Press, 2006); Adam Laats, *Fundamentalism and Education in the Scopes Era: God, Darwin, and the Roots of America's Culture Wars* (New York: Palgrave Macmillan, 2010); Susan A. Maurer, "A Historical Overview of American Christian Fundamentalism in the Twentieth Century," in *Fundamentalisms and the Media*, ed. Stewart M. Hoover and Nadia Kaneva (London: Continuum, 2009), 54–72. On competitive rhetoric in the formation of the Moral Majority, see Harding, *Book of Jerry Falwell*; Monique El-Faizy, *God and Country: How Evangelicals Have Become America's New Mainstream* (New York: Bloomsbury, 2006); Gabriel A. Almond, R. Scott Appleby, and Emmanuel Sivan, "Wrestling with the World: Fundamentalist Movements as Emergent Systems," in *Strong Religion: The Rise of Fundamentalisms around the World* (Chicago: University of

Chicago Press, 2003), 145–190; Sara Diamond, *Spiritual Warfare: The Politics of the Christian Right* (Boston: South End Press, 1989).

13. Elizabeth Castelli, "Persecution Complexes: Identity Politics and the 'War on Christians,'" *differences: A Journal of Feminist Cultural Studies* 18 (2007): 165. See also William Connolly, "The Evangelical-Capitalist Resonance Machine," *Political Theory* 33 (2005): 869–886; Melissa Deckman, *School Board Battles: The Christian Right in Local Politics* (Washington, DC: Georgetown University Press, 2004); Kirsten Isgro, "Conservative Christian Spokespeople in Mainstream U.S. News Media," in *Fundamentalisms and the Media*, ed. Stewart M. Hoover and Nadia Kaneva (London: Continuum, 2009), 94–108; Victoria Clark, *Allies for Armageddon: The Rise of Christian Zionism* (New Haven, CT: Yale University Press, 2007), 256–283; Rhys H. Williams, "Politicized Evangelicalism and Secular Elites: Creating a Moral Order," in *Evangelicals and Democracy in America*, vol. 2, *Religion and Politics,* ed. Steven Brint and Jean Reith Schroedel (New York: Russell Sage Foundation, 2009), 143–178.

14. *Dave Kubal, Dan Britton, Danny Burns, and Bethany Hermes,* "FCA's Game Plan," in *God's Game Plan: The Athlete's Bible* (Nashville, TN: Serendipity House, 2007), 1350.

15. The huddle I observed was composed of female high school athletes. These struggles indicate a gendered component that I investigate more thoroughly in part II of the book.

16. Kubal et al., "FCA's Game Plan," 1351.

17. Catherine Bell, *Ritual Theory, Ritual Practice* (New York: Oxford University Press, 1992), 221.

18. My thinking on becoming Christlike is deeply influenced by the work of Gilles Deleuze and Felix Guattari on "becoming." They write, "Becoming is not to imitate or identify with something or someone. Nor is it to proportion formal relations. Neither of these two figures of analogy is applicable to becoming: neither the imitation of a subject nor the proportionality of a form. Starting with the forms one has, the subject one is, the organs one has, or the functions one fulfills, becoming is to extract particles between which one establishes the relations of movement and rest, speed and slowness that are *closest* to what one is becoming, and through which one becomes." Gilles Deleuze and Felix Guattari, *A Thousand Plateaus: Capitalism and Schizophrenia*, trans. Brian Massumi (Minneapolis: University of Minnesota Press, 1987), 272 (emphasis in original). When applied to becoming Christlike, Deleuze and Guattari can help to clarify that this is not a full identification—one does not become Christ—but it is instead a process of proximity and alliance that connects the believer to Christ through behavior and action. This idea of becoming is also present in Deleuze and Guattari's previous collaborative work, *Anti-Oedipus: Capitalism and Schizophrenia*, trans. Robert Hurley, Mark Seem, and Helen R. Lane (Minneapolis: University of Minnesota Press, 1983).

19. See chapter 2.

20. "Athletes in Action Fall Tour Blog," November 3, 2007.

21. FCA offers programming for children beginning at age five, and many youth athletes in the United States are familiar with evangelical involvement in sport. For explorations of the role of children in constructing and maintaining religious and political ideology, see Lawrence Grossberg, *Caught in the Crossfire: Kids, Politics, and America's Future* (Boulder, CO: Paradigm, 2005); Susan Ridgely Bales, *When I Was a Child: Children's Interpretations of First Communion* (Chapel Hill: University of North Carolina Press, 2009).

CHAPTER 4

1. William James Hoverd, *Working Out My Salvation: The Contemporary Gym and the Promise of Self-Transformation* (London: Meyer and Meyer, 2004), 46–48.

2. Mariah Burton-Nelson, *The Stronger Women Get, the More Men Love Football: Sexism and the American Culture of Sports* (New York: Quill, 1995); Pamela Grundy and Susan Shackelford, *Shattering the Glass: The Remarkable History of Women's Basketball* (Chapel Hill: University of North Carolina Press, 2007); Eileen McDonagh and Laura Pappano, *Playing with the Boys: Why Separate Is Not Equal in Sports* (New York: Oxford University Press, 2009).

3. Joan Ryan, *Little Girls in Pretty Boxes: The Making and Breaking of Elite Gymnasts and Figure Skaters* (New York: Warner Books, 2000); Jill Neimark, "Out of Bounds: The Truth about Athletes and Rape," in *Sport in Contemporary Society: An Anthology*, ed. D. Stanley Eitzen (Boulder, CO: Paradigm, 2005), 180–186. Gay men who are athletes challenge prevalent understandings of masculinity and prevalent understandings of homosexuality. Celia Brackenridge, Ian Rivers, Brendon Gough, and Karen Llewellyn, "Driving Down Participation: Homophobic Bullying as a Deterrent to Doing Sport," in *Sports and Gender Identities: Masculinities, Femininities and Sexualities*, ed. Cara Carmichael Aitchison (London: Routledge, 2007), 122–139; Dan Woog, *Jocks: True Stories of America's Gay Male Athletes* (Los Angeles: Alyson, 1996); Erick Alvarez, *Muscle Boys: Gay Gym Culture* (New York: Routledge, 2007).

4. Judith Butler, *Gender Trouble* (New York: Routledge, 1990); Butler, *Bodies That Matter: On the Discursive Limits of "Sex"* (New York: Routledge, 1993); Butler, *Giving an Account of Oneself* (New York: Fordham University Press, 2003).

5 Butler, *Bodies That Matter*, 2. As Catherine Bell has pointed out, the use of the term "performance" within religious studies has been ambiguous. She notes, "Religious studies uses the language of performance to stress the execution of a preexisting script for activity (as in conducting a traditional church service) or the explicitly unscripted dimension of an activity in process (as in the spirit or quality of the service)." See "Performance," in *Critical Terms for Religious Studies*, ed. Mark C. Taylor (Chicago: University of Chicago Press, 1998), 205–206.

6. For a critical analysis of Sarah Palin's role in conservative Christian circles, see Ronnee Schreiber, "Dilemmas of Representation: Conservative and Feminist Women's Organizations React to Sarah Palin," in *Women of the Right: Comparisons and Interplay across Borders*, ed. Kathleen M. Blee and Sandra

McGee Deutsch (University Park: Penn State University Press, 2012); for an analysis of Republican female reactions to Phyllis Schlafly, see Catherine E. Rymph, *Republican Women: Feminism and Conservatism from Suffrage through the Rise of the New Right* (Chapel Hill: University of North Carolina Press, 2006).

7. Phyllis Schlafly, "What's Wrong with 'Equal Rights' for Women?," *Phyllis Schlafly Report* 5, no. 7 (1972): 1–4.

8. Betty Friedan, *The Feminine Mystique* (New York: Dell, 1964).

9. Donald Critchlow, *Phyllis Schlafly and Grassroots Conservatism: A Woman's Crusade* (Princeton, NJ: Princeton University Press, 2005), 218.

10. Ibid., 221.

11. Suzanne Venker and Phyllis Schlafly, *The Flipside of Feminism: What Conservative Women Know—And Men Can't Say* (Washington, DC: WND Books, 2011), 55.

12. On the idea of "nature" as a cultural construct, see Bruno Latour *Politics of Nature: How to Bring the Sciences into Democracy*, trans. Catherine Porter (Cambridge, MA: Harvard University Press, 2004). On the use of "nature" in constructions of gender, see Donna Haraway, *Primate Visions: Gender, Race, and Nature in the World of Modern Science* (New York: Routledge, 1989).

13. Venker and Schlafly, *The Flipside of Feminism*, 42.

14. Ibid., 11.

15. Female-led temperance campaigns of the late nineteenth and early twentieth centuries demonstrate a similar trend and decried alcohol as a threat to the family. However, many of the same women who were organizing temperance campaigns also organized for women's suffrage, whereas Phyllis Schlafly and STOP ERA used rhetoric of family to fight against equal rights and responsibilities for women. On the overlap between the temperance and women's suffrage movements, see Naomi Rosenthal, Meryl Fingrutd, Michele Ethier, Roberta Karant, and David McDonald, "Social Movements and Network Analysis," *American Journal of Sociology* 90 (1985): 1022–1054; Gaines M. Foster, *Moral Reconstruction: Christian Lobbyists and the Federal Legislation of Morality, 1865–1920* (Chapel Hill: University of North Carolina Press, 2007).

16. Chad Bonham, "D-Nasty Sunshine," *Sharing the Victory*, August/September 2010, http://archives.fca.org/vsItemDisplay.lsp?method=display&objectid=001 72C64-C29A-EE7A-E04D1CBA0C19C4D2 (accessed August 9, 2013).

17. The formation of the Commission on Intercollegiate Athletics for Women (CIAW) in 1966 and its successor, the Association for Intercollegiate Athletics for Women (AIAW), founded in 1971, drew attention to athletic inequalities at the college level. "At a typical mid-western university in the Big Ten Conference, men's athletics received thirteen hundred dollars for every dollar spent on the women's program. A mid-Atlantic university allocated nineteen hundred dollars for women's sport while granting men's athletics over two million dollars. On the West Coast, Washington State University appropriated less than 1 percent of its two-million-dollar athletic budget for women's sports." Susan K. Cahn, *Coming on Strong: Gender and Sexuality in Twentieth-Century Women's Sport* (New York:

Free Press, 1994), 250. At the professional level, women's earnings were often a small percentage of men's for the same sport. This was due in large part to the limited exposure of women's athletics, with NBC and CBS dedicating less than 2 percent of their athletic coverage to women's sports. Bill Gilbert and Nancy Williamson, "Sport Is Unfair to Women," *Sports Illustrated*, May 28, 1973, 90–91.

18. Title IX reads in part, "No person in the United States shall, on the basis of sex, be excluded from participation in, be denied the benefits of, or be subjected to discrimination under any educational programs or activities receiving federal financial assistance." Quoted in Cahn, *Coming on Strong*, 250.

19. Several factors made Title IX difficult to implement. The most important indication of compliance with Title IX is the measure of an institution's "substantive proportionality." This means that there should be the same ratio of female athletes to female students as there are male athletes to male students. Researchers have found that institutions with football teams and with high rates of female enrollment generally have more difficulty complying with Title IX. Despite these difficulties, by moving toward Title IX compliance, high schools, colleges, and universities have dramatically expanded athletic opportunities for women. See Deborah J. Anderson, John J. Cheslock, and Ronald G. Ehrenberg, "Gender Equity in Intercollegiate Athletics: Determinants of Title IX Compliance," *Journal of Higher Education* 77 (2006): 225–250.

20. Heywood and Dworkin, *Built to Win*, xxi.

21. David Andrews points out that every Olympic Games could make a similar claim because female Olympic participation continues to increase. Andrews, *Sport-Commerce-Culture: Essays on Sport in Late Capitalist America* (New York: Peter Lang, 2006), 53–65.

22. "FIFA Women's World Cup—USA 1999," http://www.fifa.com/tournaments/archive/tournament=103/edition=4644/overview.html (accessed July 1, 2007).

23. Heywood and Dworkin, *Built to Win*, xvi.

24. Yvonne Tasker, *Spectacular Bodies: Gender, Genre, and the Action Cinema* (New York: Routledge, 1993), 141.

25. Tiffany Muller, "The Contested Terrain of the Women's National Basketball Association Arena," in *Sports and Gender Identities: Masculinities, Femininities and Sexualities*, ed. Cara Carmichael Aitchison (London: Routledge, 2007), 43.

26. Heywood and Dworkin, *Built to Win*, 46, 49.

27. As Ann Braude points out, feminization is a long-standing myth in the narrative of U.S. religious history. The traditional narrative follows the decline of church power in the colonial period with disestablishment, the feminization of the church through a majority female membership and sentimental clergy in the Victorian period, and secularization in the twentieth century. In response to claims of feminization, Braude points out that women were the majority of churchgoers during all three of these periods. Construing the Victorian period as one of feminization reflects the fears and attitudes of male spokespeople, not church attendance demographics. Braude, "Women's Religious History Is

American Religious History," in *Retelling U.S. Religious History*, ed. Thomas A. Tweed and Laurie F. Maffly-Kipp (Berkeley: University of California Press, 1997), 87–107.

28. Deb Hoffman, Julie Caldwell, and Kathy Schultz, *Experiencing God's Power for Female Athletes: How to Compete, Knowing and Doing the Will of God* (Grand Island, NE: Cross Training, 1999), 76.

29. Ibid., 45 (emphasis in original).

30. Ibid., 51.

31. Ibid., 54.

32. Julie Byrne's work on midcentury female Catholic basketball players emphasizes that these women felt an obligation to their religious community to affirm the value of female modesty and demonstrate feminine attractiveness. The first national college championship women's basketball team, the Immaculata Mighty Macs, wore makeup and jewelry (when it was permitted) and had long hair tied back with ribbons or bows around their ponytails. Because these women represented Catholic women on a national stage, they were aware of the potential impact of the impression they were making; they wanted to win, but they also wanted to appear on the court in a way that affirmed gender expectations. Byrne, *O God of Players*, 108–109.

33. Hoffman, Caldwell, and Schultz, *Experiencing God's Power for Female Athletes*, 77.

34. Ibid., 60.

35. Ibid., 67.

36. Ibid., 78.

37. Laura Mulvey, "Visual Pleasure and Narrative Cinema," *Screen* 16, no. 3 (1975): 6–18.

38. Like the AIA's team, this team was also interracial but with a higher ratio of white athletes than on most elite women's basketball teams in the United States.

CHAPTER 5

1. Pat Griffin, *Strong Women, Deep Closets: Lesbians and Homophobia in Sport* (Champaign, IL: Human Kinetics, 1998); Helen Lenskyj, *Out on the Field: Gender, Sport and Sexualities* (Toronto: Women's Press, 2003).

2. Helen Lenskyj argues that lesbians in sport are doubly marginal—they are not heterosexual, and they are not male. Lenskyj, *Out on the Field*, especially chap. 3.

3. Pat Griffin, "Changing the Game: Homophobia, Sexism and Lesbians in Sport," in *Gender and Sport: A Reader*, ed. Sheila Scraton and Anne Flintoff (New York: Routledge, 2002), 193–208.

4. Luke Cyphers and Kate Fagan, "On Homophobia and Recruiting," *ESPN: The Magazine*, February 7, 2011, http://sports.espn.go.com/ncw/news/story?page=Mag 15unhealthyclimate (accessed March 6, 2014).

5. Heywood and Dworkin, *Built to Win*, especially chap. 4.

6. This is significant in the sport of female bodybuilding. See Leslie Heywood's account of female bodybuilders' self-manipulation, including breast implants, dyed hair, high-heeled shoes, and overemphasized makeup. Heywood,

Bodymakers: A Cultural Anatomy of Women's Body Building (New Brunswick, NJ: Rutgers University Press, 1998).

7. "[In 1988,] 15 percent of young Americans (born after 1965) favored marriage for same-sex couples, compared to 13 percent among the baby boomers (born between 1945 and 1965), and 9 percent among Americans born before 1945. By 2008, half of young Americans expressed support for same-sex marriage—this is 17 percentage points higher than the baby boomers, and 28 points higher than Americans born before 1945. . . . Among young people, religiosity still drives up opposition to gay marriage, but does so starting at a much lower level of opposition." Putnam and Campbell, *American Grace*, 403–404.

8. As with my understanding of becoming, the work of Deleuze and Guattari has played an important role in my understanding of desire. Deleuze and Guattari challenge psychological understandings that desire stems from lack, that humans want something only after recognizing that they don't have it. In this understanding, desire is reactionary. Deleuze and Guattari offer a different understanding of desire. Rather than as a reaction to lack, they present desire as a productive and central characteristic of being human. For them, desire exists whether or not one lacks or recognizes lack. I use the word "desire" not to imply lack but to imply a generative human condition. See Deleuze and Guattari, *A Thousand Plateaus*; Deleuze and Guattari, *Anti-Oedipus*.

9. Many liberal Protestant organizations accept homosexuality, though at varying levels. For example, some are open to congregational membership but opposed to church leadership. See Melissa Wilcox, *Coming Out in Christianity: Religion, Identity, and Community* (Bloomington: Indiana University Press, 2003); Michelle Wolkomir, *Be Not Deceived: The Sacred and Sexual Struggles of Gay and Ex-Gay Christian Men* (New Brunswick, NJ: Rutgers University Press, 2006).

10. For example, Belhaven College in Jackson, Mississippi, includes the following in its student handbook: "All relationships should reflect that of Christian character. The college upholds the institution of marriage between parties of the opposite sex as the only proper relationship for the sharing of activities of a sexual nature. Therefore, any sexual conduct not within these biblical guidelines is prohibited." Quoted in Adam Lynch, "Ceara's Season," *Jackson Free Press*, November 18, 2009, http://www.jacksonfreepress.com/index.php/site/comments/cearas_season_111809/ (accessed July 20, 2011). Belhaven belongs to an organization of Christian colleges called the Council for Christian Colleges and Universities, which has more than 100 members in North America and another 73 members in twenty-four foreign nations. While not all of these institutions police sexual behavior as explicitly as Belhaven does, the Council for Christian Colleges and Universities supports their right to do so. As it states on its website, "We place a high priority on our commitment to advocate for federal and state laws and policies, as well as for policies set by accreditation or regulatory bodies, that enable our institutions to function as Christ-centered institutions in areas such as behavioral expectations and our crucial right to hire as full-time faculty members

and administrators (non-hourly staff) only persons who profess faith in Jesus Christ." Council for Christian Colleges and Universities, "Advocacy and Public Policy," http://www.cccu.org/about/programs_and_services_office_of_the_president#Advocacy_Public_Policy (accessed July 20, 2011).

11. Janet Jakobsen and Ann Pellegrini turn this common phrase on its head in the title of their book, *Love the Sin: Sexual Regulations and the Limits of Religious Tolerance* (New York: NYU Press, 2003).

12. Pope Francis made a similar statement in a heavily covered press conference in August 2013. The pope told a group of reporters, "If a person is gay and seeks the Lord and has good will, who am I to judge him?" Translation by Zenit, http://www.zenit.org/en/articles/francis-press-conference-on-return-flight-from-brazil-part-2 (accessed August 15, 2013). This was a significant statement, but it did not overturn the official Catholic position that while homosexual attraction is not in itself sinful, homosexual acts are. Because Catholic priests are celibate, the question for ordination is not a man's sexual orientation but whether he can live a life of celibacy. This is a far different issue than Protestant ordination, particularly in conservative Christian churches where marriage and children are expected parts of a minister's life.

13. Exodus International homepage, http://www.exodus-international.org (accessed April 12, 2008).

14. Exodus International, "What 'Cures' Homosexuality?," http://exodus.to/content/view/505/186/ (accessed April 12, 2008). A search for "sports" on Exodus's main page resulted in more than ten narratives of men who turned to Exodus for help preventing and repressing same-sex attraction. All these narratives pointed to a disinterest in sport as something that set them apart from other boys/men, naturalizing the connection between gender performance (here, masculinity) and heterosexuality.

15. Exodus and other organizations with the same mission have a narrowly defined idea of homosexuality. They assume a link between sexuality and gender: women projecting femininity are therefore also projecting heterosexuality. This also assumes that the opposite is true, that a woman acting masculine is likely to experience homosexual desire. These organizations were not alone in these assumptions. In Lisa Walker's experience as a femme lesbian, she found that because she projected femininity, other lesbians treated her as an interloper in their ranks. "The femme's adaptation of what has been historically defined as a 'feminine' sexual style is tacitly constructed as evidence of her desire to pass for straight and not of her desire for other women." Lisa Walker, *Looking Like What You Are: Sexual Style, Race, and Lesbian Identity* (New York: NYU Press, 2001), 202. Interestingly, performing femininity can also result in less respect in the world of women's sports. As Kate Russell noted in her analysis of gender identities in the UK sports of rugby, cricket, and netball, "It should be recognized that women within sports also contribute to the exclusion of women who do not fit *their* ideal of what it is to be a sportswoman. One cricketer recalls how shameful it would be to be bowled out by someone she called a 'dolly bowler.' The bowler in

question was tall, slim, had long blonde hair and was not considered to be a serious competitor solely because of her physical appearance. . . . [For some,] there is as much fear exhibited by her need to avoid defeat by a 'dolly bowler' as there is for a man to avoid defeat by a 'girl.'" Kate Russell, "'Queers, Even in Netball?': Interpretations of the Lesbian Label among Sportswomen," in *Sports and Gender Identities: Masculinities, Femininities and Sexualities*, ed. Cara Carmichael Aitchison (London: Routledge, 2007), 117–118 (emphasis in original).

16. Leonard E. LeSourd, *Strong Men, Weak Men: Godly Strength and the Male Identity* (Grand Rapids, MI: Chosen Books, 1990), 50.

17. Hoffman, Caldwell, and Schultz, *Experiencing God's Power for Female Athletes*, 133.

18. Lori Rentzel, *Emotional Dependency and How to Keep Your Friendships Healthy* (Downers Grove, IL: InterVarsity Press, 1984). Pat Griffin's work describes the distribution of this pamphlet at FCA and AIA events for female coaches. Griffin, *Strong Women, Deep Closets*, chap. 7.

19. Jeanette Howard, *Out of Egypt: Leaving Lesbianism Behind* (Baltimore: Regeneration Books, 1991). This book was reprinted with the title *Out of Egypt: One Woman's Journey Out of Lesbianism* (Baltimore: Regeneration Books, 2004).

20. Jeanette Howard, *Into the Promised Land: Beyond the Lesbian Struggle* (Grand Rapids, MI: Monarch Books, 2005), 9–10.

21. Ibid., 11.

22. Ibid., 9.

23. Alan Chambers, "I Am Sorry," June 19, 2013, http://exodusinternational. org/2013/06/i-am-sorry/ (accessed August 15, 2013).

24. "Speak. Love," http://wespeaklove.org/ (accessed August 15, 2013).

25. Candace Chellew-Hodge, "Exodus 'Ex-Gay' Ministry Closes Up Shop," *Religion Dispatches*, June 20, 2013, http://www.religiondispatches.org/archive/sexandgender/7160/ (accessed August 15, 2013).

26. Famously, conservative Christians like Jerry Falwell and Pat Robertson have blamed gays and others for invoking the wrath of God and bringing on disasters like the terrorist attacks of September 11, 2001, and Hurricane Katrina. "Falwell Apologizes to Gays, Feminists, Lesbians," CNN.com/U.S., September 14, 2001, http://archives.cnn.com/2001/US/09/14/Falwell.apology/ (accessed August 15, 2013); CNN, "Pat Robertson Says Haiti Paying for 'Pact to the Devil,'" January 13, 2010, http://www.cnn.com/2010/US/01/13/haiti.pat.robertson/index.html (accessed August 15, 2013).

27. Candace Chellew-Hodge, *Bulletproof Faith: A Spiritual Survival Guide for Gay and Lesbian Christians* (San Francisco: Jossey-Bass, 2008), 12–13.

28. Rentzel, *Emotional Dependency*, 10–11, 27.

29. Susie Magill and Yvette Schneider, "Out of the Alternative," *Sharing the Victory*, http://www.sharingthevictory.com/vsItemDisplay.lsp?method=display&objectid= D3ADE24F-3516-4869-B8BB698F54235125 (accessed October 8, 2008).

30. In Romans 1:18–32, Paul describes humans who have turned their backs on God and the shamefulness of their sexual behavior. Conservative Christians often cite

this passage to argue that homosexuality is contrary to God's will. Romans 1:26–27 (NIV) reads, "Because of this, God gave them over to shameful lusts. Even their women exchanged natural sexual relations for unnatural ones. In the same way the men also abandoned natural relations with women and were inflamed with lust for one another. Men committed shameful acts with other men, and received in themselves the due penalty for their error." In response to the claim that the Bible condemns homosexuality, Chellew-Hodge argues that the Bible highlights three main instances of sexual immorality: adultery, prostitution, and rape. She notes that the Bible contains heterosexual instances of all of these immoralities but that heterosexuality as a whole is not condemned. Chellew-Hodge, *Bulletproof Faith*, xi–xii.

31. Pat Griffin explores the phenomenon of closeted female athletes in her book *Strong Women, Deep Closets*. The military is similar in its unstated demand for closeting. See Craig A. Rimmerman, ed., *Gay Rights, Military Wrongs: Political Perspectives on Lesbians and Gays in the Military* (New York: Routledge, 1996); Gregory M. Herek, Jared B. Jobe, and Ralph M. Carney, eds., *Out in Force: Sexual Orientation and the Military* (Chicago: University of Chicago Press, 1996). As queer writer and activist Victoria Brownworth notes, "The closet is the most important tool in the reinforcing of homophobia in our society, and that homophobia is cyclical in nature: the deeper one is closeted, the more fearful one is of being outed; the more power outing has, the safer the closet seems." Brownworth, *Too Queer: Essays from a Radical Life* (Ithaca, NY: Firebrand Books, 1996), 73.

CHAPTER 6

1. For some analyses of the importance of marriage for evangelicals, see John P. Bartkowski, "Changing of the Gods: The Gender and Family Discourse of American Evangelicalism in Historical Perspective," *History of the Family* 3, no. 1 (1998), 95–116; Bartkowski, *Remaking the Godly Marriage: Gender Negotiation in Evangelical Families* (New Brunswick, NJ: Rutgers University Press, 2001); Sally K. Gallagher, *Evangelical Identity and Gendered Family Life* (New Brunswick, NJ: Rutgers University Press, 2003); W. Bradford Wilcox, *Soft Patriarchs, New Men: How Christianity Shapes Fathers and Husbands* (Chicago: University of Chicago Press, 2004).

2. Rebecca Davis, *More Perfect Unions: The American Search for Marital Bliss* (Cambridge, MA: Harvard University Press, 2010), 256.

3. Ibid., 258–259.

4. On evangelicalism and family, see Heather Hendershot, *Shaking the World for Jesus: Media and Conservative Evangelical Culture* (Chicago: University of Chicago Press, 2004); Anthony Guerra, *Family Matters: The Role of Christianity in the Formation of the Western Family* (St. Paul, MN: Paragon House, 2002); Rosemary Radford Reuther, *Christianity and the Making of the Modern Family* (Boston: Beacon Press, 2000).

5. Gallagher, *Evangelical Identity and Gendered Family Life*, 171. In a similar vein, Christian Smith argued that mechanisms of distinction have allowed evangelicalism to thrive in the United States. Smith, *American Evangelicalism*.

6. Clay Meyer, "The Cove," *Sharing the Victory*, June/July 2009, http://www.sharingthevictory.com/vsItemDisplay.lsp&objectID=7DB9D890-C29A-EE7A-E38DFB7448635ECA&method=display (accessed July 15, 2011).

7. Jill Ewert, "The Richt Way," *Sharing the Victory*, October 2010, http://www.sharingthevictory.com/vsItemDisplay.lsp?method=display&objectid=309F3BF2-C29A-EE7A-E1AB2075AD260F67 (accessed July 15, 2011).

8. As noted in chapter 2, some medieval Christian women framed their spiritual lives as a marriage to Jesus and lived lives of celibacy. See, for example, Dyan Elliot, *The Bride of Christ Goes to Hell: Metaphor and Embodiment in the Lives of Pious Women, 200–1500* (Philadelphia: University of Pennsylvania Press, 2012). However, this positioning of Jesus was not common in postwar evangelicalism, and it was not until women began to outnumber men in sports ministry during the 1990s that Christian athletes (female and male) began to frame marriage as less important than one's relationship with Jesus.

9. Conservative Christians have long argued for a causal relationship between consuming pornography and sex crimes. See Whitney Strub, *Perversion for Profit: The Politics of Pornography and the Rise of the New Right* (New York: Columbia University Press, 2010).

10. Mariah Burton Nelson points out that presenting athletics as a realm of male superiority ignores sports in which women consistently outperform men, such as long-distance swimming and running. See Nelson, *The Stronger Women Get, the More Men Love Football: Sexism and the American Culture of Sports* (New York: Avon Books, 1995). Michael Messner argues that the age at which boys and girls are separated athletically is when girls are, for the most part, taller and stronger than boys. He points out that separating boys and girls at that age prevents boys from experiencing outperformance by girls, which would challenge cultural assumptions that males are athletically superior to females. Messner, *Taking the Field*.

11. Scholars have argued that new economic and social realities in the 1990s contributed to the Promise Keepers' appeal. Globalization and deindustrialization led to decreased job security, and second-wave feminists had succeeded in instituting legislation protecting a woman's right to an abortion, equal pay for equal work, and equal access to federal funding in public institutions. These laws resulted in a growing female labor force, contributing further to decreased job security for men in the United States. See L. Dean Allen, *Rise Up, O Men of God: The "Men and Religion Forward Movement" and the "Promise Keepers"* (Mercer, GA: Mercer University Press, 2002).

12. These seven promises are: "A Promise Keeper is committed to honoring Jesus Christ through worship, prayer and obedience to God's Word in the power of the Holy Spirit; A Promise Keeper is committed to pursuing vital relationships with a

few other men, understanding that he needs brothers to help him keep his promises; A Promise Keeper is committed to practicing spiritual, moral, ethical, and sexual purity; A Promise Keeper is committed to building strong marriages and families through love, protection and biblical values; A Promise Keeper is committed to supporting the mission of his church by honoring and praying for his pastor, and by actively giving his time and resources; A Promise Keeper is committed to reaching beyond any racial and denominational barriers to demonstrate the power of biblical unity; and A Promise Keeper is committed to influencing his world, being obedient to the Great Commandment (Mark 12:30–31 NIV) and the Great Commission (Matthew 28:19–20 NIV)." Promise Keepers, "7 Promises," http://www.promisekeepers.org/about/7-promises (accessed April 17, 2013).

13. Becky Beal, "The Promise Keepers' Use of Sport in Defining 'Christlike' Masculinity," in *The Promise Keepers: Essays on Masculinity and Christianity*, ed. Dane Claussen (Jefferson, NC: McFarland, 2000), 153–163.

14. John P. Bartkowski, "Breaking Walls, Raising Fences: Masculinity, Intimacy, and Accountability among the Promise Keepers," *Sociology of Religion* 61 (2000): 33.

15. Bartkowski, *Remaking the Godly Marriage*, 59.

16. Steve Farrar, *Point Man: How a Man Can Lead His Family* (Portland, OR: Multnomah, 1990).

17. Bartkowski, *Remaking the Godly Marriage*, 164.

18. Cahn, *Coming on Strong*, 224.

19. Kathleen Kaiser, "Men of Destiny," *Athletes in Action*, Fall 1982, 25.

20. Catherine Lucas, "The Swinging Nun," *Christian Athlete*, October 1970, 12–13.

21. Skip Stogsdill, "A Woman for All Seasons," *Christian Athlete*, November 1970, 12.

22. Ibid., 14.

23. Ibid., 17.

24. Chris Steckel, "Behind the Bench Exclusive," *Sharing the Victory*, January/February 2006, http://www.fca.org/BehindtheBench/Articles/2006JanFeb.lsp (accessed October 8, 2008).

25. Ibid.

26. Alex Kendrick, dir. *Facing the Giants* (Carmel Entertainment, 2006).

27. Kirk Noonan, "A Giant Vision," *New Man*, November/December 2006, 29.

28. Financial statistics can be found at the Internet Movie Database, http://www.imdb.com/title/tt0805526/business (accessed October 4, 2009). The movie was rated PG instead of G because of its religious themes. According to the Motion Picture Association of America, "Religious movies that advocate for their religion or one type of religion or are proselytizing for one religion vis-a-vis other religions tend to get a PG [in order to advise] the parents that there is something in the film that you should examine further before you take your children." See "Facing the Giants MPAA Controversy," http://www.carmelentertainmentgroup.com/News/C15A8EF0-CC2F-4447-BD1B-E33F041A198C.html (accessed October 4, 2009).

29. Noonan, "Giant Vision," 32.

30. Clay Meyer, "Linked," *Sharing the Victory*, May 2011, http://www.sharingthevic-tory.com/vsItemDisplay.lsp?method=display&objectid=A2CFB 0EC-C29A-EE7A-E7B45409AB50D2CA (accessed July 14, 2011).

31. Ritchie McKay, "My Wife, My Teammate: A Behind the Bench Exclusive," *Sharing the Victory*, June 2009, http://www.sharingthevictory.com/vsItemDisplay.lsp&objectID=AE87B5F9–16EF-4137–895C8CD400C8D11D&method=display (accessed June 14, 2011).

32. Sara Hall, "My Story," *Sharing the Victory*, October 2011, http://www.sharingthevictory.com/vsItemDisplay.lsp?method=display&objectid=3110 88F3-C29A-EE7A-E2A9CACB4E3701E4 (accessed June 14, 2011).

33. Heywood and Dworkin, *Built to Win*, xxi.

34. Jill Ewert, "Dating Game," *Sharing the Victory*, January/February 2011, http://www.sharingthevictory.com/vsPrintPage.lsp?OriginalPageOID=B2A8DB4D-0F3E-45D4–9B79C98A0F15CEB8&METHOD=display&OBJECTID=1F72A 0BF-C29A-EE7A-E8515DAB8E0D2327 (accessed July 15, 2011).

35. For explorations of women's uses of submission in conservative Christian culture, see Griffith, *God's Daughters*; Julie Ingersoll, *Evangelical Christian Women: War Stories in the Gender Battles* (New York: NYU Press, 2003); Brenda E. Brasher, *Godly Women: Fundamentalism and Female Power* (New Brunswick, NJ: Rutgers University Press, 1997).

36. Putnam and Campbell, *American Grace*, 237.

37. Ibid., 240.

38. Ibid., 241.

CONCLUSION

1. Fellowship of Christian Athletes, "2013 Ministry Report," http://www.fca.org/2014/02/10/2013-ministry-report/#.U6GwXI1dWn8 (accessed June 18, 2014).

2. Athletes in Action "Campus Ministry," https://www.athletesinaction.org/campus; Athletes in Action, "Pro Ministries," https://www.athletesinaction.org/pro; Athletes in Action, "Global Sports," https://www.athletesinaction.org/global-sports (accessed June 18, 2014).

3. For a critique of this approach, see Courtney Bender, "Pluralism and Secularism," in *Religion on the Edge: De-centering and Re-centering the Sociology of Religion*, ed. Courtney Bender, Wendy Cadge, Peggy Levitt, and David Smilde (New York: Oxford University Press, 2012), 137–158.

4. Putnam and Campbell, *American Grace*.

5. Smith, *American Evangelicalism*.

6. Quoted in Coakley, *Sport in Society*, 470.

7. Deford, "The Word According to Tom," 55.

8. Ibid., 65.

9. Cynthia Burack, *Sin, Sex, and Democracy: Antigay Rhetoric and the Christian Right* (Albany: State University of New York Press, 2008); Bartkowski, *Remaking the Godly Marriage*; Gallagher, *Evangelical Identity and Gendered Family Life*; J.

Brooks Flippen, *Jimmy Carter, the Politics of Family, and the Rise of the Religious Right* (Athens: University of Georgia Press, 2011).

10. Rather than positioning women as oppressed by their tradition's gender expectations, it is important to explore how women use gendered behaviors to their own advantage. A seminal example of this kind of work is Saba Mahmood's *Politics of Piety: The Islamic Revival and the Feminist Subject* (Princeton, NJ: Princeton University Press, 2005). Mahmood notes that, contrary to some feminist understandings, there is nothing intrinsic to women that predisposes them to resist conservative gender values. Mahmood points out that conservative Muslim women in Egypt use their piety as grounds for increasing their geographic mobility, lessening their domestic responsibilities, and increasing their political voice, but they do so within a conservative gender paradigm that they regard as essential to their faith. Mahmood's work on women in Islamist movements challenges the assumption that human agency comes only in the form of resistance to oppressive regimes.

INDEX

abortion, 5, 109, 112, 114, 163, 219n11

advertising. *See* witnessing: influence of advertising on

Afghanistan. *See* war

Agamben, Giorgio, 82–84

ambivalence, 131, 137–138, 141, 156

America: and embattlement, 83–84 (*see also* embattlement); as idealized moral model, 83–84. *See also* evangelical Christianity: and American popular culture

altar call. *See* evangelical Christian practices: altar call

apocalypticism, 84

Association for Intercollegiate Athletics for Women (AIAW), 212–213n17

Athletes in Action (AIA): headquarters, 15; history, 7, 39–40, 43–46, 56, 65; major activities, 3, 7, 100, 165, 183, 187; mission, 2; University of North Carolina-Chapel Hill, chapter 1–2, 11–15, 119, 157–158; women's basketball fall tour (2007), 17, 44, 88–100, 126–128

Athletes in Action Magazine, 17

Athletes in Action people: Abby, 48, 93–95, 97, 127; Ann, 2, 14–15; Dana, 1–2, 11–15, 22–23; Jenna, 91–92, 94; Laura, 92, 94–97, 100; Maria, 92–93, 127; Stacey, 90–96, 99–100, 189; Tanya, 93–94, 96–97, 100; Tina, 48, 88–91, 126–127, 169; Tom, 1–2, 12–15, 157

Baker, William, 204n7

baptism. *See* evangelical Christian practices: baptism

Bartkowski, John, 163–164, 168

baseball (sport), 7, 57

Baseball Chapel, 7

basketball (sport), 17, 46–47, 88–100, 113–114, 116–117, 119–120, 142, 171, 173–174, 183, 214n32

Basu, Helene, 69

Beal, Becky, 163

beauty: American cultural standards of, 104, 121–123. *See also* female athletes: and body image; femininity markers

Belhaven College, 8, 215–216n10

Bell, Catherine, 35, 88

Bible. *See* evangelical Christian practices: uses of the Bible; evangelical Christian theology: Bible; *God's Game Plan* (Bible)

Bivins, Jason, 84

bodybuilding (sport), 65–66, 68–70, 207n52, 214–215n6; Mr. Olympia, 65. *See also* weight lifting (sport)

body image. *See* female athletes: and body image

Boyd, Malcolm, 60

Boys and Girls Clubs of America, 98

Braude, Ann, 213–214n27

Bright, Bill, 37–39, 43

Brown, Tom, 202n23

Brownworth, Victoria, 218n31

Bush, George H. W., 65

Bush, George W., 82–83, 114

Butler, Judith, 107

Cahn, Susan, 164

Campbell, David, 180, 196n10

homosexuality: and abuse, 148–149; as an
affliction, 139–142; and closeting, 131,
151–153, 155–156, 191, 218n31; evangelical stances on, 10, 24, 110–113, 129–134,
139–156, 185, 190–191, 193, 217n26,
217–218n30; increasing American acceptance of, 132, 215n7, 215n9, 216n12;
and parenting, 141, 148–150 (*see also*
parenting). *See also* gay rights; lesbianism; sexuality
Hoover, Herbert, 44
Hoverd, William, 104
Howard, Jeanette, 140–141
Hughes, Thomas, 202n23
hypocrisy, 96

individualism, 40
Institute for Athletic Perfection, 56,
205n21
intimacy, 55; athletic, 22; divine, 23, 62,
67–68, 70–71, 74–75, 77, 80, 103 (*see
also* religious experience); feminine,
71, 73, 206–207n45; masculine, 71,
73. *See also* knowledge: intimate; sex:
same-sex intimacy
Iraq. *See* war

James, William, 75
Jenkins, Jerry B., 6
jewelry. *See* femininity markers
Jones, Landry, 173–174

Keating, James W., 44, 52
Kendrick, Alex, 167
"killer instinct," 46–47. *See also* problem
of winning
Knipp, Russ, 56
knowledge: embodied, 22–23, 34–35,
43, 53, 55, 76–77, 79–80, 88, 183, 193,
198n26 (*see also* embodiment); emotional, 32, 34–35; intimate, 24, 55 (*see
also* intimacy); religious, 22–23, 42, 52,
55, 75, 88–90, 95–96, 100 (*see also* reli-

gious experience); solidified through
practice, 41, 199n35
Krattenmaker, Tom, 48
Kripal, Jeffrey, 71

Left Behind (LeHaye and Jenkins), 6
LeHaye, Tim, 6
lesbianism: and female athletes, 125, 131,
134, 137–138, 143, 153, 191, 214n2 (*see
also* female athletes); and feminist
activism, 112 (*see also* feminism; gay
rights); relationship between desire
and behavior, 130–135, 139–143, 149–
150, 153, 191, 215n8; sports ministry's
approaches to, 10, 129–142, 148–156.
See also homosexuality; sex; sexuality
LeSourd, Leonard, 139–140
Liddell, Eric, 54–55, 75
Linville, Greg, 29
Lucas, Catherine, 165

Mahmood, Saba, 222n10
mainline Protestantism, 4
Major League Soccer (MLS), 183
makeup. *See* femininity markers
male gaze, 123, 125
male headship, 158–164, 167, 171–172,
174, 177–180, 190. *See also* marriage;
submission
Malinar, Angelika, 69
Malone College, 8
Maltz, Maxwell, 64
marriage: evangelical expectation of,
10–11, 24, 103, 111, 114, 129–130, 138,
141, 143, 149–150, 156–158, 169–170,
190–192, 216n12, 218n1; evangelical gender roles within, 14–15, 24,
104, 122, 148–149, 159–160, 163–164,
166–169, 171–173, 180–181, 191–192 (*see
also* evangelical Christian theology:
gender; submission); heterosexual,
110–112, 145–146, 150, 158, 170, 190–193
(*see also* heterosexuality); as a meta-

ABOUT THE AUTHOR

Annie Blazer is Assistant Professor of Religious Studies at the College of William and Mary. Her teaching interests include religion and popular culture, American politics, and gender studies.